BOJACK

When Loyalties Collide

D1127008

D A V I D   I S H E E

AND

J A C K   S A L T A R E L L I

NEWMAN SPRINGS PUBLISHING
320 Broad Street
Red Bank, NJ 07701

First originally published by Newman Springs Publishing 2020

ISBN 978-1-64801-210-5 (Paperback)
ISBN 978-1-64801-217-4 (Digital)

Printed in the United States of America

CONTENTS

PREFACE

I first met Jack Saltarelli in the fall of 1989. I was a young attorney and had been in Jackson County, Mississippi, since August of 1988 and had seen more than a few "wannabes." Wannabees did not just include criminals. There were lawyers and politicians who presented themselves as tough guys—guys who ran things or thought they ran things and liked to show their authority. There were prosecutors and cops with an "Elliot Ness" complex or criminals who wanted to be drug lords, gang bangers, or "wise guys." *Miami Vice* was about the biggest thing on television, and everybody on both sides of the law was watching way too much television.

That is what brought my attention to a guy called "Mr. Jack." He was a bounty hunter for a local bonding company, and there was something different about him. The criminals feared him; the cops, the lawyers, and even the judges respected him. His business card said, "Jack Saltarelli," but some people called him "Jack Conway." I even heard a few people use the name "Bojack." I had been around long enough to know that some people had "street names." A few had been earned on the street or in prison, but most were just nicknames—more "wannabes." I paid little attention.

There was no organized crime on the Gulf Coast to speak of in those days. Traditionally, the Mississippi Coast had belonged to the New Orleans family of La Cosa Nostra, the oldest Mafia family in America. However, they had been on the ropes since their long-time boss Carlos Marcello had gone down in BriLab almost a decade earlier, leaving a void. Santo Trafficante of the Tampa family, who ran the Gulf Coast east of Jackson County, was in his last days, so the traditional crime sources were gone. The Dixie Mafia, who had always provided extra muscle and had been partners with the wise guys, were trying to fill that void, but they too would be gone within the next decade.

Legalized gaming would soon replace the old-time bookies and sawdust joints of my youth with their own version of "Vega-style" casinos, while the payday loan companies would do more damage to the loan sharks than the police ever had. It was also about this time that the state lotteries in Florida and Louisiana would prove a death sentence to the numbers runners or "Irish Sweepstakes," as it was often called.

But this was the 1980s and early 1990s, and the I-10 cocaine corridor was in full swing. Interstate 10 runs from Jacksonville, Florida, on the east coast, to California on the west coast, passing through Mobile, Alabama; New Orleans; Houston; and numerous smaller cities and towns along the way. While cocaine was coming up from South Florida by the ton, just as much marijuana was coming up from the Texas-Mexico border on the same highway. The local papers were filled with headlines of cocaine cowboys getting busted along the interstate, which provided a good living for a young lawyer with ambition like me.

Although I had seen Jack Saltarelli and talked to him a number of times, the first time that I got to know the real Bojack was outside of the George County Courthouse on the downtown square in Lucedale, Mississippi. Lucedale is about thirty miles inland due north of Pascagoula, where the Gulf Coast ends and the Piney Woods section of Mississippi begins. I had parked on the courthouse side of the square and had gone across the street to the justice court building for a hearing. Justice court handles small civil claims and misdemeanors as well as preliminary matters on felonies.

When court was out, I was going back to my car when Jack approached two men in front of me. He called one of them by name and informed him that he had a warrant for the man's arrest from down on the Gulf Coast. The man responded, "You're in George County now. I ain't going nowhere."

Jack smiled and answered, "Yes, you are."

The other man responded, "I'm his brother. If you fight him, you gonna have to fight me too."

Jack's smile turned into "the look" as he said, "Let's get started."

Less than a minute later, Jack had the first man handcuffed and was loading him into the car as the other man lay on the sidewalk. That is when I knew Jack Saltarelli was the real deal.

Our paths would cross many times over the years. He would refer clients to me. I handled his girlfriend's divorce from her long-estranged husband so that she could become Jack's third wife. He watched my back on more than a few occasions; and when people tried to mess with him about his past, I had his back.

When he moved to Arizona the first time, after I went on the bench, we lost contact for a few years. Then one day, we ran into each other at a local gym, and I started pumping iron with him and his son John, who was a law enforcement officer. It was John who had been trying to talk his dad into writing a book about his life; that got us started. Jack had always said that he could not write a book by himself, and he did not trust anyone enough to collaborate with them.

One day, after leaving the gym, John asked his father, "Do you trust the judge?"

Jack answered, "Absolutely. He's a stand-up guy."

John's response was, "Then get him to help you write your life story."

This book is the result of numerous interviews and conversations with Jack Saltarelli; all based on his memories and recollections. Some names and incidents have been altered to protect innocent parties.

If I thought Jack Saltarelli was a complex person, going from gangster to bail enforcement agent, I had no idea just how complex the man was until he began to tell me his life story over the next two years. Beginning life in what is best described as a Dickensian childhood to stickup man and enforcer to *Breaking Bad* to *Wanted: Dead or Alive*, he has taken one incredibly wild ride. This is his story.

INTRODUCTION

The night was cold and cloudy with over a foot of fresh snow on the ground. It was winter in the Endless Mountains of Pennsylvania, and a foot of fresh snow was no big deal to the mountain dwellers who lived there. It was also a perfect night for manufacturing methamphetamine, a drug also called speed on the streets of Philly. It was also a perfect night for new beginnings, an escape from a lifetime of crime and a new start for my son and me. Unknown to the crew of five that the outfit sent up from the city to assist in the cook, those new beginnings meant they were all going to jail. Secured under my sweatshirt was a transmitter that was placed there by federal authorities to monitor and record the entire cook and any and all conversation. I felt horrible about what was going to happen, but I also knew if any one of them knew what I was doing, I would be killed or at least badly injured for sure. Though surrounded by a host of law enforcement—comprised of two federal agencies, Philly and Scranton FBI, DEA, State Police, and the local authorities, as well as FBI Swat poised above us on the side of the mountain—it was not as if they were in the room with me. And as a negative, I was not armed like I was accustomed to, and that was scary enough. I was surprised none of the crew even noticed since I was never without my gun. So tonight there was to be a tradeoff. My path to a new beginning for the seizure of the heaviest and busiest meth lab on the East Coast. All I had to do was send the word that "we are a go," where the feds wanted the cook to be to guarantee a solid manufacturing bust There had to be a finished product, weighed and bagged, workers crystalizing the liquid into powder form, and a new batch being mixed for another run.

But there was one thing that set tonight apart from so many nights over the thirty-plus-year life of crime that had begun for me at the age of eight, a life I had never chosen, a life that had been thrust upon me by an abusive stepfather before I had reached double digits in age, a life I had thought was normal well into my twenties. And now at the age of thirty-five, I would finally walk away from it—just me and my son and a new day about to dawn. But first, I had to survive tonight.

Everything was going well. The crew I had put together three years ago was top-notch, guys from the neighborhood back in Philly that I had known all my life and trusted, and guys I didn't trust as far as I could throw them. No matter who they were, they all had one thing in common: if any of them ever suspected what I was wearing under my shirt, they would have killed me on the spot.

I was wearing a loose-fitting sweatshirt to hide the listening device. The transmitter was placed in a soft cotton sleeve to reduce friction noise and was to be worn in the small of my back with a small soft antenna. The whole device was powered by a camera-type battery that had to be charged every three hours. This presented a serious problem. To get out of the cookroom that often was hard enough; to have enough privacy to pull up my shirt, turn the sleeve around, change the battery, and replace the transmitter in the small of my back took very little time, but I was completely vulnerable during those precious seconds.

I kept a spare battery in my pocket, had spares in the garage, and even one in the bathroom. Before I began the changing maneuver, I would whisper, "Changing batteries." When I finished, I would say, "Going back inside." Two innocent phrases that could get me killed. Any pause of more than a few seconds between these two statements was supposed to signal to the agents on the other end that I had been found out; and in theory, they would come to my rescue. Always in the back of my mind, I wondered if that would really happen. Wondering constantly if a dead informant might be worth more to the Feds than a live one—a murder charge carrying more weight than a manufacturing charge.

No matter what happened, this was the end of the line, the end of a life of crime and a ticket to normal life for both my son and me. All I had to do was stay alive for the next few hours.

I walked out into the garage using the excuse of needing fresh air. I opened a window and looked out into the cold black night. The moon and stars were blocked out by the clouds, but there was still enough light reflected off the snow to see a little. There was no movement, no sign of life. Was the FBI out there, or were they back at the warm hotel eight miles away, waiting for another night to take us down? I had no way of knowing. I was strictly running on blind faith as I muttered the words "changing out" and went into motion.

As I changed out the battery in the transmitter, slid it back into place, and pulled my sweatshirt over it, my hands began to shake a little. I whispered 'going back inside' praying that there was someone out there listening, and reentered the cookroom. I picked up my mask and said, "That feels better. This shit was starting to get to me," hoping my words would throw off any suspicion caused by my occasional walkouts.

No sooner than I got the words out, the whole world lit up. A floodlight came down from a helicopter that seemed to appear from nowhere; the headlights of SUVs and four-wheelers came from every direction. In the same instant, the front and back doors exploded, and teams of men in winter camouflage carrying automatic weapons poured into the house. "Freeze, you mother fuckers! Don't any of you fucking move or we will waste every fucking one of you!"

I was thrown against the wall with the rest of my crew and froze there beside them, not out of fear of what was to come, as they were, but out of relief. This was the end of Bojack.

CHAPTER 1

I was born John Michael Saltarelli on January 20, 1946, at eight in the morning. My mother delivered me at home in a small West Philly apartment and then took me to the hospital. Although I would later learn that was not uncommon in those days, I always thought that was an indication of what the first half of my life would be—everything backward.

Although I was born John Michael Saltarelli, I was raised as John Michael Conway. The reason is simple: my mother was divorcing my real father, Mike Saltarelli; and when she separated from him, she was carrying his child. She was pregnant with me. She apparently married Jack Conway immediately after I was born when the divorce became final.

Why Mike Saltarelli never stepped up to the plate and fought for me, I have no idea. I do know that he and my mother had two other sons that he won custody of in the divorce; but to this day, I have no idea why I was left behind. All of this was a secret to me until I was almost thirty, and my mother was finally leaving Jack Conway. It was then that she decided to drop this bombshell on me. It was a hell of a thing to have dropped on you. Why did my own father never come for me? Why did he not try to rescue that little boy from a life of abuse before it was too late? I will never know the answer to those questions. All that I can do is look back on my life and try to make sense of it all.

I never had any need to look at my birth certificate or to inquire as to when Jack and my mother had married. All I knew was that they were my parents, and that was all that I needed to know. Believe me, in that house, the fewer questions you asked and the less you said in general, the better off you were.

The best way to describe Jack Conway was angry—angry and sadistic—angry at my mom; angry at the world; angry at life; and most of all, angry at me. In all the years that I lived under his roof, I can never remember him smiling. He walked through life with a perpetual grimace on his face, profound evidence of the boiling volcano simmering within that could erupt at any moment for any reason or for no reason at all.

Jack Conway was not only angry and violent, he was a violent bully, which meant that he took his anger out on the weakest people around him: his wife and son.

Of all of the people whom I will later talk about, no one had a bigger impact on the first part of my life than my stepfather. None of it was good. Conway had grown up in Philly in some type of Catholic orphanage. I never knew why he went there as his mother lived nearby and even raised one of his cousins. He had entered the navy in World War II and was assigned to a Naval Construction Battalion, the Seabees, but was given a less-than-honorable discharge, which is about the time he came back to Philly and ended up with my mother. Jack always seemed to have a decent job but would disappear for long periods of time, showing back up, claiming to have been off working in Chicago, Detroit, or some other Midwestern city.

One of my earliest memories occurred when I was six years old. Conway took me on a walk with him one Saturday. I can still remember feeling so happy and excited to be going someplace with my dad. However, I can also remember a feeling of fear and foreboding, knowing something was wrong, not understanding why my father had a suitcase in his hand. We walked down to a neighborhood grocery store and sat on a bench out front, saying nothing. After a while, he went inside and bought me a ginger ale. A few minutes later, he stood up, picked up his suitcase, and said, "See you around, kid." He walked down to the bus stop, got on the bus, and rode away.

I sat there alone on that bench until it got dark and then walked home alone. It would be two years before I saw Jack Conway again.

When I was eight years old, Conway came home. All he said was that he had been doing roofing work in Chicago and had lost his job. No one asked any questions. This is when the beatings started.

A&P, the largest supermarket chain in the country in those days, had a distribution center in our neighborhood that supplied stores up and down the East Coast. Conway got a job there on the loading docks and started working his way up with the company. It was a good-paying union job. He was a member of Teamsters Local and was very active with the union. He was there for a number of years until being laid off when the distribution center was moved to another location. I later learned that during this time, Conway was also working for a local bookie taking action on the loading docks. Jack always worked hard and provided material things for his family. He just could not restrain himself from savagely beating his wife and oldest son.

One night, Conway came home drunk and even angrier than usual. Mom confronted him, and he knocked her to the floor. I tried to come to her defense and was beaten unconscious for the first time in my life at the age of eight. Over the next six or seven years, he would break every bone in my mother's face and eventually knock out all of her teeth. A few months after this first beating, I ran away from home for the first time, preferring life on the streets to this insanity at home.

Despite all of this, I always tried to do right by the man I thought was my father. I remember one Saturday sometime in the late 70s when my crew and I were working on one of our street racers getting ready to race that night. One of my neighbors came up and said my old man was down the street at a bar and a half dozen guys from another neighborhood were giving him shit. When we busted through the front door, these assholes were shoving the old man back and forth between them. I grabbed a pool stick and broke it across the face of the guy closest to me. That got all of their attention. I said, "You guys are real badasses with an old drunk. How are you when it comes to his son?" And I waded into the rest of them with the broken pool stick. When my crew and I had finished with them, I turned to the old man, who said, "Thanks, Jackie boy. You done good." That was the only compliment he ever gave me in my entire life.

A couple of years later, Conway died as a result of decades of alcohol abuse. He was broke and living in a one-room apartment. I paid for his funeral and bought him a new suit to be buried in and a tombstone. When my mother asked me why, I told her, "All the years I lived in his house, I never went hungry." It was the only good thing I could say about the man I had thought was my father.

CHAPTER 2

About Me

I know now why I have put off writing my life story for so long. I dreamed of doing so because I believe there is something to be said for people who have destroyed their lives with stupid mistakes and senseless ventures, only to continuously answer to an unforgiving society. In my case, even though I ended my reckless abandonment with an honorable bow, I had to continue to live a life of lies to be accepted. But I managed to do just that and do it well.

As I approached the writing of my story, I recognized the misery that loomed with having to relive the bad decisions I made and the fact that the price tag for my foolishness was fifteen years of my life spent in several prisons. I knew that I could and would meet the challenge in detailing for the reader my life of crime, how it all began, and my successful climb from that very doom to become the man I am today. What I cannot do is talk about my childhood in the first person.

When I look at my photos from those early childhood days, sadness pulls at my heart, and the pawing through the dust of so many painful memories takes my breath. It's those pictures of me as a child six, seven, eight years old that suddenly become a roadblock, and the only way I can continue is to speak of this youngster in the third person.

This innocent young boy has no idea of what he is about to experience and what his life will encompass, yet I know what I did to destroy his beautiful existence. Instead of growing up surrounded with all the joys and wonder of an adolescent, I compromised his youth and sent him on a protracted journey. I created a world that was void of warmth and love, hope and promise, and replaced it with a need to survive. Imagine you're eight years old and in an institution for boys because you ran away from home, and your very first lesson was to assault another youth who attempted to take your breakfast. There is no excuse for what I did to this child's future.

The greatest ache that strains my heart is the knowledge of how he was beaten so many times by a man he believed early in his life was his father, and I cannot reach into these photos and protect him. I want to. Oh, God, I want to. I see him before the beatings come, and I cannot intervene. This frail child will be beaten with a strap from back to hamstring; and when the drunk who is lashing him finally gets winded and quits, his body is welted and discolored. If he wasn't being beaten, he usually had to listen to the screams and cries of his mother as he beat her. In the years to come, his dad would eventually break every bone in his mother's face and knock out most of her teeth.

His dad occasionally made sport of his punishment. One evening, the fragile youth tried to sneak in the house after dark to avoid contact with his father. He mounted a flight of stairs to the second floor where he lived, and crouched in the dark was his father, waiting for him to reach the top step. Just as he did, the darkness became a bright flash as he was viciously punched and went airborne, landing on two bikes leaning against the wall on the bottom floor. I cannot believe his back—my back—wasn't broken. Fortunately not and the beating episodes went on until that kid just would not live there in that house with him and began to run away repeatedly.

How I would like to reach into this kid's world and take hold of this villain who could relish punishing a child and a naive woman with such vicious beatings. I could cry just looking at this child's pictures and knowing the damage is done, and I did it. I need to say now that I love him and want very much to cradle him in my arms and tell him I will never let anyone ever hurt him again. His survival from that era on became my survival, and so we did together. I was that boy, and he is this man.

Learning to Survive the Mean Streets of Philly

The 1950s were a different world than today. America had just come through the Great Depression and the Second World War only to find itself in a cold-war-turned-hot in Korea. After almost two and a half decades of war and economic hardship, America had passed from adolescence into adulthood and leader of the free world. There was another side to America in those days, a side that still exists on an even greater level today, one far removed from our father-knows-best image of that decade.

Juvenile justice was designed to deal with petty theft and street fights, not broken families and destroyed lives.

CHAPTER 3

Mastering Survival as a Juvenile

1954–1958

When I first started running away from home to escape the insanity that festered there, I didn't fear the challenge of surviving long nights as an eight-year-old on the street. I would seek shelter in someone's unlocked car or a building that was either abandoned or presented a lock that I could easily open with a penknife or screw-driver. Locks were not much of a challenge in those days. As far as cars were concerned, people rarely locked their automobiles.

The challenge was to avoid the police cars that occasionally roamed the deserted streets of my neighborhood; and if I spotted headlights in the distance, I would lie alongside a parked car or hug an alley wall and wait for them to pass. I can still remember the sound of those slow-moving police cars that had a particular ticking sound to them. I believe they were Fords then; and when they coasted down a quiet street, barely moving above idle speed, that ticking sound would warn me not to raise my head and peek because I might be seen and surely get taken into custody for being out so late. I would wait patiently for the car to leave the area before I would get up or come out of the alley, whichever the case.

The great thing about the city was it was a mass of alleyways and rooftops that were great for travel, depending on how far you were traveling. For instance, if you intended to cover several blocks or more, the alleyways were safe routes because there was no risk of being seen until you ran from one row of homes to the next and back into that alley. Rooftops were great for immediate travel. Smaller alleys that separated a section of buildings were fairly narrow and easy for a fast and agile kid to leap. When you imagine cities like Philly and New York back in the day—my day, the 1950's—it was not only a source of travel, but many activities were common on rooftops. Raising and racing pigeons and growing gardens was big. Neighborhood gangs sought refuge high above the streets and the reach of the law.

Usually, if I crawled into someone's vehicle and was still sleeping when they came out to get into their car, I would get, "What the hell are you doing in my car kid?" I would use an assortment of stories, but the best was that I got locked out of my house. If everything looked in order with the car, I was sent on my way. No one called the police; they were heading out to work or needed to go.

Getting into a building to find shelter was another matter. It was, even for an eight-year-old in 1954, a burglary offense. If I found an abandoned building, then I was not as apprehensive about entering it without consent because it was abandoned and unlikely that somebody would come there early in the morning to start a work shift. All I had to do was make it until early light, and I would stalk the grocery stores in the area for food. Trucks would deliver boxes of goods and stack them outside the front door. If a delivery was made at seven in the morning and the store opened at nine o'clock, I would have all kinds of goodies to choose from. Large grocery stores would have milk, butter, eggs, bread, cakes, and a host of other food items. I would usually grab a quart of chocolate milk and a box of donuts and find a safe spot to enjoy my breakfast. I only took what I ate, so I supposed that a small amount of loss was accepted, considering that routine was never altered. Plus, I moved from one store to another and never made one particular store my regular morning stop.

During the day, I naturally skipped going to school since I was a runaway. I would wander through the Fairmount Park area, which was pretty massive in size back then. It was also the storage site for a lot of the old locomotive trains, and I would climb on them and imagine what it would be like to actually drive one. Fairmount Park was a wonderland to me in my innocent youth. I would get a stick and either play soldiers or cowboys and Indians. There were paths for horseback riding, and I would imagine the riders were Indians galloping past me. I would let my imagination go wild. I would hide in the tall growth that bordered the riding path and imagine myself taking out the wild renegades that rode past me.

Fairmount Park has become totally commercialized now. I don't think there is even a park anymore. I recall the police on horseback that had their stable close by. I would walk from West Philly to the Philadelphia Zoo and down to the Schuylkill River and look across to the art museum that was on the Ben Franklin Parkway, a section of Center City.

As a youngster, I traveled miles upon miles walking. I recall when the work to construct the highway along the Schuylkill River first started—Schuylkill River Expressway, Route 76—so long ago. I spent a lot of time alone.

I would be picked up for being a runaway many times by the year 1958. I was twelve years old and by now a true survivor of the streets. I was taken to the Youth Study Center on Ben Franklin Parkway eight times. Some of those times I was charged with theft and breaking and entering. Running away and seeking shelter led to petty crime. There were times when I entered the building of a business and came across cash. I took it to eat and travel the subways from West Philly to downtown Center City where all the action was. Market Street was the host of novelty stores and arcades, and I love the pinballs and other machines that were set up in the arcades.

Now, every time I was taken to the youth center, I was good for a stay of up to two weeks or a couple of months. It was a call that the center's supervisors made after you had a hearing to view your case. In the beginning, I was always sent home with my mom, but I never stayed home long. The shit would start again, and the insanity would showcase itself once more. How could anyone live like that? I spent more time petrified than I did relaxed. I was gone again.

So as I began to accumulate repeated runaways, my stays at the center were longer. By October 31, 1958, Halloween Day, the

Philadelphia Common Pleas Court said they had had enough. I was taken before Judge Julius Hoffman and sent to the Catholic protectory located in Phoenixville, Pennsylvania. I was twelve years old and was given a year to serve, providing I didn't do anything to add to it, like escape. In four years, I had come a long way from a terrified eight year old to a habitual delinquent.

When I got a little older, around ten or so, I put together a small gang from the West Philly area of Fifty-Fifth and Jefferson. None of them stole things that I ever knew about, but they loved hanging out with me when I was treating everyone. Not every ten-year-old would carry a hundred dollars or more to spend on rides, food, and games for his sidekicks; grown men didn't clear that much money at the end of a workweek in 1956. But my ability to gain entrance into shoddily locked businesses was uncanny. I was small and slim and would squeeze through transom windows that were left slightly cracked open above entranceways for airflow. I managed to go through skylights and drop to the interior of some businesses.

Banking was nothing like today. You were guaranteed to at least find a ton of change in a business, and small bills were always left as well for opening purposes. I learned how to find store owners' hiding spots that would serve as their stash so they didn't have to carry money home at night. I would sit on the floor of the business, well out of sight of anyone passing by, and I would study every inch of the store.

I always found the money in the least expected places: under a trash bag placed in a trash can as a liner, cash rolled up and stuffed in the toe of an old pair of beat-up work shoes. A popular spot was in the pockets of work clothes that were hanging on a nail in a back storage room. I would go to the obvious cash drawer or register first and bag the change; and if there were bills, I took them too. But if there were only ones and no large bills, I owed it to myself to scour the store for the larger bills. Sometimes, the smaller amount was all I got, but I had at least forty or fifty dollars.

I didn't start out to burglarize or to break and enter into someone's business. I was looking for a place of refuge and shelter. The first time I found money and associated it with a quick way to have cash to survive on was when I used a screw-driver to jimmy a center door open that was built into a garage door of a neighborhood auto shop. It was a Saturday night, and I knew they would be closed on Sunday. No stores were ever opened on Sunday; all that operated on the Sabbath were churches. So I gained access and picked a clean car that was parked inside awaiting work or pickup and decided I would sleep in it.

The only light inside the shop was coming from a blinking light in the office section of this garage. I couldn't get to sleep, and I remember I was cold. I looked into the small window of the office, and I saw an old ceramic heater glowing. It must have been left on to keep the small office warm. Fires were frequent back then with those heaters being left unattended, but I was cold. The door was unlocked, so I went in, and I will not forget how it was that I discovered my first cash stash.

There was nowhere to lay down, so I sat in an office chair and put my feet up on the desk. I was a little warmer and comfortable but not where I could sleep. So nosey me started opening the desk drawers out of boredom. I was probably about nine years old, and like some big shit, I'm going through some business owner's desk drawers. I never expected to find money. The office stunk of oil and chemicals; and at my young age and ignorance, I did not associate mechanics as an expensive cost and a good trade to be in. When I slid the top drawer open, I could see dollar bills spilling out of an envelope. There was over a hundred dollars. And that's when I realized that depending on the building I decided to seek refuge in, there could be a bonus for the taking.

I still slept in cars from time to time; and many a night, I slept under a bridge that a local train would pass under. I kept an appliance box up under the bridge in which I climbed into to rest. I got around; I was versatile.

When I revisit my young juvenile years and think back to the havoc I created for a bunch of hardworking people, the local milk delivery guys come to mind. I terrorized those poor men driving those milk trucks not just in my neighborhood but practically all of West Philly. I stalked them on Saturdays. I knew that they would do their deliveries early in the morning while people might still be asleep or just stirring and drop off the milk, eggs, butter, whatever it was that particular stop requested. A lot of times, there would be notes in empty bottles telling the milk man what to leave or what not to leave. In any case, the driver would take care of his deliveries, and after lunch or just about that time, he would return to the start of his route and begin collecting for the past week's deliveries.

In the beginning, when I first discovered that milk trucks carried and left money in their trucks, I had jumped into one to grab a hunk of ice to wet my mouth in the summer heat. When I opened the icebox, I saw the sack and moved it to reach a hunk of ice it was covering. I heard the sound of coins; and when I lifted it up, it was super heavy. I ducked down because this was not an ice raid anymore, something easily smoothed over if the driver saw me and raised hell. I was hanging onto a bag of cash that I didn't even know how much it contained, but I knew I was taking it with me when I exited the truck. I peeked through one of the rear-panel windows and could see that the milkman was fast about his work, a distance away, and involved with a customer at their door with his back to me. Embracing the heavy canvas bag and holding it close to my chest, I walked away from the truck and turned the corner. I was gone in a heartbeat.

I zeroed in on several of these milkmen. I would rob just one, and that was usually sufficient for me. But I scouted several of the milk trucks in the event that if the driver of the one I was going to target didn't travel far enough from his vehicle for me to safely search it, I could abandon that one and track another. There were at least three in the immediate area; and though they didn't all carry the same brand of product, their systems were pretty much the same. And collection time was good from one in the afternoon to three; or better yet, around two in the afternoon. The reason being there was too much cash to carry on his person at that time of day. The cash flow was the prize, and the driver had nowhere to put it other than in his truck. A popular place was in the ice cooler and always in a canvas sack with a company logo on it.

The way I would do it was I would never let the driver notice me spying on his truck or his movements. I'm just a kid and no threat to him. If it was possible, I would pick a store window—and in those days, we had stores on every corner—and act like I was looking at something in the window, but I would be watching his reflection as he started his method of collection by climbing over the wooden railings that divided the brick row homes and knocking on doors of his clients. Usually, they were ready for him, and he'd get paid and climb the next railing, all the time getting farther and farther away from where his truck was parked. Rarely did they interrupt this routine to move the truck because in many cases, the driver would start the same procedure, returning back on the other side of the street and end up where he was parked.

I terrorized these guys for quite some time. It became my Saturday operation. No milkman was safe, and I got them all at least once and some more than once. The repeats would attempt to find new hideouts, and I would crawl around in their truck and locate the money. I would move into another area of my neighborhood and target other carriers because I was sure that once you ripped off several carriers in a given area with the same company, they were more than alert and probably sharing ideas on how to catch who was doing it.

These rip-offs were always good for no less than a hundred dollars, but I got as much as three hundred in a single grab. If you think about it, most customers in those days probably owed five or six dollars. Now that may not sound like a lot, but the carrier is delivering milk, butter, eggs, and some other dairy items and delivering some of that every day, like milk. If he was taking in lots of small bills, then it became a chore to pack all of them in his pocket.

I know that when they started their day, they left the payroll area with rolls of change to make change for customers. All that added up. I actually went to the company late one Saturday and entered the counting room where the milkmen came in from their day and counted their money before handing it through a gated teller window with their paperwork. I pretended I was using the vending machine and restroom. I just wanted to know how it worked and how it ended. I wonder now how many of those poor guys came back short and had to make good for the money they lost—the money I stole from them. I suppose the Saturday reign of terror ended for those milkmen on October 31, 1958, the day I was sent to the Catholic protectory in Phoenixville, Pennsylvania.

The Catholic protectory was just that; it was all about discipline, education, and religion, with emphasis on the teachings of the Catholic church. I was taught catechism and made my first Holy Communion while I was their guest. Discipline there was fine-tuned. In time you learned to hear the snapping of the brother's fingers, the clicking of his two fingers, pinched and released to make a crisp snapping sound. You learned in short order to hear that sound, even over the noise of a hundred kids, and freeze in place until you were instructed to either speak softly or not talk at all.

I also saw what rebelling against their system would get you. You couldn't win; those monks ruled you with intimidation. Picture being in a room with a mass of kids making the normal noises with small talk and other movement sounds and with your back to the brother, where you cannot see him make the finger snap gesture, yet you hear it and freeze in place. You are in a room the size of a ballroom and a finger snap reaches you because you have been fine-tuned to respond. That's conditioning to the max. That's bordering on brainwashing.

qBrother Gabriel was a tall, thin Franciscan monk who never smiled, always sporting a frown, always looking to add a new name in his little black book. If he called for total silence, I swear the man could detect a whisper. The scary part of his black book was if you were in line movements or in church or somewhere he couldn't deal with you right then, then he wrote your name down for Saturday night, what we all called a "Bendo Party."

The problem with not being called out on the spot and at least being able to say you were not the one whispering was that when Saturday night rolled around and your suspicions were correct in thinking he looked at you and put your name down when the kid behind you was the culprit, well, you could forget about any denial or on-the-spot explanation. Saturday night consisted of showering in the basement and then moving upstairs to the dormitory. There in the bathroom, which was a very large room, we shined our shoes and set out our clothes for church the following morning. Once all that preparation was completed, before Brother Gabriel would dismiss us to go to the end of our beds and prepare for night prayers, he would produce that infamous black book and, with a scowl that scared the hell out of us, would announce, "The following people remain here and form a line in the order that I call your name."

Monks did not wear pants and shirts. Their garb consisted of long tunics that began just under their white neck collar and stopped just at the tie part of their shoes, all black with slits on the sides for their arms to move in and out of. You prayed you weren't on his list. You swore to everything holy that you would be a better person, just please don't call my name. You have to imagine and place yourself there to understand the extent of the fear such an event instilled in you. All you were wearing were very thin pajamas, tissue thin material between your flesh and his bendo stick.

All the brothers at the protectory, which was made up of three divisions according to age, used these sticks, which were baseball bats that were shaved on both sides to do away with the rounded part and were about an inch or a bit thicker in the center. These altered ball bats were then drilled with holes and taped the entire length of the bat They were designed not to break, and I never saw one do so. While the boys who weren't called were permitted to go to their beds for evening prayers—all breathed a sigh of relief—the remaining boys stewed in the horror of what lay ahead.

If you were in the basement during recreational activities and got called out for an infraction, you usually received bendos right then. The positive part of that punishment was that you were wearing heavier material, like regular pants. And for some reason, the amount of bendos weren't as many, and it was over with as quick as it started. There were occasions, like the day I arrived on Halloween, that corporal punishment was being illustrated while boys were exiting the shower, still wet, and being hit across the buttocks with no protection at all.

The first thing I noticed when I entered the third division was evidence of the abuse taking place there. Practically every ass there was black-and-blue. The boys lined up for their showers had their backs to me, and I was horrified. Then, as a couple of the boys exited the shower, they were told to stop, bend over, and grab their knees. Brother Gabriel was at least six feet two inches or six feet three inches, and he had extremely long arms. I watched as he raised that bendo stick and listened as it whistled its way to its target, sending a heart-shattering crack as it met the youngster's wet flesh. This place was all about discipline, and I was facing a year of it.

Now the Saturday parties were different. It was as if Brother Gabriel had waited all week for this with much anticipation. It was an actual ritual. The problem at this gathering was the absence of justice for whatever you may have done to get on his list. An infraction that may have gotten you four bendos normally, your being a guest of the party meant you were going to get what everyone else got. Everyone got the same amount. The history of these events was there were usually ten to twelve bendos.

The session began with the first in line to step up and bend over. Most boys knew the drill. If you moved or jumped away as the brother struck his blow, whether he made contact or not, it didn't count. You had to return back to the line and repeat the ritual. Everyone in line just wanted to get it over with. I can attest to the fact that after having attended these sadistic ceremonies on more occasions than I wish to admit, you get numb after the third or fourth lick, and those who knew this wanted to keep the line moving. Once you received a blow, you were to run around the sinks and get back in line. You didn't rub your ass because you wanted it to stay numb. You did this dance in place and hissed with the sting. If a new kid screwed around and caused us to wait longer, we let him know about it later. I remained black-and-blue most of my stay. My last month at the protectory went without bendos because the idea was to send us home with an ass that had its original color back.

Bendos were one punishment, but there were other painful activities the brothers could muster up when not in an area where they could swing their bats. Handshakes were horrible. Employing the use of a radiator brush that had an extended wooden handle, the brother would demand that you put your hand out in front of you, palms up and fingers stretched out clear of your palms. Then from a position high above his head, he would bring the wooden handle of that brush crashing down on your palm. My god, they stung. I would go into a crouch with the pain of each whack. After a few of those, your palms swelled so bad, you could not close your hand to make a fist.

And lastly, the round wooden ball on a stick. These jewels had to be designed by some real sadistic fuck. Unlike a bendo or a handshake where the pain is away from you, the wooden ball on a stick would be used in the following manner. Imagine being in school doing your assigned classwork, and your teacher, a Franciscan monk like the rest of the caretakers, eased up on you and looked over your shoulder to see how your work was coming along. He then decided you needed a wake-up call because your work was off the mark. You would be struck on the top of your skull, that wooden ball coming into really hard contact with the bone of your scalp, and the pain would travel right through your brain to your jaw. Good lord, where did these monks get these tools of pain and the right to torture and terrorize children? That's all we were. I was twelve, but our division had kids ten and perhaps younger staying there. Only in the 1960's could you get away with that.

I visited the protectory in 2007 during a visit to the East Coast from Mississippi. There are no monks now; they have been gone for some time. Today, the institution is run by civilians. I often wonder how many kids left that place with mental issues that surfaced later in their lives, or worse, prevented them from being able and equipped to live a normal life from the time they left there.

Being a product of the Catholic protectory would explain how I survived seventh grade at St. Francis de Sales Catholic School under Sister Assumpta Mary, my seventh grade nun and teacher. She always saw me as a hard case; and according to her letters in years to come while writing to me in prison, she saw me as someone who needed reaching. She would paddle me to no avail. She meant to humiliate me in front of the class by making me face the students, attempting to make me cry from her paddling. I never even felt her blows. She would swing away until she was out of breath; and when she told me to take my seat, as instructed after punishment, I would say, "Thank you, Sister."

It was while writing to her in the following years that I told her about the protectory and the cruelty that the monks savored there. It wasn't that I meant to embarrass her in front of the class by failing to teach me a lesson. It was just that I felt nothing; I was numb. You can't make someone cry who is void of any real emotion other than the necessity to survive.

I wasn't home long enough from the protectory to even begin to recognize normal, but I did adore Sister Assumpta Mary. I only attended that one grade, seventh, because I was arrested again and went before Judge Hoffman, the judge who sent me to the protectory. This time, he sent me to Glen Mills for boys.

I forget how it was that Sister Assumpta Mary and I began to write. I think I wrote her first, and that began our correspondence. Later, she became what is referred to as a traveling teacher. But wherever she traveled to, she kept in touch and kept me abreast of her activities. What I remember most about her is that she always told me that deep down inside my hard exterior was a warm and kind person, and that one day I would be okay, that I had to let go of the need to be defensive all the time and be able to trust again. She was so right, I realize it now. Defensive and unable to trust anyone or anything, she saw right through me.

I lost contact with Sister during my stay at Holmesburg Prison in Philadelphia where I was serving a state sentence for three armed robberies—1966–1968. I know it was not because she gave up on me; she wouldn't do that. Perhaps she became ill. I truly loved her. How ironic that a Catholic nun who was assigned to be my seventh grade teacher zeroed in on me and was relentless about it. And all the while I thought she was targeting me to break me and show her class I was not a tough guy and could be broken, when all she was trying to do was to save me from myself.

Along with my loving grandmother, I hold Sister Assumpta Mary to have been a paramount source of comfort for me. I know she is in God's kingdom now, and I hope she is looking down on me and, though it took me a while, she sees that I finally made it. I'm okay now. It would be great if my grandmother and Sister Assumpta Mary were together in His kingdom. I lost them both around the same time while I was in Holmesburg Prison.

CHAPTER 4

June 8, 2016

The early years of Jack Saltarelli were defined by a time when the government often overlooked children. Despite today's criticism of the government's interfering with people's personal lives, and we have certainly gone too far in a loss of personal freedoms, Jack's formative years were determined by the idea that a man's home was his castle, and how he treated his wife and children was his business. There were no specific domestic violence laws protecting women and children as well as few social workers, and those were overworked, undertrained, and grossly underpaid. One would hope that in today's society, a child like Jack would be placed in foster care, his mother given access to a woman's shelter, and his stepfather put behind bars.

However, after twenty-five years in the criminal justice world, I still see kids like Jack. Most go off to prison by the age of twenty-one, a large percentage are dead before the age of thirty, with maybe one in a thousand turning their life around either on their own or with the help of the military. Jack is not just one in a thousand; he is one in a million. Given up on by his family as well as society by the age of fifteen, he turned his life around at the age of thirty-eight, and has led a law-abiding, productive, and (to say the least) interesting life ever since.

Despite his ultimate success in life, the long road to today has left its scars. The two-year narrative that resulted in this book has obviously had its painful moments filled with both regret and sadness and feelings of "what could have been." These feelings were rarely set out in words, only in his eyes. To the contrary, Jack has never complained or whined or blamed his mistakes or misfortunes on others during all of the years that I have known him. Other than one lost love and the current estranged relationship with his two children, the only time I have seen Jack go to a dark place is when he talks about "that little boy," and he always blames himself.

In short, everyone failed Jack—his family, the government, and even his church; the very institutions constructed and designed to be the foundations of society. They were supposed to be the protectors of the weak and oppressed, and, especially, of the children. The only saving grace in his young life was his grandmother Conway and Sister Mary Assumpta. Both of them reached out to him in their own way. I am convinced that it is their influence that ultimately saved Jack Saltarelli. They instilled in him the beginnings of a moral compass that would prevent him from becoming a killer and a sociopath; and after decades of strife and turmoil, this influence would make him into the man he is today.

CHAPTER 5

Camp Hill Prison

Five years at Camp Hill were the final touches of turning Jack Saltarelli into a hardened criminal. Prior to that, his "crimes" had consisted of running away from home, trespassing, petty theft of food, and breaking and entering—all of which would have been handled through the youth court system and juvenile detention centers in today's justice system. However, after spending the better part of the three years in the Catholic protectory and Glen Mills farms, Jack's childhood, such as it was, ended when he was told by a judge that the system had "done all it could to help him" and sentenced him to Camp Hill Penitentiary at the ripe old age of fifteen. The previous years in juvenile institutions had taught Jack the fundamentals of surviving on the inside, and the beatings doled out by his stepfather and the brothers at the Catholic protectory had toughened him to a hard edge.

Jack has told me on many occasions, "You can't be a punk in one jail and a tough guy in the next one. Once a punk, you were always a punk. Reputations were important, and you knew who was solid and who wasn't. Now I'm not putting down guys who came to jail and just wanted to be a model inmate and get out as soon as possible, and a good number of them did. But as a whole, you were going to be called on, and you either answered the call or you were forever labeled a punk.

"Even if you chose to allow another convict to degrade you and call you out, and you accepted the consequences of not wanting to fight, many times, you took a beating anyway. I used to shake my head in disbelief. 'Just put your damn hands up and try to tear the jerk getting in your face to pieces.' I always had a saying: 'slide 'em and deal 'em.' In other words, land that first punch and let them rip because you would normally be met with a half a dozen guards pulling you apart in short order. The principal thing to do was inflict as much damage as possible before you were separated, and hopefully the dude you were engaged in combat with decided that he got in the wrong guy's face.

"A lot of white boys got called on because not many would go toe to toe with another con. But there were a lot of hard-ass white boys that made the grade, and they walked side by side with the brothers in the jail, and we respected each other. Standing strong came with a price in the form of an extended stay, but I personally didn't care. I had nothing to go home to. As far as I was concerned, I was home. So the way I saw it, I could either stand proud and do a few days in the hole from time to time and be respected, or I could be weak and suffer the consequences.

"I will point out that in those days, there was not a lot of racial divide. We were segregated by cellblock, but everyone seemed to see each other as sharing the same fate. You just could not appear weak. Jail hustlers could smell it, and they would hone in on it.

"After arriving at Camp Hill and completing orientation, just a few hours into my prison schedule, I had my first situation there. That evening, when our block lined up in the chow hall for supper, I noticed this big white dude who was from another block scouting our line. Then he looked at me, and he was smiling as if to say, 'Yeah, you.' I was new and only fifteen and was assigned to 'J Block,' which was known as 'sweet boy block' because all of the inmates were young first offenders. I might have appeared young and innocent, but that impression was about to change.

"All line movements were controlled and orderly. You were required to follow the inmate in front of you, and you were not allowed to break the line formation for any reason. The guards were positioned throughout the mess hall, so I knew I had very little time to make my move. I watched to see where he was finally seated and knew that I would have to travel quite a distance to reach him from where I would end up seated. As I made the rounds along the food line, I loaded up my tray with all of the extras allowed and started for the assigned tables for 'J Block.'

"That is when I just broke loose into a run. And when I reached his table, he was looking down at his tray about to shovel down a portion of food. I slammed him across the face with my tray and started to beat him with it. Eight pissed off inmates with mashed potatoes and gravy all over them rose up and wanted to kill me, but the guards were all over me that fast and wrestled me down to lockdown. Now this infraction was extremely serious to the warden, whose name was Snare, because a metal tray is a weapon, and so I was given ninety days on Labor Five, an intense work detail inside the lockdown section. When Warden Snare asked why I had assaulted another inmate, I used my standard answer: 'I don't know.'

"During this time, I found out that the inmate whom I slammed with the tray was Big Bill Wilby, a hard-ass from North Philly and a banger with the Irish mob. He wanted to kill me, and probably would have, but while I was in Labor Five, I met up with one of my homeboys that I grew up with in South Philly Mike Palumbo. It turned out Mike was a friend of Wilby's, so he negotiated a meeting in the yard between us when I got out of lockdown. Later on when I was back in general population, we met up a couple of times and had a few nervous laughs. The important thing was the message I sent, a very necessary message, and what better place to send it than in the mess hall in front of hundreds of convicts to let them all know what I was about.

"I have known some solid guys during my travels from one institution to another. But today, I can recall six really tough white boys at the Hill. Now I'm not being racial in any way by singling them out as white, but it was an absolute fact that a lot of the young white guys under those circumstances were lacking balls, so it was refreshing to encounter guys that would stand their ground because having heart is something inherent in you and something you cannot fake.

"Dave Humphrey was my number one go-to guy. I met him when I was assigned to the craft shop three months after arriving in 1961. He had been there for a while and had established himself with a tough-take, no-bullshit reputation. This is a good time to explain how 'body boxing' worked. They had organized boxing at most prisons in those days, but it was a privilege that had to be earned, and getting thrown into the hole for fighting could cost you that privilege. However, if you liked to box, and many of us did, then you had to sneak in a session of 'body boxing' whenever the guard walked to another are of the wood shop due to the fact that any kind of physical contact was forbidden.

"Body boxing was actually an art since no headshots were allowed because if the guard came back ten or fifteen minutes later and somebody had a black eye or a busted lip, everybody around would be questioned. And when no one had seen anything, we would all be written up and lose privileges. This was a sport, not a fistfight. The art of it was to block punches and be able to move fast and avoid accidentally hitting a guy in the face. Squatting, slipping, and sliding, a moving body required some precision to find opponents' openings and score shots to his torso. Of course, this was all bare-knuckle, no gloves or mouthpieces or cups. Sounds crazy, I know, but if you boxed enough in this manner, whenever you had a real match, you were a very well-rounded body puncher and not just some wild head hunter.

"If a guy like Dave Humphrey challenged you, and you declined, well, you were at the bottom of the respect pool amongst the work crew, and then you had real problems. If you did not know how to box, but you gave it an honest shot, you were at least looked upon as a guy with some moxey, and you gained a little respect. If you were cool and kept giving it a shot, someone on the crew might teach you.

"When I arrived in the craft shop, I was approached by Humphrey, who asked me if I knew how to box. I assured him I did and would be happy to oblige him. When the guard left the building to go next door, we began to thump, and man did we thump! Humphrey was thick and short and solid, a real powerhouse. I was lean and fast but hit with a snap. And so we danced. We went for over ten minutes, which would be three rounds in a sanctioned fight, only without any rest periods in between. Finally, the inmate watching the door yelled, 'Guard,' and we all quickly returned to our work tables sanding wooden furniture.

"I liked Humphrey right away, and I could tell he respected me too. He actually told some of the other cons at his table that I was good and fast as well, and that he liked my technique and the way I threw combinations. After that night, Humphrey and everyone else in the shop was about to respect me even more.

"That evening when I lined up with the rest of my tier for showers, the block guard walked past me and stopped. He told me to step out of line and asked me point-blank, 'Where did you get those bruises?' I looked down, and sure enough, my chest and ribs were turning black-and-blue. I told him it must have happened when I ran into my cell door. I refused to involve another inmate and showed everybody that I was a stand-up guy.

"I was sent to disciplinary section and held for a hearing in front of Warden Snare, my second in less than ninety-five days, ninety of which I had spent in lockdown on Labor Five.

"I spend three days in the hole before I was taken before the disciplinary hearing and told to remove my shirt. By that time, the bruises were turning purple, but I stuck to my story and refused to give up another inmate. I went back to general population and my job at the woodshop. My respect level at Camp Hill was growing.

"Billy McBride was another solid guy. He had been one of the older guys when I was at Glen Mills farm as a juvenile, and Billy and I were like brothers. We put our time in together at the Hill and continued our friendship back on the streets of Kensington in North Philly. Billy was a freelance burglar by trade and worked with a lot of different crews off and on. We were close friends right up until he was murdered in a North Philly bar on a bullshit rumor that he was talking to the district attorney's office. I knew Billy would never rat on anybody, but I was doing time in Terre Haute Federal Prison and could not help him.

"Someone put out a bad wire on him, and somebody else acted on it. At last call in a neighborhood bar, while Billy went to the restroom, someone tampered with his drink. And when he returned to the bar and tossed down his last shot, whatever he had been given caused him a horrible death. No sooner had he swallowed his drink than he went into immediate convulsions. The bar quickly cleared out, and Billy was left writhing on the floor in pain, foaming at the mouth, and choking to death. He finally succumbed to a heart attack. That rumor was later cleared up, and people got straightened out, but Billy McBride was gone. So much said for living the life.

"Another good friend from my Camp Hill days was James Riley. He was a South Philly boy who could fight, and had the heart of a warrior. He was not a big guy, but I never saw anyone that could hit as hard as he did for his size. We boxed a lot, and I respected his hitting power. Plus, he was incredibly fast. Once he left the Hill, we lost contact, and I never saw him again. Like James, most of the tough guys and true bangers were Irish and came from the mean streets of North Philly, mainly in the Kensington area. This was the domain of the Irish Mob who were juiced in with the Roofers Union, which was part of the Teamsters. No matter who says what, these were the toughest guys in all of Philly. These guys would show up in and out of my life as my true life in crime would grow.

"Camp Hill was the first place to have an impact on my life, sending me down the road to a life of crime. This is where I earned the name of 'Bojack.' I say earned because it had once belonged to a tough old Irish con who had been one of the most respected guys in the joint and had been released shortly before I arrived. When I was first processed into Camp Hill, I was told that if I obeyed all of the rules, I would be home in thirteen months. However, fighting got your stay extended by thirty days, so I ended up serving twenty-two months before I made parole. During that almost two-year period, I fought at least once a week, either body boxing or real fights, so I guess getting caught eleven times was not a bad average.

"Now, you would think that I would have been happy to be getting out, but I really didn't care. There was really not much of anything for me to go home to. If there had been, I would not have started running away at age eight in the first place. But I did know one thing: after almost five years in juvenile and adult jails, I was not going to be Jack Conway's punching bag anymore. However, like most things in my life, even getting out of jail could not go without a hitch.

"The procedure for being released from Camp Hill was that you went to all of the departments in the prison and got your release papers signed. That way, each of the departments could remove you from their files. And by signing your release, they showed that you had been there, and your release had been acknowledged. At first, everything went well.

"My final stop was the nurse's station in the prison infirmary. We had two doctors working at the prison, Dr. Wilson, who was a decent guy, and Dr. Zerbe, who was an obnoxious jerk. Zerbe was known to make inmates stand in front of him and drink large amounts of castor oil no matter what medical problem brought you there. Of course, the doctor on duty at the time I entered the medical department was Dr. Zerbe. He must have been bored or just in a mood to give someone a hard time because instead of the usual, 'Are you feeling okay?' and then signing off on my release, he started looking at my face. Like most seventeen-year-olds, I had some teenage zits but nothing unusual. The jail diet was not the greatest, and lots of the guys had zits. He then refused to sign my papers, which meant I could not go home the next morning.

"After this bit of bright news, he took black drawing salve and covered my entire face. I looked hideous. He then made me return every two days to see if he was going to approve my release. I went through it for two weeks. And by the time he approved my discharge, I had full-blown acne. Huge red bumps, swollen and weeping, that were so bad, it was a painful chore to shave. I had severe acne from that day until I went to Holmesburg Prison in 1966, where the University of Pennsylvania had a dermatological study going, which cured me.

"I cannot emphasize how much this acne contributed to my feelings of being ugly and worthless. Girls thought it was gross, and guys made wisecracks about it, but only once. In ways, it deterred me from establishing any normal teenage relationships with girls that I was interested in. I am not saying that some did not find me interesting, but I had been considered a good-looking kid before I went in, and now I was not. That creep of a doctor really caused me a lot of pain. And not being a crybaby about it, I will tell you that acne gave me a horrible hang-up and an awful complex as I went back out into society.

"Feelings of worthlessness and depression, like everything else in my life up to that time, just cemented me into a no-give-a-shit attitude and started me drinking heavily for the first time in my life.

"I left the Hill in the summer of 1963 and was back again in September of that same year. I would end up doing my entire five-year sentence there. Being out only a couple of months and drinking all of the time, I let my tempter and drunkenness instigate the very circumstances that sent me back to the Hill. In those days, we called ourselves 'corner boys,' and anyone coming up in those days knew what that meant. Philly was an accumulation of gangs that were made up on neighborhood grids. You had the 'old heads' who were older and had pretty much cut their teeth coming up and had their own individual reps. And then you had the 'young boys,' my age and just coming into their own.

"I was a young boy but with so much experience. I actually had more time in the joint at the age of seventeen than any of the older guys in their late twenties who sat around and bragged about doing thirty days here and there in the county jail for some bullshit misdemeanors. We were the fifty-first and Baltimore Crew, which was the corner we hung out on, and our numbers were respectable. Anytime there was a problem involving another corner crew, we could quickly amass the numbers.

"On this hot summer day, my friend and partner was Mike McGille, known as 'Chops' in the neighborhood. Both of us were drunk on whiskey when I decided to purchase a new pair of slacks. The clothing store was located just half a block from my mom's apartment. They were known for good prices, and being so close by, we decided to walk over. Now, this was the street that I lived on, and everyone knew me. I may have done some stupid things in my life, but I did not plan the insanity that was about to take place that afternoon.

"When we entered the clothing store, there was only one other customer, a lady who was making a large purchase. I was only getting one pair of slacks, and after going right to the shelf that I knew they were on, I made my way to the counter. She stepped up behind me before the clerk had rung up my purchase, so taking into consideration that she was cradling an armload of items, I stepped aside and told her to go ahead of me. I have no reason to lie at this stage of the game. I truly meant well and was a perfect gentleman in the manner that I did so. She gave me a look of disgust and tossed her items in a pile on a rack to her left and, with her nose in the air, stormed out. I was a young guy who stunk of booze, so maybe she got offended. I don't know.

"I watched as she exited the store, somewhat amused by it all, and turned back to the clerk to see him glaring at me. What a look! Hell, I was just being nice, and here was this clerk staring at me like I was something he had scraped off the bottom of his shoe. So I laid a shot square on the side of his jaw, and down he went. I can still see him lying on the floor, coming around, and looking up at me. Only this time, his look was that of fear. All I heard coming from him was, "Take the money. Take the money." He said it twice, so I did.

"I reached over the counter into the already-open cash drawer and grabbed a large handful of bills. In my mind, this was not a robbery. This guy was just offering me an apology for treating me like dirt. We simply walked out of the store and down the street to where I lived. We did not even run. We walked, and it was hot as hell out.

"Not long after we went into the house, we heard a lot of commotion up the street, so we went up on the roof and worked our way along the rooftops until we were above the store where I had just decked the guy. We were looking down on the crowd that had gathered around the clerk who was talking to the police when, for some reason, he looked straight up at us and yelled, 'That's them!' It was only then that I realized I had screwed up.

"The block was surrounded, and a three-hour search was carried out. We pulled up a tarred down opening into a ceiling and pulled the top back in place. We lay there while several sets of footsteps tread back and forth over us, almost passing out from the heat in that ceiling. Chops threw up, and I came close to it. The police must have figured that we got off the roof before they were able to get it surrounded and figured we were long gone.

"It was just a matter of time before I got drunk again and got picked up by the cops. So instead of buying myself a new pair of slacks, I purchased a trip back to the Hill where I would do two and a half more years.

"I had only been to Pennypack Bounty Jail once. It was used as our county lockup until 1964, when they opened up the adult detention center on State Road across from Holmesburg Prison. I was housed for a couple of days before being transferred back to the Hill. The only incident arising during those few days came not long after I was assigned to my cell. I had arrived in the early morning hours and noticed that I had two cellmates who were fast asleep. It had been a long day, and I was coming off a bad drunk into a bad hangover combined with a heavy heart for my stupidity, so I crashed hard.

"That morning, I awoke to two Hispanic cellmates staring a me. I figured they were curious about what I had gotten busted over, and their stares were just curiosity. I swung my legs over the side of the bunk and looked down where I had put my shoes. Instead of my brand-new pair of high-top comforts, a popular shoe back then, there was a pair of beat-up, broken-down, worn-out shoes. I looked at the one who had my shoes on, and I became insane. All the rage I felt for having fucked up struck me, and I rose up and went for him at the same time telling him that I was going to tear his fucking face off. Suddenly, I was not the sleeping, maybe scared, white kid who had come in during the early morning hours, which I am sure was his impression as he checked out my shoes and sized me up.

"I only got in one shot before he was curled up on his bed in a fetal position, trying to get my shoes off while his friend kept saying, 'Chill out, man. You'll have the guard down here.' I told them to screw the chitchat and get my shoes off, or they would both be screaming for the guard. Needless to say, I got my shoes back. And to try and save face, he tried to pass it off as a joke. I am sure they thought I would call for the guard like scared inmates do, or pick up his raggedy shoes and put them on for everyone to see. That was not, nor was it ever, in my playbook.

"A couple of days later, we had a severe thunderstorm. This same inmate crawled under his bunk and cowered like a child. I told him to knock it off because I thought he was screwing around, and it was freaking weird. He was so serious that he almost cried. It took some convincing, but he turned out to be for real. And needless to say, he was embarrassed when the storm passed. Some tough guy. He gave me an explanation that his mother told him it was God causing the thunder when He was angry.

"Later on, he was eventually sent to the Hill, but I never acknowledged him. I did not like him. And now that he was new to my nest, thinking about him attempting to take my shoes may have caused me to revisit the incident and act on it. I did not need any more time over a punk like that. Screw him.

"A few days later, I was shipped back to Camp Hill Prison where I had to hear all about how the ink on my release was not even dry yet. I was given my original number, G-6432. I was back home."

CHAPTER 6

Camp Hill, Round 2

The next two and a half years went well for me. There was an occasional beef here and there but nothing I could not handle. I went back to work in the prison furniture factory; and if you had a problem with someone, a fight could be arranged without its being reported or broken up. We were only paid sixteen cents a day, but it kept you in snacks and smokes, which were the real prison currency. Since I never smoked, I was a wealthy man inside.

After a while, I was offered the position of Cadet Officer or CO. This was simply another term for trustee, and it meant working on your housing block in a position of trust and enforcement. We were required to "get the noise" if it got too loud on the block or if any inmates got out of hand. COs wore blue pants and shirts with a "CO" patch on the sleeve, while regular inmates wore khaki outfits. Our blues were starched and pressed in the prison laundry, and we looked great.

The COs also had a good understanding with the other cons because we were in a position to run a lot of favors for other inmates. If you wanted any position of respect on the inside, you had to have a solid contact out on the deck to communicate with after lockdown. As COs, we were only locked down after the late night count, so we were always out and about. Inmates were always asking you to deliver smokes or snacks or other necessities to other cons after lockdown. These could be payoffs or protection or simply part of the regular prison commerce. Sometimes, you took a percentage; sometimes, you did not. We liked doing it because it was a "you take care of me, I take care of you" thing. Plus, being a CO in blue automatically got you a lot of respect all over the institution no matter where you went.

There were about 180 inmates on each block, and six COs had to be relied on to get the respect of the rest of the population. One of the key requirements (besides not being a screwup, like I was my first term in) was that the officer recommending you for the position had to know that you could fight, and that you definitely would fight.

In the early days, if you were a CO and were called out by another inmate, a belt was laid out on top of the trash can outside of the shower room. Both inmates went in, and whoever came out and put on the belt was the CO. The difference later was if an inmate called you out, you had your backup stand watch, and the inmate's door was clicked open, and you went in on him and straightened him out. I remained CO the rest of my time at the Hill.

Out of the six COs on my block, there was me and one other white guy; the other four were black. The other white guy was in his late twenties, was a severe jazz head, and came across as being laid-back. He was well liked by the other inmates but could throw down if he had to. Of the four black COs, two were from West Philly, making them practically neighbors. One guy was from Forty-Ninth and Woodland, a grid that bordered my own neighborhood back home, and the other guy was from the "moon" section of West Philly. I had known both of these guys during my first stretch at the Hill and had even engaged in some body boxing with both of them, and now we had each other's back. As a result of doing so many years away with these guys, there were few areas in "the hood" that I could not visit when back on the streets in Philly.

CHAPTER 7

Back on the Streets a Second Time

When I went home for the second time after an almost five-year stay at the Hill, I was a little more inclined to enjoy the freedom of the streets and what it had to offer a twenty-year-old who had spent the majority of his life in one institution or another. I was back with the "2Cs." We had a pretty robust crowd in our neighborhood, and we partied a lot. Jack Conway was not around much; and when he was, he now knew better than to lay a hand on my mother or me. Other than drinking and fighting, I pretty much went straight for a while.

I got a job at a place called Repco, a carburetor rebuilding shop that was close to the house. I was making two dollars an hour, eighty dollars a week; but when Friday rolled around, and mom got her hands on room and board, there was not much left. I would mention that one positive note on my second stretch at Camp Hill was that I managed to obtain my GED, a general education diploma, through the Department of Public Instruction out of Harrisburg, Pennsylvania. I want to say that 1964 was the start of that program, but it was definitely the first time for Camp Hill. Nevertheless, two dollars an hour was the best it could get me.

Cheap wine and booze and hanging out with girls was a brief reward for a long week of standing at a work bench assembling springs, gas jets, and gas bowls. I started going with a girl named Fran Mahan, whom I had a serious crush on even before I went off to Camp Hill the first time. She was the first woman to make love to me, and make love to me is just what she did. Other than heavy make-out sessions, I had not yet been with a woman due to my long periods of incarceration. Fran told me that she would guide me through the moves so that I would not be clumsy or shy. I was comfortable with her, and the act of making love to her was amazing for a twenty-year-old kid whose life had been geared toward violence, not love.

We made love every day, and several times a day if we could get together. This was not just making up for lost time but because I was crazy about her and could not keep my hands off of her. We spent a lot of time together, and that kept me off the streets and home with her to some degree. She lived with her dad, whom I really liked. And despite my history of getting into trouble up until then, he treated me with respect, and I think he really liked me. He was a good man and was good to Fran and all of her siblings. Despite this, when Fran told me that she was pregnant, I was petrified.

I already knew that Fran had had a child prior to getting pregnant with me, but being only seventeen at the time, her mother took over and arranged for Fran to have the baby at a Catholic center, which would keep the baby afterward and adopt the child out to a good Catholic family. Fran had been seeing a neighborhood guy from our neighborhood crowd who, for whatever reason, had broken up with her or she with him, depending on who was telling the story. So instead of getting married, he went to Vietnam and never came back. This had all happened while I was at the Hill, but I knew all about it from neighborhood gossip, and I was okay with it. Knowing how her mom had dealt with things three years earlier, I asked Fran what her plans were. Though she was scared, and rightfully so, she said she wanted to keep our baby. My heart did leaps and bounds.

My daughter was born on August 2, 1966, and I was on cloud nine. I went to visit my daughter, and I was very nervous; but the moment I laid eyes on her, I fell in love with her. The magic of this moment was complicated and short-lived with all of her family members encircling me as though I was going to steal her away. Fran's brother, who was away at college on a football scholarship, had come home and was breathing down my neck like some goon. I was not bothered by him and thought, *Jesus, can Fran and I just share some time with our daughter together?* They said I could not even hold her because she was sleeping.

Now Fran's father was a different matter. He would gladly have welcomed me at any time in the hope that Fran and I would get married and become responsible parents. However, Fran's mother rose to the occasion and, showing her true colors, took over again. She made it clear that she did not want me in Fran or the baby's life. She thought she knew it all, yet when I look back on her situation, she was a failure as both a wife and a mother. She was both judgmental and extremely treacherous.

Not long after Charlene was born, I was offered a job as a mechanic's helper, sort of an apprenticeship that could have led to a great job. A friend of my mother's offered to drive Fran and me to Maryland where we could get married at age twenty without both of her parents' consent. Fran and I were both ecstatic. We were at this friend's house in Lansdowne, Pennsylvania, packed and ready to go when Fran decided to call her mother. Fran was warned that if she married me, she could never come home again. If it did not work out or if we fell on hard times, she could never again come to her family for help.

I was devastated. I begged Fran to have faith. I was already seeing us raising our daughter together; and with my working as an apprentice in a good profession, we would soon be putting a great life together. However, Fran panicked and not only let her mother throw a monkey wrench into our lives but into the life of our daughter. After that, everything changed. Not only did we not get married, but I was no longer welcome in her parents' home, and everything went downhill from there.

I started hanging out with the local misfits again, which Fran did not like one bit. Trouble between us began, and we started to see each other less and less. Our group would go to the clubs in downtown Center City, Philly; and after a while, we were known well enough by the owners and the assigned bouncers that if there was a problem with another rowdy crew, we were asked to help out. We were a rough crew, and I cannot count the number of fights that we got into. Even on the subway going home in the early morning hours, we would come into contact with other gangs and crews that were just as worked up as we were, and it was on. Many a night, the police had to board the subway trains and ride the route just to keep us separated.

I still saw Fran and Charlene but not very often. I no longer felt comfortable around her family, so my visits consisted of showing up with a little money and taking a walk around the block with the two of them. Then one night, it all started again for me. I had lost my job and was tired of being broke. So I got a pistol off of my sister's fiancé and paid a visit to "Uncle Nick's," a neighborhood supermarket.

I waited until after dark and watched from a distance as the local foot cop made his rounds. Once he disappeared around the corner, I made my move. I stood in line at the store, waiting on the woman in front of me to complete her transaction. The woman had two children with her, and I found myself wishing there had been another register open, but it was late, and this was the only one. I had no money in my pocket, so once I got to the counter, I could not call it off by making a simple purchase of some small item. I was all in.

Before the woman in front of me could leave, the clerk, who was an older woman, asked if she could help me. I leaned in close to her and pulled the .45 from my pocket, keeping it down by my side but only where she could see it. I told her to step back from the cash drawer. I leaned over the counter and grabbed two handfuls of large bills and started stuffing them into my pockets. The drawer was full, and as I grabbed a third handful, a really large man who was stocking shelves noticed what was going on and stopped to look. I turned toward him so he could see my weapon, and he went back to stocking canned goods. The lady in front of me just pulled her children close to her, told them to stay still, and looked the other way.

I was a mess, and my heart started racing like it would blow out of my chest. After grabbing all the cash, I went to the front door and stepped on the black floor mat that controlled the automatic door and nothing happened. I thought that the clerk had hit a switch to turn it off, but I just was not stepping all the way onto the mat. The clerk yelled, "You have to stand all the way on the mat." I did, and the door opened.

I was less than five blocks from home and had planned an escape route. I was out the door and around the corner through a schoolyard. I crossed an open field, scaled a fence, and I was home. I ran so fast that I think I was home before the store clerk was off the phone with the police. I counted the money and found that I had eight hundred dollars—ten weeks' pay with no taxes taken out. That was a gold mine to me.

I had never done anything like that before, an armed robbery against an innocent citizen; it was really scary. I knew in my heart and mind that I would never have shot anyone in that store. If I was cornered, I would fight anyone and try to get away, but I knew that I could never take the life of an innocent person. The gun was just to scare the clerk and the other people in the store, and it did the job.

It was not long before the police were looking for me. At first, I wondered how they figured out it was me as I had no previous record for armed robbery. Then I remembered that earlier that evening, while I was waiting for it to get dark and for the store to clear out, I happened to run into a guy I knew hanging out in front of his house. We talked out on his stoop for about an hour and at one point noticed my gun. Hell, a .45 hanging out of your pants pocket is pretty hard to hide, even with your shirt pulled out. He asked what I was doing carrying a gun, and I made up a story that I was going to sell it to a guy that I was to meet later than night.

I guess that had made him suspicious, so it was only natural that when he saw the cops speeding down the street to the supermarket, he walked down to see what was going on and figured out it was me. He was a John Q. Citizen, not a guy living the life, so I was not surprised when I found out later that he was the one who ratted me out. Of course, he knew my name and described my weapon and what I was wearing, all of which matched the description that the clerk had given them. The cops were on to me from the start. In fact, in the next couple of months that it took the cops to catch up to me, they were showing my mug shot to every robbery victim in that part of the city.

There was way too much heat in my neighborhood, and I was not about to hang around to catch any of it. So I headed to North Philly up to Kensington where my friend Billy McBride lived. Billy was a freelance burglar and a great second story man. He was apparently doing pretty well and had a nice apartment. He lived alone, so it was a safe place for me to lay my head. As I said before, I knew Billy when I was away; and since he had never come down to my neighborhood, no one there knew him. It was like I had just disappeared.

I just laid low, and everything was quiet for the next week or so. Then Mike Palumbo showed up. Of course, Mike and I had grown up together and had been in the Catholic protectory together. He had been the one to square things up for me after I had dealt with my problem back at Camp Hill with Big Bill Wilby. We had all three done time at the Hill together, had a strong history, knew we could trust each other, and were really close. Mike and I did some stickups to keep us in petty cash while Billy set up a string of burglaries that we would all pull off together. We were definitely living the life. No one in this neighborhood knew me, so as long as I avoided the cops, I could run the roads and do what I wanted.

Every now and then, Mike and I would sneak back down to Southwest Philly and visit his sister and brother-in-law. We would just hang out there a few days, visiting and partying and catching up with what was going on in the neighborhood. Then one day, Mike got the bright idea to hold up a hardware store that was only about three blocks from the supermarket that I had stuck up a month or so earlier—not a bright idea. On top of that, the only weapon we had was a blank gun. For some reason, I went along with it. In those days, I figured my life was on temporary anyway, and I was beginning to think my time was becoming severely limited. Never thinking that I would live to see twenty-five, I said, "What the hell."

That hardware store was right in the middle of a busy block of stores. It was the middle of the afternoon, and everyone was out shopping. The plan was to do the robbery, blend into the crowd, and quietly walk back to the house. We did not want anyone to see us running, and no one would have noticed where we went.

When we entered the store, we noticed that the only person in there was a young male clerk about our age, so we thought it was going to be simple, a quick in and out deal. However, the moment Mike stuck the gun in the kid's face, he said, "Yeah, right, a blank gun."

I almost broke out in a fit of laughter, but Mike then got real serious with him. Like I said before about Mike Palumbo, he could and would hurt you. I heard him say, "Open the fucking cash drawer or when I'm done with you, your own mother won't recognize you."

We were at the rear of the store, so we could not be seen by the people out on the street, which was busy with pedestrians. The kid was stubborn, and I still can't believe another customer did not come in. Finally, after a little more convincing from Mike, the kid opened the drawer, and I scooped up the cash while Mike kept a hold on him and told him to stay in the store.

Mike and I walked out of the store calm as you please and started zigzagging through the traffic. No sooner than we were across the street, the kid came out of the store, beaten up and screaming that he had been robbed. A crowd quickly gathered around him, so he was unable to leave the front of the store, which was lucky for us; otherwise, we would have been caught out on the street in open daylight. As it was, we were able to blend into the crowd across the street, and within just a few minutes, we were safely back in Mike's sister's house. Within seconds of closing the front door, the neighborhood was crawling with cops, no doubt showing my picture to the clerk.

His sister's house was right on the railroad and backed up to a four-lane track system. As we peeked out through the curtains, we could see the neighbors pointing toward the tracks. Apparently, no one had noticed us walk into the house; and since those tracks were heavily traveled by people on foot, they must have thought that we had run out of the neighborhood along the rails. The cops must have thought so too because we braced ourselves for a house-to-house search that never came. We stayed inside for the next twenty-four hours and then got Mike's brother-in-law to drive us back to North Philly the next night.

During this time that we were hiding out in Kensington at Billy's place was when I noticed Mike was starting to get into heroin. I was shocked at first. None of us had ever used drugs. The only partying we did involved drinking, not dope. I did not know anything about heroin, but I did know that putting a needle in the crook of your arm was not cool. Mike swore he was just "chipping," a term used when it was a once-in-a-while thing. Then I started to notice other guys doing it. This was the late 1960s, and the shit was turning into an epidemic. Hell, it seemed Billy and I were the only two not doing it, and we wanted no part of it.

I saw Mike getting worse and worse on the poison and knew it was a matter of time before it took over his life, but he would not listen to anybody. Billy knew it was just a matter of time before the drugs would bring the heat down on all of us, so he moved on. Mike and I did one more job together, along with a guy named Tommy Becker, at a small variety store; but after that, I was not going to work with a guy that I could no longer trust, so I decided to get away from that environment. I sure as hell was not into watching all these dudes shooting up and then sitting around nodding for hours until it was time to go out and get another bag, so I went back to Southwest Philly and hid out at my sister's apartment.

I should mention that Mike had met a wonderful girl and had gotten married just before he had gotten back together with Billy and me. I felt sorry for her. She was living alone out in Darby with him never there and her working to pay the bills. Mike also had a fantastic set of loving parents who went to bat for him every time he got into trouble. They hired Charles Peruto, one of the top criminal lawyers in the city of Philadelphia, who had a reputation for being a mob lawyer. Both of Mike's parents worked, and I think it took every penny they had to keep Mike out of jail on more than one occasion.

Not long after I got to my sister's house, Fran showed up with our baby for a visit. I still do not know if she suspected that I was there or if she was just trying to locate me, but we spent a great afternoon together. It was just Fran, our daughter Charlene, my sister, and her husband. It was great seeing the baby there at my sister's place with no pressure from Fran's family, no standing of the guard monitoring my every action. It was probably the best afternoon that I had spent with Charlene since she had been born.

Less than an hour after Fran left, we heard footsteps racing up the stairs. It sounded like a herd of wild horses. I knew what it was and who had orchestrated it. We were on the third floor, and there was nowhere for me to go. I climbed into the closet, still hoping it was not a raid but knowing in my heart and mind that it was all over. When my sister opened the door, the police said that they had a call about a disturbance in the apartment and needed to check the place out. They went straight to the closet.

Fran had been made to believe that she could not get assistance for the baby unless I was brought before the family court. She knew that I was running from the law on a robbery charge and should have known that turning me in was not going to get her anything, just me sent to prison.

I was charged with the robbery of Uncle Nick's Supermarket and held without bond. I was surprised to find out that that was the only charge. No one even questioned me or asked me about anything else at all.

CHAPTER 8

Holmesburg

November 18, 2015

Holmesburg Prison was a shithole of a prison even by prison shithole standards. Built before the Civil War, it resembles a midlevel fortress more than a twentieth-century correctional facility. After a series of riots beginning July 4, 1970, the prison was finally closed in 1995.

Bojack went into Holmesburg in December 1966 at the age of twenty, having already spent most of the last five years in and out of adult prisons for a series of robberies. Prison was not a big deal for the young gangster. Most of the inmates were from the Philadelphia area and hung out in "neighborhoods" while in prison, just as they had on the street. The practical effect of this was that after a year or two, an inmate would have connections all over the city. Having spent the last fifteen years living on the streets and in various correctional institutions, the opportunity was not wasted on Bojack.

The ability to network and put together an organization was nothing new to Bojack, as evidenced by the tattoo "2C" on his right wrist. The 2C crew took its name from the intersection of Second Street and Cumberland Avenue, the largest intersection in the crew's neighborhood.

After being released from Camp Hill State Prison in 1965, Bojack started putting together this crew. By the time he went back inside in December 1966, a dozen members wore the "2C" mark, establishing themselves as potential young up-and-comers in the Philadelphia underworld. Today, Jack Saltarelli is the only living member of the "2C" crew.

During his two-year stay at "the 'Burg," Bojack would get two more tattoos, including "Charlene" on his inner forearm to commemorate the birth of his daughter—or as he explained, "the only girl I would put on me." He made that statement to me in August of 2014. By November of 2015, he was planning on having it removed. "I'm sixty-nine years old. I gotta live with memories. That's all I got." Such is the life of Bojack.

At the same time, he had "Bojack" and a pair of boxing gloves inked on his outer forearm. Years later in Terre Haute Federal Prison, he would have a woman tattooed on his back after paying a Mexican inmate two cartons of cigarettes to tattoo him. Appropriately, the woman is nameless, simply an image picked from a book of samples the inmate had to choose from.

Holmesburg was used to process prisoners to other facilities around the state who were serving long sentences, so most of the guys who were there doing their time were "short timers," doing two to eight years. Bojack describes it as "a cold ass place," surrounded by stone walls, concrete, and iron bars. According to Bojack, survival in Holmesburg was no different than any other prison. "You went in with a decent name, and you survived." The basic rules of survival were, "Don't get in people's business. Don't be an ass. Stand up for yourself."

Holmesburg also offered boxing, and Bojack got involved, rising up in the middleweight division. A number of outstanding boxers came out of the 'Burg, including a heavyweight named Jessie Smith who "dropped Sonny Liston," one of the most underrated champions in history who had also gotten his start in Missouri State Penitentiary while serving two concurrent five-year terms for armed robbery. Boxing was a fast way to win respect on the inside. Although there was no money to be made, it established your place in prison society. However, there were other legitimate ways to make money and do easy time.

Jack started painting on a maintenance crew, which did their work at night when the other inmates were on lockdown. This enabled the painters to sneak into the kitchen for extra food. Scrambled eggs and bacon were what Jack went after, and there was even an occasional steak left over from the guards or for "special" inmates. But the real cash cow for inmates was the University of Pennsylvania.

The Perelman School of Medicine at the University of Pennsylvania, through its department of dermatology, was running tests on inmates. The tests were under the supervision of Dr. Zerby and ran the gamut from soaking your hands in dishwater for an hour to being injected with skin cancer. The inmates exposed to cancer were paid a flat two-thousand-dollar-fee. Jack was paid 150 dollars to be injected with blood poisoning, but most of the jobs paid a dollar a day. Despite the risks, these jobs were popular and hard to obtain. You had to give the inmate who assigned the jobs a taste of what you were paid, usually five dollars out of every thirty dollars you made. Bojack volunteered for every job he could get and sent hundreds of dollars in child support home to Charlene and her mother.

Holmesburg Prison was a medieval and morbid place. In the 1800s, it was designed with one idea in mind: to beat you down both mentally and emotionally. Although I can only speculate at what the ultimate intention of the founders was, I can tell you it was certainly not rehabilitation.

I was sent to Holmesburg in December 1966 at the age of twenty on a four-year sentence to be followed by six years of postrelease supervision. This meant that I could make parole in two years, be on parole for two years, then finish out the other six years on PRS.

Unlike a lot of people, I wanted to do my time at the 'Burg. Parole was a lot easier to make at Holmesburg because the prison was not designed for lengthy sentences, and most guys were doing two- to eight-year hitches. If I had been in Graterford State Prison or any of the other five Pennsylvania state prisons, the parole board would have probably denied at least once or maybe both times that I would come up for parole during a four-year sentence. They would have known that they would have to supervise me for an additional six years after making me serve the whole four years on the first charge.

So it was in my best interest to take a split sentence, four years to serve on the armed robbery of Uncle Nick's Supermarket to be followed by six years of probation for the assault and strong-arm robbery of the hardware store. So even though I was getting what amounted to a ten-year sentence, I could be a model prisoner and be out on the street in just two years.

There was also the chance to make money doing regular prison jobs and as a test subject for the University of Pennsylvania medical school. Besides, I would be doing my time right there in my hometown of Philly, and I would be able to see my mom, brother, two sisters, and hopefully my daughter on occasion. However, the last one never came to be.

Despite these advantages, I knew Holmesburg would not be a cakewalk. I was in the company of Philly's worst offenders. In some respects, they were local celebrities. But we all had one thing in common, and that was all of our lives and futures were balanced on a very fine thread. Violence could erupt at any moment, and you always had one eye on your back.

As I said before, your reputation follows you from one prison to another. I had just spent the better part of five years in Camp Hill Prison, three of those years as a CO, and the name "Bojack" all came with me. Besides, I was there on charges of armed robbery and assault, both violent crimes that marked you as a guy to be treated with respect. So all in all, I found myself surrounded by good neighbors.

In the two years I spent in Holmesburg, I noticed that there was a rash of union guys getting whacked and others getting arrested for murder as common as catching the flu. Rocco Turra, whom I admired as one of the toughest dudes in the city, was in and out of the 'Burg in those days. They say that Rocco was connected with Angelo Bruno, who they say was the godfather of the Philly family. Either way, the charges on Rocco would disappear, and Rocco would leave us.

Years later, they said Rocco turned informant, and I guess he could not live with it because he hung himself in his cell. Rocco was never afraid of anything and was the kind of guy who loved life and really lived it. I cannot fathom him taking his own life, but he was found hanging in his cell from a rope made out of sheets, and it was ruled a suicide. Life is what it is.

Another guy awaiting trial for murder was Jack Lopinson. Jack was a nightclub owner from downtown Philly and was told that his business partner was having an affair with his wife. Jack hired a local shooter known as Phelan to come into the club's office and kill the partner and wife and to make it look like a late-night robbery. However, Jack was planning a double cross and busted in on Phelan with the intent of killing him and making it look like he had happened to walk in and kill a robber. But Phelan must have smelled a foul deal and was ready for Jack, shooting him in the face. Jack survived and went on to face murder for hire charges.

One of the more infamous guys charged with murder that I walked the tier with was Anthony "Mad Dog" DiPasquale, who was charged with the murders of two union reps. He was found not guilty on these and other charges over the years. After all, I cannot imagine anyone wanting to testify against "Mad Dog." I heard later, in the mid-70s, that he was running amuck in the city, robbing drug dealers. I sent him word where I was working, and we never had a problem. We had always respected each other in the 'Burg, and that spilled over onto the street when he got out.

When I look back on the life that I lived and the environments I lived in, I wonder how I ever considered my life anything close to normal or acceptable. My life was what it was from the age of eight right up to fairly present times. Sharing a tier with the city's most infamous killers and mobsters seemed like a natural flow of life for me. I guess it was no different for their sharing the same tier with a young armed robber who would have killed anyone if provoked. In that world, what goes around comes around, and I kept my good name—Bojack.

CHAPTER 9

One More Time Around

"I was released from Holmesburg Prison in December 1968 after making parole in two years, but like I said, 'The 'Burg wasn't designed to rehabilitate anyone.'

"One of the first things I did when I got out of the 'Burg was to look up my old running buddy Bobby Borshell. Bobby was a professional burglar from out in the Kensington area of Philly. He was a freelancer but had a lot of connections with the old K&A Gang, with whom he had done a lot of work, and had learned to perfect the crime of burglary down to an art."

The K&A Gang, which is alleged to be the forerunner of the current Northeast Philly Irish Mob, was an almost-all Irish-American criminal organization who took its name from the Kensington and Allegheny Street intersection. The gang had formed shortly after World War II, and this type of naming technique became popular among street gangs all over Philadelphia for the next three decades from guys wanting to emulate their success. This was the inspiration for Jack's 2C crew that he organized after his first release from Camp Hill.

Although the gang is reputed to have started out exclusively as a burglary ring, it is alleged that it did not take them long to expand into loan-sharking and gambling; and by the 1970s, they were alleged to be the main source and muscle behind the methamphetamine explosion that took over Philadelphia. By the late 1960s, the K&As had established professional burglary rings in every city along the East Coast and were the muscle behind John McCullough, president of the Philadelphia Roofers Union Local 30, a close friend and associate of Jimmy Hoffa as well as that of Hoffa's closest friend, admitted Mafia enforcer and hitman Frank "The Irishman" Sheeran.

It is also reputed that several members of the K&A Gang moved into North Carolina where they began a collaboration with the Dixie Mafia and jointly spread their influence across the south. Their fearlessness and reputation for violence allowed them to gain respect and form alleged ties with the Philadelphia Greek Mob and even the Irish Republican Army. This reputation and network led the Philadelphia family of Les Cosa Nostra to form an alliance with the K&As rather than take them on directly in a war, which is said to have led to other alliances with the Genovese and Gambino families of New York.

* * * * *

Jack Saltarelli

The Kensington area in North Philly was the toughest neighborhood in the city. South Philly was all Italian in those days. And for the most part, still is, except for a large black community that started moving up from the south after the war. The Italians ran their businesses and their neighborhoods, and there were guys who would shoot you down in a heartbeat. But for sheer physical toughness, the real badasses were the Irish. They didn't need a gun. They were big and strong and would beat you to death with a ball bat, a pipe or even their bare hands. If you got into a jam with the Italians, you had a chance to get someone to negotiate for you and to buy your way out of trouble. But not with the Irish. If you got turned around with them, you were gone right there on the spot or at least before the next morning.

When I looked up Bobby, he and three other guys were putting together a five-man burglary and walk-in team. Bobby and I had done time together, and both knew the other to be a stand-up guy. We also both knew that they had found their fifth man. Bobby had learned a lot through his affiliations with the K&A Gang, who were the most professional burglars on the East Coast and were known for "working on insurance policies." This meant that they had people working on the inside of insurance agencies, sometimes the agent himself, who knew exactly what was covered under a particular policy. Everything had to be listed individually on the policy along with its value; this included jewelry, coins, stamps, and even art work. It all had to be verified by the agent. The agent had to know what kind of alarm system was in place, if there were any security cameras or dogs, as well as how many people lived in the house. All of this had to be proven to qualify for a lesser premium on the policy.

A lot of these homes were in Philly, but many of them were upstate with a lot of rich people having two or even more houses, so it was nothing to travel a couple of hundred miles to do a job. The beauty of this was that you knew everything there was to know about a job before you ever left home. It sure beat the hell out of entering a house blind, hoping to find something of value while not setting off an alarm or being eaten up by an attack dog in the process. We also had professional fences to move anything we heisted.

We each got shares with another share going for "expenses." Whoever was on the inside with the insurance company got ten percent right off the top. You would be out of business without that guy, so you had to keep him happy. There were also other people who had to be taken care of, whether it was protection from crooked cops or the K&A Gang or the Italian Mob—I did not know, and I did not want to know. Bobby Borshell took care of all that. All I knew was that once the job was done, I got my share, and it was never light.

I said before we were both a burglary and a walk-in team. The purpose of a dual team was that you had some guys who were burglars and did just that. They got you into the house or business, past the alarms, and into the safe. However, we also had walk-in guys, or stickup guys; that way, if you traveled a couple of hundred miles to do a job only to learn that the people were home, the trip was not wasted. You just turned the burglary into an armed robbery. I always thought that the robbery worked better anyway, because the chances of getting what you came for were better. If the people had gone out of town, they may have taken their most expensive jewelry and furs with them. Also, if your guy had trouble opening the safe, well, you just convinced the owner to open it.

I had been with Bobby's crew about three months, and things were going well. I should have known it would not last. Sometime in March of 1969, I was approached by a guy named James "Jigs" Cordisio about a robbery that promised big money. Jigs was a gambler and small-time hustler from South Philly who wanted to move up in the world. I had met Jigs a couple of times through my sister Lil as he was a friend of her husband's. He was occasionally dating a friend of Lil's. The girl was young and very attractive, and she would use his car when he was off on two- and three-day card games. I had started seeing the same girl off and on and had been told that Jigs had been pretty upset when he found out about it; but for some reason, the subject never came up between us.

Then one day, out of the blue, Jigs comes to me with this robbery. A guy named William Hildreth was a small-time gambler whose day job was at the Philadelphia Quartermaster Depot on Oregon Avenue. The guy owed Jigs a lot of money and knew Jigs was starting to lose his patience. The guy had bartered information to Jigs to pay off part of his debt. Every morning, a car left the Quartermaster Depot, crossed Oregon Avenue, and went through a residential neighborhood on its way to the bank. The car had a driver and an armed guard in the front and two or three civilian employees in the back. The civilian employees were carrying bags of cash to the bank and supposedly had one hundred thousand dollars or more every day. According to Hildreth, the car took a different route every day; and for some reason, they never locked the doors. We scouted the government vehicle and followed it every time it rolled off the compound headed for the bank. Sure enough, true to our information, they never took the same route two days in a row, but they only had about three routes that they used.

Looking back on this, I cannot believe I was stupid enough to get involved in this. After all, what faster way can you bring the government, especially the federal government, down on you than taking their money. But, hey, I was young, just twenty-three years old, and only out of prison for a few months. I wanted to make up for lost time, and a hundred grand in cash split four ways sounded pretty damn good to me. Jigs also said that he came to me with this because I was the only guy he knew "with the balls to do this thing." Well, being young and dumb, that swelled my ego, and I was all in.

Like I said, Jigs was a "downtown guy" looking to make a bigger name for himself, and he ran with a young sidekick called Ray. Ray was to be part of the crew for this robbery because Jigs wanted another downtown guy watching his back. I did not blame him; we had never done a piece of work together, and the only person I trusted watching my back was Bobby Borshell.

The four of us took turns scouting out the payroll vehicle and decided that one particular route was best for a robbery in broad daylight. It took them down a narrow Philly street in a residential neighborhood. All of the people around here were old-school Italians, so we knew when the cops came around, no one would have seen anything. There was a two-block long park at one point with trees down both sides and very little traffic. We agreed that we would set up on this one route by the park and every morning be ready to go when the car came our way. We had set up two days; and when the time for them to come by had passed, we went home.

On the second night, the temperature dropped, and a fresh layer of snow fell. As we stood around in place on that third morning in freezing weather, we saw our target turn onto our street. It was go time.

The car was moving slow because of the icy roads and stopped at the intersection next to the park. They eased on through the stop sign and came down past the park. About halfway down, Jigs and Ray were waiting in a car parked parallel to the curb. When the target car got to the right point, they pulled out blocking their way. At that moment, Bobby and I, who were hiding behind large trees on opposite sides of the road, jumped out and went into action. Bobby snatched open the driver's door, stuck a gun in his face, then reached in and shut off the engine. At that exact moment, I snatched open the passenger door, stuck my .45 in in the guard's ribs, and relieved him of his weapon.

This is the part of the job where your intel can make you or get you killed. Hildreth had worked as one of the passengers and, like I said, knew that for some reason, they never locked the doors. If this had been wrong, we would have been standing in the street pulling on doors that would not open, and the driver could have simply thrown the car in reverse and backed out of there; or Bobby might have shot him, and we would have all been facing a murder charge. We also knew that the guard in the front passenger seat was the only one with a weapon, and it was a handgun in a holster on his right hip. If in fact he had been armed with a shotgun or a Thompson across his lap, he would cut me in half when I yanked the door open. As it was, I took him completely by surprise; and with my gun in his chest, I was able to easily grab the gun off of his right hip. Bobby grabbed the canvas bags of money off the back seat while I told everyone to stay in the car for ten minutes and not get out. That fast, we were gone.

We took off down a side street where we had a car parked less than a block away, facing the opposite direction. As we neared the car, we slowed to a casual walk, got inside, and drove away. Our plan was to meet up at Jigs's place on the lower side of South Philly and split up the loot The problem was when we got to Jigs's, the only thing we had was two canvas bags and the guard's gun. That is when it dawned on me that there had been three people in the back of the car, so there should have been three canvas bags. We only had two canvas bags, mostly stuffed with checks, only about twenty-five thousand dollars in cash. Right off the bat, I could tell that Jigs had his doubts that we had only taken two bags and thought we were holding out on him.

All I knew was that I had done my job. I had snatched open that door, faced down and disarmed the only armed passenger, and drove the second getaway car that Bobby and I had made our escape in. We were later vindicated that night when the evening news carried the story, and the joke was on us. One of the rear passengers had been a woman. When she saw us charging the car, she shoved the third canvas bag under her and had sat on it throughout the robbery. Not only had she saved the bag, but it had been the main bag with over fifty thousand dollars cash inside. She thought she was funny that she had outwitted her robbers; but sitting at home watching the evening news, I think I laughed even harder than she did. But the laugh did not last long.

It does not matter if you get one dollar or one million dollars in an armed robbery. What matters is that it was armed robbery, which is a capital offense. And in any case, the victim is pissed and wants their money back. If the victim is the United States Government, you are in a world of hurt. The response was unbelievable.

FBI Agent Buck Revell, head of anti-terrorism for the state of Pennsylvania, was assigned to hunt us down. This was the late 1960s, and there were a number of left-wing terrorist groups hitting banks and armored cars to finance their terrorist activities against the United States Government, so this case was made a major priority. When none of these groups stepped up to claim the robbery, Agent Revell started going after every heavyweight mob guy and stickup man in the city. However, it would turn out to be an absolute quirk how he lucked up so fast and got my identity.

It turned out that Bobby Borshell's kid brother Mike knew about the heist. Bobby had been promising Mike a place in our crew, or at least one of our jobs. We had put those jobs on hold, thinking this would be a really big all-cash job, until this one was behind us. We did not invite Mike in on this job because he clearly did not have the brains or the balls for this type of robbery; plus, we only needed four people. Bobby had also promised to toss Mike something out of his end for waiting if this federal job turned out to be as big as we thought. Myself, I never would have told Mike anything. But Bobby was his brother, so he trusted him.

When Mike could not get in with us, he joined another crew of rank amateurs involved in sticking up a doctor and his wife in their home in Northeast Philly. The crew took the doctor and his wife by surprise and succeeded in getting everything that they wanted, so the result should have been leaving the house quietly with the doctor and his wife tied up and getting away to steal another day. However, one of those idiots, the one who later ratted out Mike Borshell, was nice enough to let the wife use the bathroom and close the door for privacy. He was also stupid enough not to check for a telephone in the bathroom first. Needless to say, the police were waiting outside when they exited the house, and a shoot-out took place right there on the front lawn. A police officer was killed by one of the robbers, and the robber was taken out by the other officers. Jesus, what an insane mess.

Mike had gotten out on bond despite the charge of murdering a law enforcement officer. This was a fresh standout case when Agent Revell looked at who might know something about our job. It turned out to be a great break for Revell; he got our only weak link right from the start. All they had to do was threaten to take away Mike's bond, and he started to sing. All Mike had to do was keep his mouth shut and sit in jail a few days until his lawyer could get his bond reinstated, but he ratted on us all—even his own brother.

I had never liked Mike Borshell and sure as hell never trusted him. Months before the federal payroll heist, I had seen his true colors. Some of us from our crew went out drinking one night with some other friends, and Mike had tagged along. We were in a neighborhood lounge. I was seated at the bar, and the rest of our group was playing pool in the back when some of the K&A Gang busted through the door, demanding to know where in the hell was a guy named Mickey who hung out with us. The guy at the front announced that Mickey had tried to rape one of their female relatives, and he was there to set it right and for no one to interfere. He then grabbed a pool stick and went to town on Mickey while the rest of his crew kept everybody at bay.

Now as far as I was concerned, I was not going to protect any rapist or other type of pervert or sex offender. Even if he had been part of our crew, he was on his own on this one, no matter how close I was with his brother. The problem with this was that the K&A Gang did not know this. The guy who stepped up behind me was a character named Charlie Devlin.

Charlie Devlin was reputed to be the number one button man and enforcer for the K&A Gang and had a reputation for being an animal. He was about six feet four inches and over 250 pounds of solid muscle. He had already had a reputation for being a tough, ruthless street fighter as well as a cold-blooded killer when two guys tried to make a hit on him. One guy's gun jammed, and Charlie took it away from him and beat him to a pulp with it. Meanwhile, the other guy, who had pumped two bullets into Charlie, panicked and ran. Charlie, who was unarmed, chased him down and was beating him to a pulp when Charlie finally passed out from the loss of blood. Charlie had a rep as a guy who could not be killed.

I had met Charlie during my time in Holmesburg. He had been in and out on several charges, all of which he had beaten. So we knew each other on a casual basis. Every time he was brought in, his head was bandaged, and it was said that it took four to six cops to bring him in. I do not know if they had told Charlie to watch me or if he had selected me out himself. Either way, here I am at twenty-three, sitting at a bar, staring into a mirror and into the eyes of the most ruthless hitman in the city.

His face reflected the fights he had been in with scars and a deformed ear. He had the coldest and most menacing eyes that I have ever seen. There was no mistake; this guy was a flat-out stone killer.

I was wearing a leather trench coat, and when the K&As had busted in, I had slid my hand inside and around my Colt .45, and I was not about to turn loose. He could not see my eyes as I was wearing a pair of mirrored sunglasses, but I felt like he could look straight through them and into my soul. I don't know how long we just stared each other down through that mirror, but it seemed like forever. I was just sitting there, knowing that if he made a single move, my only chance would be to empty that weapon into him and hope I didn't miss.

Finally, the guy came out of the back room and said, "let's go."

That's when Charlie said, "We're cool, Bojack."

And I said, "We're cool, Charlie."

And he walked out.

A few years later, some guys finally did hit Charlie. He had gotten into a beef with another Irish Mob guy, an old-time con who would not let something go. The guy and his crew shot Charlie five times in the back after luring him to a house where a party was supposed to take place. When they were carrying him out to the car to dispose of the body, they realized that he was still alive, so they chained his feet to the bumper and dragged him up and down the street. At this point, he was still alive, so they finished him off with ball bats.

Regardless, I was the first one picked up by the FBI and charged with armed robbery for the Quarterhouse Depot hit. I denied everything but was taken to the Adult Detention Center on a parole violation since I was out on paper. As I was being processed in, before I got to lockdown, I saw Mike Borshell, who was being released. The first thing he shouted as soon as he saw me was, "I didn't rat on you guys."

It hit me. *Why would he say that?* I had no idea who had turned us in until that moment. Now I had no doubt. I was held in the ADC for a couple of days then transferred to Holmesburg Prison as an escape risk. I sat there for the next year, awaiting a court date before I finally pled guilty.

I was more than ready to get sentenced on my charges and get transferred to a federal institution. With the year that I had just put in at Holmesburg, plus the two I had just done for the 1966 robberies, I was over the place. I knew everybody that mattered at the 'Burg and had no safety issues, but I knew federal time would be much better. Not just better food and more comfortable facilities but actual programs to further your education and prepare for life on the outside. The dark-gray stone walls of Holmesburg were starting to close in on me, especially since I knew there was something better awaiting.

CHAPTER 10

Doing Federal Time

Playing with the Big Boys

This was my fourth time to go down on a felony; and since my first three times had involved multiple charges, I knew it would not go well. I was given twenty-five years with a B number and sent to Lewisburg Federal Prison. Twenty five years. Christ, I had just turned twenty-four years old awaiting sentencing; this was longer than I had even been alive.

Lewisburg was a maximum security prison located in upstate Pennsylvania and was made up of some of the East Coast's most celebrated mob guys. The first impression I got of this place was when I was being delivered to processing on the day that I arrived. One of the first people that I saw was Jimmy Hoffa. Hoffa worked in the mattress shop, making mattresses, doing his time like everyone else. I worked making deliveries to the various shops around Lewisburg. I often delivered rolls of canvas and other materials to the mattress shop, and there was Jimmy processing the paperwork. There were plenty of mob guys there: Anthony "Tony Pro" Provonsono, who is reputed to have been one of the people responsible for Hoffa's disappearance years later, as well as a guy named John Gotti, who was nothing big at the time but would later go on to his own fame and fortune in the 1980s, only to die on the inside a decade later.

Lewisburg would be made famous in the 1990s by the movie *GoodFellas,* based on the life of Henry Hill. True to the movie, the mob guys lived a lot better than the rest of us in their own section. For the rest of us, Lewisburg was strict rules and lockdown. The rules in Lewisburg were the same as any other prison. You had to stand up for yourself; but with so many mob guys around, you had to be careful and know who was who. The mob guys usually stayed to themselves; and if you had a beef, you negotiated. You could not just take a made guy's head off like he was any other con; there would be repercussions. Besides, Lewisburg was not a fighting place; it was a killing place.

As I said, I had been given twenty-five years with a B number. The "B" number that accompanied my sentence meant that after four to six months, I would be returned to federal court in Philadelphia to appear before my original sentencing judge for a possible reduction in sentence. I was fortunate in that I was assigned to Judge Masterson, who was known for being fair.

In those days, there were no Federal Sentencing Guidelines, and judges were given free rein. I had heard stories about judges asking a defendant to count the pigeons on the window ledge outside of the courtroom and then giving them either that many years or maybe even twice that many years. Who knows if that was true. It was a different time.

Since I was going in front of Judge Masterson, I asked to speak, and he listened to everything that I had to say. I was the youngest member of the robbery crew. My partner Bobby had been given four years; Cordisio, two; and Ray, a first offender with a good lawyer, had gotten off with probation.

The judge was thinking about giving me five years, so I explained that I had a detainer from the Pennsylvania state parole board, which would require me to do the two-year balance from the 1966 charges, which in fact would mean a seven-year sentence. Normally, a federal sentence does not take into consideration other pending state time, but I had to take my chance. The judge took pity on me and gave me a three-year sentence. I knew that my crime was serious, and that I would be maxing out my sentence—no parole—but three years beat the hell out of twenty-five. I did not know it at the time, but my luck had started to turn for the better.

While I was awaiting resentencing in the summer of 1970, I was being housed in the Philadelphia Adult Detention Center. After my resentencing, I was to be transferred to Holmesburg and then eventually back to Lewisburg to finish my federal time. While at the ADC, I managed to work my way into a job in the inmate processing room, operating the camera for mug shots, which meant that I could stay in the ADC until the federal marshals came to take me back to Lewisburg sometime in the next one to three months.

My job was to photograph all of the inmates as they came into the facility. I would also take down all of their information, what they were charged with, and once I developed their mug shot, I would assemble it all onto an inmate card and deliver it to central control. No one entered or left the facility without being identified, so it was very important to get this information to central control as soon as possible.

Working that position meant I never had to return to a cell if I wanted to keep working. I could even answer the daily count right there in intake. There were long periods of time during the day when no one was brought in, so I had time to read and could even take a nap at my desk. Besides, there was always a pot of coffee going, and a lot of guards would bring in doughnuts and other snacks, which they always shared. It was a great gig; and when I did have to return to my cell, a fourteen- or fifteen-hour day made a mattress on a steel slab seem a lot more comfortable than it really was. Information is an important commodity in prison, and I had the lowdown on everybody who came and went.

I have no doubt that being the intake worker at that time changed the course of my life for many reasons. I would see that more over the course of the next few years; however, the first evidence was to come in only a few weeks. Had I not been the photographer for the ADC, I would have been in Holmesburg Prison on July 4, 1970.

With July Fourth being a holiday, we were geared up for a lot of people coming through intake. It was during the noon hour when all of the alarms sounded, putting the ADC on high alert and the prisoners on immediate lockdown. Every available guard poured out of our institution and across the street to Holmseburg, leaving us with only a skeleton crew. I was one of the first people to become privy to what was happening since I was held in intake instead of being sent back to my cell. Wires were coming in, and the guards were talking in front of me. Holmesburg was in the throes of an all-out, full-blown race riot The only difference was that the white inmates had no idea it was coming until all hell broke loose.

It has been alleged that certain radical elements of the Muslims had put together an extensive plan to coordinate with different areas of the jail and successfully took over the dining hall and all of the workshops at one end of the prison. During the midday feeding time, a large percentage of the inmates were in the dining hall while others were being taken to a movie in the auditorium. At a predetermined time, an orchestrated fight broke out in the movie. When the majority of the guards rushed to the auditorium, that was the black inmates' cue to turn on the white inmates in the chow hall.

It had all been well planned out. In addition to what I heard over the police radio that day, I read other accounts; and after my release, I talked to a lot of friends who were in there that day. As the convicts had been moved in lines to the dining hall, they passed through gates that separated the different sections of the jail. The black inmates, most of them either Panthers or Muslims, had taken plastic combs and broken the teeth off in the locks as they passed. This prevented the guards form locking down the jail in sections; and once the rioters closed the gates to the part of the prison they had taken over, the guards could not get back in to stop the riot.

The rioting inmates first took over the butcher shop and the woodshop, attacking the civilian employees who worked there. This gave them access to all types of weapons, and they began to cut up any white inmate they could find along with the few guards who were trapped inside. During this time, they also took over a downstairs welding shop, and some of these maniacs set several white inmates on fire with welding torches. A line of Black Panthers had fashioned blades to the ends of broom and mop handles and were jabbing them through the gates to keep the guards at bay when they tried to force their way back in. I had a lot of friends in there during the riot, many of whom were maimed, crippled, or killed. One of them told me of watching his closest friend hacked to death with meat cleavers. They all said the same thing: "No matter how tight you were with the black inmates, you were fair game." They had come with a plan: to kill whitey, and whitey was taken by surprise.

Frank Rizzo, who was later mayor of Philadelphia, was the commissioner of the Philadelphia Police Department, and he arrived with busloads of what he termed as his "elite warriors." Rizzo was a bull of a man with a twenty-two-inch neck and all of the muscle to go with it. He told the warden, "You have fifteen minutes, and then I'm taking over," and started getting his men into place.

The first thing Rizzo did was put his sharpshooters up on the rooftops on both sides of the dining hall. One particular account from a sharpshooter was that once he was in place, he saw a black inmate holding down an older white inmate and chopping his hand off with a meat cleaver. When he raised the cleaver to take off the other hand, the sniper shot him through the window. Rizzo announced that the rioters had ten seconds to get on the floor, and then his officers started shooting live rounds two feet high into the walls. The same technique was used for the rest of the prison.

Frank Rizzo did not play games and he had the riot quelled in a matter of minutes. Once the riot was ended, the detention block was opened up. The troublemakers were made to strip naked to make sure that they had no more weapons, and then they were marched to the lockdown cells through a line of pissed off police officers with batons. If they even looked cross at an officer, they were beaten to their knees.

Although that ended the problem that day, the violence in Holmesburg continued. In 1973, the warden and one of his captains were stabbed to death by inmates who were alleged to be Black Muslims. After several more smaller riots over the next twenty years, Holmesburg was finally shut down in 1995. It still towers alongside Interstate 95 in the middle of the city like a giant ogre, reminding people just how sinister prisons can be.

As a result of the riot, the Feds took all of their prisoners out of Holmesburg and shipped them to other facilities. They even came and got me from my cushy little job at the ADC; but instead of sending me back to Lewisburg, I ended up in Terre Haute Federal Prison in Indiana. Going to Terre Haute would have dramatic changes in my life, but the trip there would be an interesting ride.*

---

* This riot was the result of long term racial tensions and deplorable living conditions. Some of this information was obtained from The New York Times article, "Philadelphia Warden and Aide Stabbed to Death by Two Inmates", June 1, 1973.

CHAPTER 11

The Road to Terre Haute

Sitting in the ADC in Philly after the Holmesburg riots, I was still scheduled to be returned to Lewisburg Federal Prison in Pennsylvania. All I was waiting on was my paperwork to be processed through the Bureau of Prisons (BOP), and nothing would take place without their approval. It only took a few days after the riot for the federal lawsuits to start pouring out of Holmesburg. When this happened, the federal government went into crisis mode, and the BOP started pulling all of their people out of the Philadelphia Prison System and shipping them to wherever there was available space or an empty bed.

Every day, a group of federal inmates were shipped out. When they were moved to the holding cells to wait for the US Marshals, they would ask where they were going, and the answer was always, "Your guess is as good as mine." So, like all of the other inmates, I was not given a clue as to where I was going or with whom. That morning, I was loaded up with eleven other prisoners—all of them black and most of them Muslims.

When we loaded up that morning, things were a little tense with not knowing where we would be ending up. But after a few hours of riding, things got pretty relaxed; we were just federal convicts being temporarily relocated. I found out that none of these inmates had been charged with any crimes stemming from the riots. That was the first time that I learned that not all of the black inmates had been involved. These guys were like me, just wanting to get somewhere and do their time the best way possible.

We ended our journey in the mountains at a coal mining town called Pottstown in Pennsylvania. The bus pulled up in front of the Pottstown County Jail, an old stonewalled prison that looked like a miniature Holmesburg Prison. The walls were not nearly as high but were constructed of some serious stonework. It was one of those places that cast off a cold and lasting impression. However, unlike Holmesburg where the bus pulled inside the compound and the gates secured behind you before unloading the prisoners, we were unloaded out front onto the sidewalk two at a time and walked into the foyer of the jail. Once we were all inside, our paperwork was checked in with the warden. After what can best be described as a hearty briefing from him on the rules and regulations of his facility, the marshals left us there.

There was a massive barred wall that separated the foyer from the cellblock. On the foyer side was the receiving area and the warden's office; on the other side was a long, wide hall with cells on both sides facing each other. There was also a second-story tier where we were each assigned a cell.

There were no guards in this facility. During the day, it was run by trustees who were all locals doing county time. At night, they had a civilian that came in; and after lockdown, he performed the nightly head count. If there was a call for alarm, he would call the local police or, if it was serious, the state police. It was truly a relaxed environment from what we were used to. I say "we" because the twelve of us pretty much hung out as a team. We were all from Philly, and being city tailored, none of us were too comfortable with what we considered the hicks in the jail. We just did not see any attraction in building friendships with people we would only be seeing temporarily. We also knew that we had nothing in common. I do not recall a serious charge among any of the locals; most of them were in for simple assault or petty theft or even DUI. We were all sporting federal offenses such as bank robbery, mail fraud, and my charge of armed payroll robbery. It was clear that these hicks did not like us, but they were not about to make any trouble. We had put race aside and formed a strong crew.

We had no idea how long we would be there, and there were other factors that brought us together. It only took a couple of meals, especially breakfast, for me to start making waves. I started to get loud about how shoddy the food was as well as the amount being served. Naturally, I voiced how I was sure that the warden was getting a pretty penny under the emergency agreement to take federal prisoners on a "per prisoner, per day" agreement; the least he could do was give us a decent meal. It did not take long for word to reach the warden through one of the trustees that I was making trouble.

One morning not long after I first voiced my discontent about the food, I was called to the front, and the warden faced me from the opposite side of the bars. He wanted to know what my problem was. I explained that a cup of oatmeal and one piece of toast in the morning was a scant way to start the day, especially with the rest of the meals not being any better. We were hungry all the time. I let him know that we were restless with the treatment we were receiving and were going to request to be moved by the BOP. That got his attention. I do not know how much he was getting paid to house us, but I did know the Feds were paying big bucks. At the time, he had twelve of us and was probably open for more federal inmates because he had the room. I also knew his jail was now on the map for traveling federal marshals to stop while in transit with prisoners and house them for the night.

Surprisingly, he asked me what I thought was a suitable breakfast I thought about what breakfast was at Lewisburg and told him bacon and eggs, a piece of fruit and toast, as well as a choice of cold cereal and fresh milk. I was shocked when he said, "I'll take care of it. Tell your crew I need a day to put it all together." This was the first reference he made toward all of us from Philly being "my crew." I wondered if the man was color-blind. Not only were they all black, but most were labeled Muslims or Panthers on their paperwork. How were they "my crew"?

Within the week, the warden delivered on his promise not only to us but to all of the other inmates as well, which was the right thing to do. As you can imagine, the local inmates loved the changes, and they knew who had gone to the man with the request. It was not long before they started coming to me with their requests, thinking of me as the leader of our crew. Not wanting to cause any dissention, I took every complaint before our crew of federal prisoners, and if everyone was in agreement, I would talk to the warden.

We had been there a few weeks when I received a visit from a girlfriend. She had visited me often in Holmesburg and then later at the ADC, but now she was driving to Pottstown. Although trustees were allowed to go outside of the bars and have visits in the foyer, we were only allowed to talk through the bars. While these were non-contact visits, we would hold hands and touch each other's faces. What were they going to do? The only guards were inmate-trustees; and if any of them got on my case, I would remind them that we all lived together, and it was a small cellblock. Needless to say, they left us alone, which allowed her to pass cash to me. This was money that I had left with her, and she usually brought forty dollars.

The reason the Philly crew followed me was because I always found a way to make things better for us. That is why I wanted the cash from my girlfriend. We all had money on our accounts up front; and as you purchased items from the commissary, it was deducted from the money on your books. The problem was, not everything we wanted was in the commissary.

It had not taken long after our arrival that I learned that the night civilian was both a hustler and a hard drinker. I stopped him one evening not long after I got the contraband cash and struck up a conversation while he was doing his rounds. He was clearly afraid of the federal convicts and told me that he did not want any problems, and that he was not making enough money to risk getting hurt on the job. I told him that this was my crew, and that he would be okay.

I had also previously learned that he brought liquor to the head trustee on occasion, so I went a step further: "Why don't you do my guys a favor. They'd really appreciate it and so would I. I can assure you, you do this favor for us, you'll have the best support in here anyone can have." I have no idea what he thought the favor was going to be, but I could see the look of relief on his face when I said,

"I need two pints of whiskey. I give you a twenty, and you can keep the change." In those days, a pint ran between three and four bucks, so he could buy the pints and have enough left over for a fifth for himself. I slipped him a twenty and waited. Sure enough, the next night, he delivered the two pints.

The next morning, while we were walking the yard, I assembled the federal guys and told them I had arranged a treat for them. I explained that there were only two pints because I did not want them to get drunk and screw things up. There would only be enough for a buzz and crash for the night. I did the whiskey treat several times during our stay at Pottstown. Needless to say, I was the sharpest white boy on the planet.

A couple of months later, the warden summoned me to the front of the block and spoke to me through the bars. The warden just stood there looking at me, then said, "I want you to shave that hair off your face."

I had a small goatee at the time, and I kept it very neat and trimmed. I might add that all of the black prisoners that had made the trek with me from Holmesburg were also sporting facial hair of some kind. I just laughed and asked him why. "Because if you shave then so will the rest of your buddies," he said.

"They're not going to shave just because I do, shit, warden. Why all of a sudden do you want us to shave? None of the locals do." Most of the locals had facial hair, and it was not even neat. Some of them resembled the guys you see today on Duck Dynasty. I knew he was just testing me to try to put me in my place after I won the confrontation over the food. He was trying to put me at odds with the Philly guys, but I was not getting played by him. I simply told him that I was not going to shave, and that was that.

The warden threatened me with lockdown, but I still refused. He said, "Go to your cell immediately," and motioned for the trustee to escort me to my cell and told him to lock me down.

I told the warden, "I'm not going to lockdown. I didn't do anything wrong. This is all bullshit." I also looked at the trustee and told him that he was going to have a hard time putting me in my cell.

The poor guy just sighed and looked at the warden. We just all stood there and stared each other down.

The warden finally blinked first. "You have to go back to your cell sometime, young man. And if you try to stay out after official lockdown, the police will be brought in, so enjoy the run of the block while you can."

I then walked back to the cellblock on my own. I remained on the floor for the rest of the day and into the evening. I noticed the warden visiting the front bars from time to time, looking to see where I was and if I had gone into my cell or not. The trustee did not want any trouble and was staying to himself, content to wait until lockdown; and then if I refused to go to my cell, it would be a police matter, not his problem to deal with. When everyone returned to their cell for the nightly lockdown, I returned to mine.

The cells all had a huge padlock, which secured a slotted handle that locked the door in place. Every cell worked off a single master key. Each morning, the trustee would start opening the individual doors and fasten the doors into a locked position so your cell remained open all day. In the evening, they would reverse the process. As the lock snapped closed that night, I asked the trustee, "How long do people usually stay locked down for?" He did not know, it varied from inmate to inmate. He did tell me that he thought it was odd that I was singled out to be told to shave, and that the warden must really have it in for me.

When the cells were unlocked the next morning, mine was not. I had been on lockdown before in other places, but it had always been for a good reason. This bullshit pissed me off. I had no idea how long I would be singled out and punished for not shaving and being the only inmate told to do so. Some of the crew stopped by to talk and ask if there was anything I needed.

Soon after the inmates were unlocked, chow was called and the block emptied out. The other inmates all walked across the yard to a separate building that served as the dining hall, and I was left alone to the silence of an empty cellblock. I was hungry and started thinking that being on lockdown might mean not getting fed either. Shit, were these hillbillies going to starve me to death?

It was almost half an hour before I heard movement on the tier. The trustee was coming my way with a large breakfast tray. Before he even got to my cell, I realized that it was too big to fit through the hole in the bars. This was the same trustee from the day before, and I could not believe it when he set the tray down to unlock my door. When he opened the door and reached down to pick up my tray, I stepped out and looked at him. The expression on his face told me he knew it was on all over again. "Come on, man. Don't do this," was all he said.

I understood his position, but I was not going back on lockdown. I told him, "Tell you what. You leave the lock undone, and I'm going to eat out here on the tier. Afterward, I'm going to stretch my legs, and then I will lock down on my own."

He explained that no locks were to be left unfastened, and he was going to have to close it in a locked position whether I was in my cell or not. It was a serious rule so that the lock would not be lost or stolen and used as a weapon. I just told him to do what he had to do, figuring if the door was locked open, I could always step in and out and avoid the warden. The trustee backed off, and all went well for most of the day.

When the warden did appear, he simply gave me a dirty look then stood at the bars, staring at me in disgust. He clearly had a real problem with my challenging his authority. Once again, I repeated the lockdown scenario from the night before and figured they would be prepared the next morning. I did not expect to get out of my cell for a long time to come. What I did not know was that was to be my last night at the Pottstown Jail.

The next morning, breakfast came in small portions and was easily passed through the bars. So much for getting out. However, not long after breakfast, the trustee showed up with my street clothes and told me to get changed; I was leaving. When I asked where, he did not answer. I guess he had enough of me too. A little while later, he came back and opened my cell door. All he said was, "You are wanted up front. You need to hurry. It's the warden and some US Marshals."

What I did not know was that two federal prisoners had been dropped off the previous evening for overnight housing, and the marshals had gotten an ear full from the warden about me. I later learned from one of these prisoners that the warden told the marshals to either take me with them the next morning, or he was going to put all twelve of us out on the street. He had laid it on so thick the night before, they got on their hotline to the BOP. One of the prisoners was bound for minimum security prison at Ashland, Kentucky, and the other for the maximum security prison at Terre Haute, Indiana. Needless to say, my next destination became Terre Haute, Indiana.

When I arrived out front, there were two Deputy US Marshals waiting for me in the foyer. They were both tall and thick and had a no-nonsense look about them. They also seemed pretty disgusted to have to deal with me. The marshal-to-prisoner ratio had now changed from two to two to three to two with the third prisoner being labeled a troublemaker with a long string of violent priors. They were definitely in a "take no shit" mode. The first thing one of them said was for me to take my Catholic medal off. When I started to protest, they told me I could either hand it over, or they would rip it off and throw it in the garbage.

They then placed me and the other two prisoners in leg shackles, handcuffs, and transport chains. We were loaded into a transport van and forbidden to even whisper. It was obvious that everybody in the van thought I was a real danger. Even the other two prisoners would not dare make eye contact with me. Within five minutes of leaving my cell, I was headed down the long road to Terre Haute.

We made it as far as Dayton, Ohio, that first night where we were housed in the county jail for the night. There, I tried to get to know my traveling companions. The younger guy going to Ashland did not say much, and I don't recall anything about him. The older guy was named Bruce; and since he was going to the same place I was, we struck up a friendship.

The next day, the marshals lightened up a little and let us talk once we got into Indiana. This was the first time I had left the state of Pennsylvania in my life, and I started to welcome the thought of breaking new ground. I also felt that as far as prisons go, they were all pretty much the same or at least the rules of survival were. What the hell, change is good, and I was okay with it.

* * * * *

Terre Haute would become one of the turning points in Bojack's life. A turning point without which he would have probably not lived to see the age of thirty. This would not be some sudden epiphany that put Bojack on the right track—that would come later. This was simply the beginning of a slow process.

First of all, the trip to Indiana was the first time that Bojack had left the state of Pennsylvania, or, for that matter, the greater Philadelphia area, with the exception of his time in Lewisburg and Camp Hill. It was his first real introduction to people outside of his previously tiny world of Southwest Philly. This was the first time that he would make friends with people who were not small-time street guys living from one minor score to the next in a violent and deadly world. These were guys who thought about next year instead of guys who did not even think about next week. Here is where the seed of wanting to go straight was first planted. It was here in Terre Haute that Bojack would come to meet the first three mentors of his life: Big Joe, Jerry, and Slim.

* * * * *

Bojack

Big Joe was from a large Midwestern city and was of pure Italian descent. I later learned that he and his brother, who had also done federal time, owned several restaurants in that city. Everyone had a job in Terre Haute, just like in Lewisburg, and Big Joe was head of the kitchen in the correctional officers' dining room. This was a very secure area, for obvious reasons, so you had to be one of the very top cons in the joint to get that job.

Joe was a big man and got a lot of respect from both the cons and the guards and not just for his size. There was something about the way he carried himself. I always figured that he was a made guy and probably pretty high up, but you did not ask a guy like Joe any questions and sure as hell not something like that. Joe never even said exactly where it was he was form, just referring to it as "back home" on the few occasions he mentioned it. One thing that I learned doing my previous stints was that you did not pry or ask somebody about their business. That's just the way it was back in the day. Nowadays, it seems like everyone wants their business known because they are enveloped in a need for notoriety. Everybody wants to be famous. I always believed, and still do, that still and silent was the best course to pursue when doing time, at least until it was time to make your niche.

When I first arrived at Terre Haute, I was assigned to the prison bakery, which was the perfect job for me. I would report to the bakery in the early morning hours before the other inmates were even up; and after several hours of mixing, sectioning, and placing dough into containers for baking, I would get a couple of hours' break before returning to the bakery to start over for the next meal. That is when I would head for the yard and the weight pile to start my lifting routine. This gave me privy to the yard during the day when most of the inmates were working and gave us bakery and kitchen guys exclusive access to the weight pile. We could get a really good workout in without a bunch of other cons standing over you asking, "How much longer you gonna be?" Night yard was a literal nightmare trying to work out with so many guys trying to squeeze in a session on the iron. It was at Terre Haute that I truly became addicted to exercise, and that continues up through today.

The bakery and the CO's dining hall kitchen both shared the same entrance into the eating area, so I saw Big Joe several times a day. One day, we happened to take a break at the same time, and he said "You're from Philly. Why aren't you doing your time back east?"

Several of the guys working in the bakery with me were supposed to be wise guys, so I figured that was where he got his information from. I knew that you did not ask Big Joe questions, but you certainly answered his. I told him that I originally had a twenty-five-year sentence and had gone to Lewisburg on a B number going back for resentencing and the riot at Holmesburg and how I had landed here in the Midwest.

When I finished, Joe told me, "When you finish your morning shift, come to the kitchen in the officers' mess. I want to talk to you some more. You can do your workout later."

I answered, "Sure thing."

When my morning shift ended, I did as Big Joe said; and to my surprise, I was able to walk right into the kitchen of the officers' dining room. As I said, this was a very secure area; every officer in the prison ate there, so all of the workers had to be trusted one hundred percent. As I walked in unchallenged, Big Joe motioned for me to stand by his side as he worked to prepare lunch for the guards. Joe asked me what I was charged with, breaking a cardinal rule in prison that simply did not apply to him. When I told him armed robbery, he just shook his head as if to say, "Yeah, that's what I thought."

"You need to stop that stupid shit. There are easier ways to make money," he replied, and we never discussed my case again.

Joe told me that he liked the way that I carried myself, and that he had been told that I did not whine and complain like a lot of cons do. He also told me that the inmate in charge of the dishwasher was being released in a few days, and that he wanted me to take over the job as he could not trust just anybody back there in his kitchen.

I told him that I would request the job change with my current boss in the bakery and ask my counselor to approve it. That was the normal procedure; that way, I could get first shot at the opening. Joe just cut his eyes at me and said, "Don't worry about it. It's done." So from that day on, I worked in the officers' dining room.

My time had been going just fine when I worked in the bakery, but it got much better the next morning. When I reported to work, I was told to go across the hall to the officers' mess. From now on, I would be working there. My schedule remained the same, and I still had access to the yard and the weight pile while everyone else was working, and I never ate in the inmate dining room again. I ate the same food that the staff enjoyed, cooked by Big Joe. I was now part of his crew. I was living my life as Conway in those days and often wondered what would have happened if Joe had known my real name was Saltarelli. Hell, he might have adopted me.

At the time I started working for Joe, there was a powerhouse of a guy working there too named Jerry. Jerry was a tough Irish street kid from Chicago, and he was massive. I hate to say that he was antisocial, but all he wanted to do was lift and eat. This was before Arnold Schwarzenegger brought weightlifting and bodybuilding into the mainstream, and all of this was very new. In fact, the first time I saw Jerry, I thought he was deformed. Then I saw him working out, doing squats with over five hundred pounds, and realized hope powerful he was. This was all without the use of steroids or even any type of special supplements; he was just a thick monster who ate like a horse.

Jerry and I started talking one day while we were both out on the weight pile, and I noticed that he liked lifting by himself like I did. We hit it off pretty well and, like Joe and me, I think we recognized a certain level of character and respect that was lacking in a lot of cons, which brought about our close friendship.

Jerry and I ended up as training partners and lifted every day for the rest of my time there. We always worked out as a team and never let in a third member. I loved the feeling of well-being that the weights gave me as well as the fact that it took commitment, something up until then I knew nothing about. I had boxed in every joint I had been in since I was twelve, but this was something different. This was not just about tearing some guy's head off for status or for releasing hostility. This was me against myself, trying to create a better me. It was not just that Jerry was the strongest guy in the prison, and I was his workout partner, he pushed me constantly; and under his influence, I gradually began to develop not just physically but mentally, which for the first time in my life gave me a boost in self-confidence and a sense of accomplishment. I always look back on that time spent in Terre Haute as a turning point for me. I started to like myself; and with liking myself, I began to want more out of life than one petty crime followed by another jail stint.

Then there was Slim, one of the most pressing people that I have ever met. Slim was a tall, lanky kid from rural Tennessee who was doing a short stint for taking stolen cars across state lines. I always wondered what the rest of his story was; I could not figure how a small-time charge like that could land a guy in the maximum security section of Terre Haute. But unlike Slim, I never asked questions, figuring that was his business.

Although he was not a serious weight lifter like Jerry and me, he just showed up one day on the weight pile and struck up a conversation. Slim and I started talking on our off time, and he turned out to be a smart and interesting guy, not just the hick I first thought him to be. He would talk to anyone and seemed to be liked by all the cons who knew him. Plus, he hung out with Jerry and me, who were both part of Big Joe's kitchen crew, and that certainly did not hurt his status any.

My friendship with Slim was unlike the one with Joe and Jerry. Slim was a thinker, and he would start to ask me the important questions that the others did not. Like, "What are you going to do when you get out?" and "Where are you going with your life?"

The first time that he started this type of conversation, my answer was that I had a detainer on me from the Pennsylvania Parole Board for a two-year balance on the 1966 robberies. "So I have plenty of time to worry about the future later." However, Slim was persistent and returned to the subject on other occasions. This persistence would get under my skin, but I put up with him for one reason: I knew that he was sincere about every question. He spoke to me like he was planning to crack my exterior and get inside to me; it was his way. Eventually I did engage him on the topic of my future and where I was going in life. It was a short response to say the least: "Hell, I don't know."

His response was quick and thought-provoking: "You really need to think hard about what you are going to do when you hit these streets and need to fend for yourself. Are you going to steal again? Put a gun in some innocent person's face and take what they worked their asses off to earn?"

I can still hear these words like it was yesterday. For the first time in my life, I was feeling remorse for what I had done to people in the past.

"You need to start preparing now, Bojack. Detainer or no detainer, you will eventually walk back into society. And from that first day, you will have to make ends meet, and it had better be by legal means, or you will be right back here or in some other prison. So if that's the case, why even go home in the first place if you intend to take what you want from innocent people?"

It was the first time in my life that I thought about right and wrong, and that there really was a difference.

Before I go any further, I do not want to paint my time at Terre Haute as some kind of picnic. I was institutionalized in a maximum security prison. The fact that I had been on the inside for so many years had taught me to survive on a day-to-day basis and not just with situations that involved me directly. There is always the danger of serious violence, and it does not to take a lot for one inmate to exact violence on another; and you have to be on constant guard not to get yourself dragged into it one way or another. One such incident happened in the late fall of 1971. It was during football season, and the tragedy was all over a lousy carton of cigarettes, commonly known as a "box" on the inside.

I was sitting on my top bunk reading *The Godfather*, of all things, and enjoying some relaxation time on a Sunday afternoon. Dinner was being served, and inmates could come and go to the chow hall down on the first floor. Some inmates went down as soon as they opened, and others waited until the crowd thinned out. The building was three stories tall. My "dorm" was on the second floor with three rows of bunks that stretched from the "dorm" entrance to the rear of the building. My bunk was right near the front entrance. At the very front of the dorm, right before you got to my bunk, was the dayroom where you could watch television, play cards, or just hang out. I had already eaten and was reading and letting my food settle. Being that time of year, football season was in high gear; and though I did not follow it much or gamble on games, it was a big activity in prison.

A tall, thin black guy in his later twenties known as Cano came out of the dayroom, complaining about losing on a game. Cano stopped to talk to a group of his buddies who were playing cards at the end of someone's bunk straight across the aisle from mine. He was standing there, bitching about the game when a Mexican about his age asked him something that I could not hear. What I learned later was that he was asking Cano about getting paid since his team had won the game, and he was owed a box.

As far as I am concerned, Cano made two mistakes: one, he told the Mexican kid to get the fuck away from him, that he was not paying him shit; and two (what I regard as a really egregious offense, as would any inmate), he told the Mexican to pack his shit and to get the fuck out of the dorm as there wasn't enough room for both of them. I can tell you that back then—and I have no doubt it's the same way today—if you tell a man to pack his shit, and he does, he will be disgraced as a punk for the rest of his time. Cano's friends started laughing, which did not help matters, and the Mexican kid hung his head and sauntered off to the rear of the dorm.

I could not believe that this kid would take shit like that, so I kept an eye on him. He crouched down in the back of the dorm with another Mexican inmate. Meanwhile, Cano was enjoying his victory over this kid and was running his mouth about what he would do if the dude tried to remain in the dorm. Suddenly, the Mexican charged from the back toward Cano, who was standing in between the bunks. Cano's buddies yelled for him to watch out; the guy had a shank. The Mexican had a long shiny object in his hand and was stalking Cano, who was now leaping over the lower bunks, trying to get away, but there was no place to go. Everyone in the dorm froze, watching this strange dance of death. All that moved were the two players; the only sound was the hum of a large hurricane fan in front of the dorm.

I could not have cared less about either one of these convicts; but as far as I am concerned, Cano had asked for this, and I am not sure if he even realized. He was so preoccupied with getting away from this shank-wielding assailant, he may have never accepted that he would be dead in a matter of seconds. Cano had leaped over several bunks toward the back of the dorm, and I am sure he was tiring, so when he broke free from the sanctuary of the bunks and attempted to run up an aisle toward the front with his back to his attacker, in his panic, Cano made the mistake of running up the aisle with the hurricane fan at the end. When he realized his mistake, he turned to face his attacker.

Cano was not wearing a shirt. He was lean, and his skin was tight across his chest. When the shank struck him square in the heart, the blood shot out like a fire hose. As I watched him fall backward with his eye rolling back in his head, I slid off my bunk and slipped my feet into my shoes and went straight for the door. Blood had sprayed as far as the foot of my bunk, but luckily none of it got on me.

Just as I cleared the dorm entrance and started down the stairs, I heard the huge fan crash to the floor as Cano fell backward into it. I hit the first floor and headed for the chow hall when the guard at the bottom of the stairs heard the commotion and raced to the second floor. I had just made it to the chow hall when the alarms sounded for emergency lockdown. I noticed an empty tray on a table and sat down at it as though I had just finished eating and knew nothing about what had just happened upstairs.

I had done nothing wrong, but I had been around long enough to know that when the guards started taking names as to who was where when the murder went down, I wanted to be listed as in the chow hall because anyone who was in that dorm when names were collected for questioning was going to pay a price for being there.

The FBI investigated murders in federal prisons; and innocent or not, you would have to make a choice. Claim you were asleep and had seen nothing and be labeled as uncooperative and a liar at your next parole hearing, or say what you saw and be labeled a rat by the other inmates. Oddly enough, it turned out that there were rats to spare.

All of Cano's buddies who had been playing cards across from my bunk ratted. They used the excuse that he was one of theirs, which I thought was total bullshit The Mexican kid who stabbed Cano ended up getting fifteen years added to his sentence of five years, which he had already served over half, and the guy who had provided him with the shank got five years. The most ironic thing was that Cano had less than two years left on his sentence; and if he had just handed over the box, he would have walked out of Terre Haute instead of going home in a body bag.

Not being on that witness list was a smart move, but it also made me take further stock of the life I was living and the situations that I was exposing myself to. I was scheduled to be released to the state of Pennsylvania at the end of June 1972. In March of that year, Slim and I were talking, and he again brought up the subject of what I was going to do when I eventually got out. He knew that Cano's murder had a sobering effect on me, or maybe it was just the moment. But his next remark shattered me, and I did not know what to say: "Bojack, what are you afraid of out there? What is it that terrifies you so much that you sabotage your freedom almost immediately after you are released to come back to prison? When have you ever given life out there a chance?"

Slim buried a seed in my head that day. He asked the right question at the exact moment that it needed to be asked. I had never given life outside the walls a chance. I had never worked at anything good long enough to reap results. I have all the respect in the world for that man. I don't know what became of him. We lost touch after Terre Haute. I hope he had a great life. He certainly had an impact on me. He walked onto the weight pile one day and took aim at me as if he was sent there for the purpose of getting my attention.

Over the previous months, I had been writing to the Pennsylvania state parole board, letting them know that when I was released in June, I was going to fight extradition back to state prison in Pennsylvania on the balance of the 1966 charges. Now I knew that the state of Pennsylvania was almost bankrupt at the time, and they would not waste the time and money to bring one guy back just to do a couple of years on some charges from six years ago. I softened all of this in my letters to the board by explaining that I was not the same man that I was in 1969 when I violated my parole, how being sent to Terre Haute in faraway Indiana had turned my life around by getting me away from all of my old associates. I never expected any results from all of this and figured they would be coming for me upon my release by the Feds.

I was down to about my last two months at Terre Haute when I was sent for by my counselor. I just figured it was an official visit preparing me for my upcoming release. There was not much to plan on. I was maxing out on my federal time, and there was a state hold on me. I would simply be held until my release date and then transferred to the county jail in Terre Haute where I would be held for seventy-two hours or until the Pennsylvania authorities came for me, whichever came first.

When I entered the counselor's office, he told me to take a seat across from him. I noticed he had a legal-size paper in front of him, and he flipped it over to me, saying, "How would you like to go out on the farm?"

"The farm?" I wanted to be sure that I had heard him right.

He pointed to the letter in front of me, and I noticed it had a Pennsylvania state seal on it. Before I had a chance to read the document, I heard the words I had been dreaming of for months: "Pennsylvania has dropped its hold on you." What he said next came as an even bigger surprise: "Since you are going home in a couple of months, I think that you should get out of maximum security and into a more relaxed atmosphere. I am transferring you to minimum security and sending you out to the farm."

The farm was for short-timers and definitely not for anyone with a hold from another jurisdiction. Walking into my counselor's office, I was "short," a term we used for someone nearing the end of their sentence. Even though I was going to state prison in Pennsylvania after leaving Terre Haute, I was still "short" on my time there with one sentence down and one more to go. Now, suddenly, I was less than sixty days from a bus ride home. As of this moment, I was "short-short."

I only had a few minutes to visit with Big Joe and Jerry back in the kitchen and then to get with Slim to thank him for all of his time and friendship. They were processing me immediately for transfer that afternoon to the farm, which was outside of the main prison on surrounding acreage. I packed what few belongings I had and was taken to records to have a trustee ID made. That quick, I was outside of the maximum security perimeter of the prison for the first time in over two years.

They assigned me a cubicle where I was to sleep, and I began to feel that freedom was all around me. What I found especially great was that you were permitted to walk the entire property, which was acres and acres of land. I visited all of the animal pens and even witnessed livestock being born. I got to see firsthand what farming was all about. For a guy who had spent his life on the outside in the city and who had never even owned a dog, this was incredible.

After a day or so, I was assigned to work at the powerhouse and would be working the night shift from midnight to eight in the morning. That suited me just fine. The guy who processed me said it was because of my size and build. My job was to shovel coal from the delivery port into large coal carriers on tracks, which took about two hours. Then I would read gauges and record their levels. I would then push the coal carriers down the tracks to the front of the huge boilers, which took another two hours, and then shovel the coal from the carriers into the boilers, which generally took another two hours or so. It was a very old power system even in 1972, but it generated power for the entire prison.

At the end of an eight-hour shift, another crew would replace us, and I would go back to my dorm, shower, and pass out on my bunk until lunch. After a huge lunch, I would go out onto the weight pile where I would be allowed to work out for an hour and a half. I would then take another nap and hang out until midnight when I reported back to work. There were easier jobs on the farm, but this was perfect for me. I knew nothing about farming, having grown up in Philly, and the hard, brute work felt good to me.

CHAPTER 12

Back Home from Terre Haute

After I got home from Terre Haute, I knew that I wanted to straighten out my life. I got a job with a paint contractor working on the campus of the University of Pennsylvania. My brother-in-law, my sister Lil's husband, was working there and had helped me get on. He and I even started doing some painting jobs of our own, working after hours on the weekends and at night doing small jobs. I worked hard and stayed clean, but even working ten or twelve hours a day, six days a week, I was lucky to clear $120. That's when I met a guy named Tommy "Monk" Oteri.

Monk owned a successful club in our neighborhood and was known for moving a lot of drugs. He did business with both the Irish out of Northeast Philly and the Italians out of South Philly. He made a lot of money and seemed to be juiced in with just about everybody. Our company was painting his nightclub, and he asked my brother-in-law and me to do his apartment as one of our side jobs.

I was over there at his apartment one day, getting ready to finish up, and I could tell Monk was upset about something. Dressed for work in a white T-shirt and painter's pants, Monk commented that I looked like I kept myself in great shape. I answered, "Yeah, I work out every day. Something I picked up in Terre Haute."

He said, "That's right. You did some time, more than once. I bet you can handle yourself."

I did not answer.

Monk went on, "I need you to take a ride with me. You don't have to do anything, just sit in the car. There's fifty bucks in it for you."

I hesitated. I had no idea what he was up to, but I knew it was illegal. But hey, fifty bucks was two days' pay. As I hesitated, Monk repeated himself, "Fifty bucks and you don't even have to get out of the car."

What the hell; I was in. We climbed into Monk's Cadillac and drove over to another neighborhood and rode around until we saw a guy standing out on the corner. Monk parked his car next to the guy and said, "This guy owes me money. Just sit tight and watch my back."

Monk stepped out of the car and said, "Hey, Rocco, you got it?"

That was when I realized I knew the guy. Rocco was a small-time thief and dope peddler, and we had been in Holmesburg at the same time. He was a decent fellow, but he was no tough guy. About this time, Monk and Rocco started to argue, with Rocco putting his finger in Monk's face. I thought, *Aw, shit. Looks like I'm going to have to earn this fifty.* I stepped out of the Cadi and slammed the door.

That was when Rocco recognized me. "Bojack. Shit. I didn't know you were with Monk."

I didn't answer. That's when he turned back to Monk and said, "Look, I've got most of it right here." He reached inside of his coat and pulled out an envelope full of cash. "I know I'm a little short, but I can give you the rest of it in the next two or three days. I just gotta move the rest of what you gave me."

Monk took the envelope and said, "You got two days, and then we're coming back."

"Sure thing," Rocco replied. "Two days. Good to see you, Bojack."

Monk and I got back in the car and drove away. He turned and looked at me. "Who the hell are you? I'm juiced in with half the wise guys and a lot of made guys all over this city, and the asshole gets in my face. You step out of the car, don't say a fucking word, and the guy hands over the money. So just who the hell are you?"

"He and I were in Holmesburg together," I said. "When you've done time in the same joint with a guy, you know all you need to know about him."

Monk pulled a hundred-dollar bill out of the envelop that Rocco had given him and handed it to me. Geez, almost a week's pay for a half an hour's work. "Come to work for me, and there will be plenty of those in your pocket," he said. I was twenty-seven years old and had been to prison four times. I should have known better.

I kept my painting jobs and continued to focus on going straight. Monk kept calling me more and more to collect for him. After about six months, I hung up my paintbrush. Like I said, "I should have known better," but I was twenty-seven and had never owned a suit of clothes, let alone a car. Now, I was driving a Cadillac of my own with a closet full of expensive clothes and never left the house without at least a grand in my pocket. That was ten weeks' pay for an assistant painter. I was back in the life and in a bigger way than ever before.

* * * * *

In the 1970s, Philadelphia was the undisputed meth capital of the country, and Monk was establishing himself as a major player. Monk had his own labs and employer "cookers" of his own and was getting hold of enough phenyl 2-propanone (P2P), a major ingredient in meth, to sell to both the Irish and the Italians to run their own labs. Monk was also selling a lot of finished product to the Warlocks Motorcycle Gang. The Warlocks were a statewide gang who about this time were "patched over" or merged with the Pagans, a national gang known for being ruthless and sadistic even by biker gang standards. This was a violent and dangerous world where you never knew who your friend was and who was out to get you. To make matters worse, about half of the people moving the meth were using it themselves and becoming more whacked-out and paranoid by the day. Bojack saw it as his ticket to the good life.

* * * * *

Bojack

It must have been sometime in the summer of '73 that I went all in with Monk. My job was simple: Monk delivered large quantities of product to various guys around the city; they either cut it and sold it themselves or, in most cases, delivered it to other dealers further down the chain in Philly or some other East Coast city. I would come around a few days later and collect the money owed. This may seem like a strange deal—dope deals on the honor system—but it worked.

Sometimes, guys would claim not to have the money, and I would have to help them remember where they had put it. Like I always say, "Some conversations are best ended with a ball bat." It worked well enough that I was visiting Monk every three or four days and delivering twenty to twenty-five thousand dollars every trip; and of course, I always got my cut.

During my early days with Monk, one of the guys I collected from was a huge biker they called Lurch, like the butler on *The Addams Family* television show. Lurch hung with a guy named Marco. I had grown up with Marco's nephew and had spent more than a few nights sleeping in Marco's car when I was a kid living on the streets. Lurch always seemed like an honorable guy, and I knew he was completely loyal to Marco, so it seemed strange when he approached me about ripping off Monk.

This really pissed me off. Monk was the boss, and I worked for him. I don't bite a hand that's fed me, so I went to Monk and told him that we had better watch his back even closer. I was already acting as Monk's bodyguard, and he never went out without me, so it surprised me when Monk blew off the info that I had just given him.

Later that night, on the way home, it dawned on me that the whole thing had been a test. Monk had wanted to find out if he could trust me, if I would rip him off. I wrote it off as part of the business, but in the back of my mind, a light went off. If Monk did not trust me, just how far could I trust him.

If all this sounds paranoid, it was. Anytime you are dealing with criminals, everybody has some paranoia in them; it's the nature of the game. But anytime you had a lot of money into the mix, things get really bad.

I remember one night, I went down to one of Monk's labs where a cooking was going on. Even though I was on the muscle end of the business, I knew the easy money was in becoming a "chemist" and cooking the stuff up yourself. When I got to the house where they were cooking, all the lights were out, and there was no sign of anyone inside. I went around to the back and went in with caution. No one was in the kitchen, and they had apparently stopped right in the middle of the cook. There was half done meth all over. The four guys who were supposed to be cooking were all gathered at the front windows, peeking through the blinds. The minute they started talking, I could tell they were all loaded. Mike Brabazen, who was in charge, said that a couple of hours earlier, he had noticed a car parked out front with two people in the front seat, and they were still out front watching the house.

I told them, "I just came in, and I didn't see anybody out there."

Mike said, "I can't believe you missed them, Bojack. They are right out front."

I went to the window; and as my eyes adjusted to the light on the street, I looked at the car they were talking about. The headrests of the front seat were both pulled up; and in their stoned-out minds, they thought it was two people sitting in the car. They had been staring at an empty car for over two hours. I was not happy. I told the rest of the idiots, "Get in the kitchen and clean up the mess. If this had been a surveillance, they would have raided the place and caught all of you dumb sons of bitches red handed while you were staring out the front window." I hauled Mike Brabazen down the street and loaded him on a bus and sent him home. I then went back and helped finish cleaning up and cooked a fresh batch to take to Monk.

As mad as I was, I started to think. I had known Mike Brabazen for a while. He hung out at a bar on that I often went to. Mike was a tough guy and always seemed to have it together. If this stuff could turn him into an idiot, what would it do to weaker people.

I had been on board with Monk for probably a little over six months when I started to have my doubts. It all started when he began to tell me about a partner he had before we met. The partner's name was Louie Agnes, and he was off doing a long hitch on a federal drug charge. Apparently, Agnes had gotten involved with some guy in New Jersey who got popped by the Feds, and the guy ratted Louie out. Louie hired a hit man known as "Killer" who was supposed to be the top button man for Mike Marrone, who was alleged to be a captain in the Bruno family.

According to Monk, Louie Agnes had made arrangements to pay Killer ten thousand dollars, five thousand dollars up front and five when the job was done, to take out the fed's witness. Sure enough, the guy was blown up starting his car outside of his home in Cherry Hill, New Jersey. It did not really matter as the Feds had enough other evidence, and Agnes went down anyway.

The way I found out about all of this was that I happened to be at Monk's place on the day when the Feds paid him a visit. They told me to step outside. Of course, having been their guest for the last three years, I obliged. After they left, Monk told me about Louie Agnes for the first time. The Feds had been there to find out if Monk knew anything about the hit. He claimed he did not, and I believed him because if he had, the Feds would have pursued it further.

That's when Monk dropped a bombshell on me. Agnes still owed Killer the other five grand for the hit, and since Agnes was in prison and could not pay, Killer had started shaking Monk down for the money. It did not matter that Monk had nothing to do with the New Jersey deal. The fact that Monk and Agnes were partners in Philly was enough for Killer. He expected Monk to pay up. That's why Monk had me not only collecting for him but also acting as his bodyguard. That's when Monk asked me if I would take out Killer.

Of course, my response was, "Are you out of your fucking mind? If Killer ever found out you had even thought about killing him, he would whack you and everybody around you. Even if you did get to him first, he's not only a made guy, but he's Marrone's top enforcer. Every Italian in the city would be gunning for us. There wouldn't be one place we could lay our head." I went on, "It's a lousy five Gs. I bring you either five or ten times that much every week. Just pay the man."

Monk agreed to pay him, and I never brought the subject up again. But the whole conversation left a really bad taste in my mouth as far as Monk and his judgment were concerned, a taste that would only get a lot worse over the next year.

Not long after this conversation, I discovered Monk's problem. Like most dealers, he had begun to use his own product. I have never used drugs. In fact, being a health freak, I have never even taken a pain pill that was prescribed by a doctor. Putting any kind of chemical into my body has always been taboo. I rarely even drink alcohol and then never more than two.

As time went on, Tommy Monk became more and more open with his drug use and began to use on a regular if not daily basis. I had to stand there and watch him snort meth up his nose or inject it into his veins, and the whole thing made me sick. I had seen other friends and partners use heroin, and I always viewed any kind of drug use as a weakness and vulnerability that I wanted no part of.

Over the course of the next year, I watched Monk change dramatically as a person. You would think that he would want the man watching his back to have his wits about him, and that he would be happy that I was always straight. But at times, he seemed to resent it. They always say that meth makes you paranoid, and I saw it firsthand with Monk. He read a lot of misconception into everything that people did and said and became completely delusional. For example, he would suddenly believe that we were being followed, and nothing I did or said could change his mind. He would keep driving around the same block over and over to see if there was a car following him. There never was. I was riding shotgun on these occasions, and it drove me nuts. During this time, Monk was hanging out with his biker buddies, getting high, and going to wild parties with them. He was getting into a lot of things I wanted no part of. The bikers for the most part sold the dope they got from Monk but also used a lot of it. They also gave a lot of it to young girls at the parties they threw.

The Pagans had an old mansion they had bought called the Dupont House. Whether the Dupont family had ever actually owned the house, I have no idea. The house was in rural upstate Pennsylvania and was built to look like a medieval castle. It was said to have been over a hundred years old and was filled with hidden rooms and passages.

I remember making a delivery there once, and the guy I was supposed to meet just appeared out of nowhere. I was in a room facing what I thought was the only door, and this guy was suddenly behind me out of nowhere. Needless to say, I rarely went there, and then with somebody I could trust to watch my back.

There were all sorts of stories about the parties that went on there concerning young girls—a lot underage, some of whom died from drug overdoses or from brutal sex games. I wanted no part of that place. When Monk went there to party, he was on his own.

The more Monk got high and hung out with his entourage of bikers, the more of the daily business fell to me. It got to a point that I was doing everything. Meeting the sources for the P2P, overseeing the cookings, cutting up the product, and delivering to the dealers. The less Monk was seen, the more people asked me about him. Even I only saw him once or twice a week when I had to hunt him down to give him a bag of money. As I said, other people were noticing, and it did not take long before one of them pointed out to Monk that since I was now doing everything while he was just hanging out getting high, he really was not needed anymore. I could just put him in a hole somewhere along the highway, and I would be making all of the money.

We had been together about a year and a half when Monk showed up at my house unannounced in December of 1974. He told me it was inventory time and to pull out everything that I was holding. We went down into the basement, and I pulled out everything, including a couple of pounds of product, scales, and other items. I could tell Monk was loaded, and I was not in a mood to put up with any shit. But he started taking the small bags I had set up for delivery and pouring them into bags for weighing and after a few minutes announced, "You are off a gram."

Talk about ignorant, trivial crap. Anytime you move product from a big bag to smaller ones, then back to a bigger bag, you will lose some weight because some residue will get left in the bags. This really pissed me off. "A fucking gram. Are you fucking kidding me?

I handle pounds of this shit every month and have never come up short once. First of all, I don't do drugs, so I didn't use any. Second, I am too loyal to steal from you. And with all the weight I move, you are going to bitch about one gram?"

Monk just looked at me with a dumb stoned-ass expression on his face. "Give me my gun back," was all he said. He had supplied me with a .38 revolver in the beginning of our arrangement, so I got the gun from its hiding place and gave it back to him. Without a word, he started to pack everything into a leather satchel he had brought with him. The only thing that he did not pack was the scale.

And when he started to leave, I asked, "What about the scale?"

He responded, "I'll send someone for it later," and walked up the stairs and out of my house.

Now this last bit of craziness sent me a bad signal. Who was he sending over here and when? A couple of days later, my neighbor and good friend, a guy named Rich, was leaving his house when a guy stopped him and asked, "Is this Bojack's house?"

"No, he lives next door."

The guy was dressed in a long dark trench coat and big oversize sunglasses; and as he started to walk away, that's when Rich noticed that the guy had a brown paper bag over his right hand. Rich went on his way; and as he started down the street, I turned the corner on foot with three other guys. The stranger was about to knock on my door when Rich, unaware of what was going on, yelled back, "Hey, here comes Bojack and some of his boys now." The guy then turned and saw us coming his way and immediately ran to his car, which he had left running in the street and took off.

About this time, I reached Rich and asked, "What the hell is going on?"

He told me what had just happened and about the paper bag over the guy's hand. When I saw the guy running to his car, I knew he looked familiar. But then it dawned on me that it was the guy they called "Killer." I told Rich we need to catch this guy, and all of us piled into Rich's car that was parked there by the curb.

Rich's car was a Dodge Super Bee with a worked-up 440 Magnum engine in it, so it did not take long to catch up to the guy in the Valiant even though he was running every red light to get away. His effort paid off because he got out of our neighborhood and back into South Philly where he knew the streets better than us; and if we did catch up with him, he would have a lot more friends around than we would.

As we headed home, it all became clear. Monk was going to have me whacked. If I had been home and had opened the door, he would have put two in my head and been gone in seconds. The only thing anybody would have known was "some guy in big sunglasses and a black trench coat," which would have been all that they remembered.

I went inside and got Monk's scale, and we delivered it to that little piece of shit personally. He was hanging out at his place with a couple of his biker buddies when I explained to him there was no need to visit my house again and for him to call his friend in South Philly and put an end to their business or I would tell him about Monk's previous plan. It must have worked because I never saw Killer again. That conversation with Monk was one I did end with a ball bat.

When word got out about what Monk had done, a lot of people quit doing business with him. Philly was the meth capital of the country in those days, so there were plenty of people to cook for and a lot of people to keep you supplied. So why deal with some paranoid little lowlife who already tried to whack his last right-hand man? Besides that, he no longer had me to collect for him, which is where a lot of his strength came from; people quit paying, and he soon lost everything. The last time that I saw Monk alive, he was nothing but one more insignificant druggie living from one fix to the next.

What a waste. Monk had been a decent, stand-up guy and a friend, but he let the dope take over his life. Despite the way things ended, Monk had been good to me in the beginning and had introduced me to a business and people that would come to be my world in the decade to come.

One of the people that I met during this time was a top criminal defense attorney named Bobby Simone. Simone was known as a topnotch lawyer for the Philly family and would represent me more than a few times. Monk and I spent time in Simone's office, and some of it was on behalf of a guy named Steve DeMarco. DeMarco was a member of the Pagans and was one of Monk's main distributors. Apparently, DeMarco had been in the army and came home on leave and decided not to go back. I have no idea how he did it, but Simone took care of it somehow, and DeMarco never had to go back to the army and never went to jail either. After Monk's fall, DeMarco came over to me and was one of my biggest movers, and Simone would represent me many times over the next decade.

After my split with Monk and his crew, I started to go straight. I found a job at a salvage yard and started putting my personal life on track. The place I started out with was called Oscar's Salvage Yard. I met Oscar the first time while I was still with Monk, and he seemed like an honest guy who minded his own business. He started me out at $125 per week, less than five percent of what I had been making with Monk. This is when I began my lifelong love affair with cars and racing. This is also the time I met my best friend Mike Corsetti, who introduced me to it all.

We got a good engine from the yard at Oscar's and rebuilt it, then put in another car for street racing. Mike was a born motorhead, and it did not take him long to turn me into one. We would organize these street races at night and place bets on who would win. They were often on neighborhood streets, and we would pay the cops off to keep traffic away. These would usually run around three in the morning, so there was little or no traffic to begin with; but every now and then, you would come across a cop that did not like the street racers or who just wanted a bigger piece of the pie. They would turn on the fire hydrants around midnight and flood the streets so we could not race. As we started out, Mike did most of the driving and took care of the engines. But as time went on, we started splitting the driving and mechanics work.

During these early days of street racing, I was working mainly at Oscar's on Peashuck Avenue. There are many salvage yards up and down that road, and many of them are controlled by the Italian mob. I found this out as I started working at other yards on occasion to pick up a little overtime. More than once at these other yards, a car would suddenly turn up out of nowhere, often a new or late model car, and we would be told to "put it in the shredder now." We never asked questions; we just ran it through. I wondered what—or probably more likely, who—was in the trunk of that car. I never asked questions. That was why I tried to work exclusively at Oscar's. That sort of thing never went on there. Like I said, I was trying to go straight.

It was not long into this period of my life that fate took a hand. I was getting tired of long hours and little money when my sister Lil was in a terrible car accident Not only was she badly hurt, she never really completely recovered from that wreck. There were thousands of dollars in medical bills, more surgeries needed, and no money and no insurance. Well, after about a year and a half of having worked for Monk, I knew how to make a lot of money fast.

Now I am not trying to whine and cry and say, "I had no choice. I did it for my sister." I was a grown man, had a choice, and I made it. Unlike today, in those days I did not look at things as right or wrong in a normal sense. I just did what needed to be done. I really did not even think there was anything wrong with the drug trade in the way that I had come to realize there was a problem with robbery and burglary. The way I looked at it was there were people who wanted dope; it was their decision, and I was providing it to them. I had spent most of the last twenty years either living on the streets or in a correctional facility. Now, at twenty-seven years old, I did not have much of a moral compass.

The best way to look at my way of thinking in the 1970s is to take a look at my arrest record.

CHAPTER 13

Pick Up the Pieces

Like I said before, Mike Corsetti and I cemented our friendship in the world of street racing. We hustled together throughout the seventies and the early eighties. He was godfather to my son, and I was godfather to both of his.

In the summer, we would head out to Delaware Avenue, South Philly, where much of the street racing took place. We started out going to see the "heavyweights," guys who would tow their rides out there and race for money. These runs usually took place in the late hours when there was no traffic, and most of the young "hot dogs" left to take Mom and Dad's car home. The early hours were for the young couples just out to catch some action who had to get both their car and their date home.

Then there were the really sharp looking rods that looked great but were not for racing, just for show. Lines and lines of these good-looking cars would drive up and down the strip, showing off their custom looks. Occasionally, you would hear the purr of a cam coming from under a hood, but they were no match for the tow-ins that started rolling in around midnight.

This was the hobby I fell in love with. I loved the roar of the horsepower and the brute strength of these machines leaping forward from a dead stop like a beast pouncing on its prey. I knew I had to build one, and I knew it was going to be a small block Chevy. Mike was a very skilled mechanic, and I was learning quickly. Work the junkyard for over a year and you will learn enough about auto mechanics to insure that you will never need a mechanic for your own repairs.

In those days, most work under a hood was simple; all you needed was the tools. Mike and I teamed up to build what we decided early on was to be one badass small block that could hunt down and destroy any big block out there. The advantage of running a small block against a big block was you were spotted two car lengths in a race. I liked the edge you got as well as the shifting advantage as opposed to the big blocks.

When we finally reached our goal three years later, we were unbeaten and had taken everyone's money. We spent thousands and thousands building the cars I designed. I was especially close to a speed shop owner who raced pro stock cars, but he was strictly a track guy. His partner was probably the best in the city when it came to setting up the rear of a car. I would get all the latest tips from him as well as good prices and the firsthand pick of the latest in high performance equipment. He was a small-block man like us and raced a Vega, a popular choice back then.

In 1973 and 1974, he was running 10'0's. That was fast for that time, and he eventually broke the high 9's. He loved the fact that we kicked the ass of all of the big-block guys that would come into his shop and rag him about small blocks. As soon as I would show up on Monday mornings, he wanted to know whom we had dusted over the weekend and for how much money. Mike was my driver, and I can truthfully say, I never saw anyone that could shift a gear and stab a clutch like Mike. I never once heard him miss a gear, which is why he always won. If you pulled up to the line, got the go from the flagman, and you broke or missed a gear, it cost you the race. Even worse, it cost you the money.

By the second year, we had named my Nova "Express Yourself," and she sure as hell did. The third year, we unveiled it for the summer season; the reason for the new name was obvious: "War Boots." You could not have gotten a bigger slick on that car: thirty-three inches high and fourteen inches wide. She also had blowproof Summer

Brothers axles, Moroso blowproof posi, and a set of 617 Pro Gears for the rear.

There was 660 actual horsepower launching a '64 Nova that had been gutted and weighed hardly anything. We kept the front end down with wheelie bars along with 90-10 lockdown front shocks and 50/50 lockdown shocks on the rear. We had also used Brandywine heads, a 660-lift roller cam, and tunnel ram with two 660 Holley center squirters that had been milled and worked to the max. The car was a true beast, and everybody was talking about it. We had a huge following. It was Southwest Philly running against South Philly rods, a bunch from North Philly, and even as far away as Norristown; we had become local celebrities. These were some of the best days of my life.

The whole time I was consumed with racing, I was financing it all by dealing speed. I had a very select number of customers that I dealt with personally. They, in turn, had hundreds of customers of their own who had to go through them to get my product. I only personally dealt with people I knew I could trust and who had built a personal alliance with me. I never made the mistake of getting greedy and selling to someone I did not know personally just because I did not want to lose out on a sale. My regulars appreciated that as well because they knew if one of their customers tried to approach me, they would be told, "Get the fuck out of here," or possibly knocked on their ass for even suggesting that I sold dope. The people I supplied knew that their customers would stay their customers.

When I started dealing after falling out with Tommy Monk, I picked up some small amounts from dealers I had become familiar with. I did not do dope, and I never put a cut on it, so even before I started getting it straight from the lab and had to depend on the street suppliers, I would still have a decent product.

Of course, as time went by and I was allowed into the inner circles, no one could touch my product, especially after I became my own chemist. I was asked on occasion why I put it out so pure, and my answer was, "So no one can compare to me, and all those that rely on me know that they will never see anything like mine anywhere." That way, everybody makes money. You allow the customer under you and under him to both make money, and the whole operation grows in size.

However, if you cut your product, you limit how far it will go and stunt the growth of your business. I did small pieces because that is where the money is, but I did it carefully. You could make four or five grand every weekend by dealing small pieces; and if I had to deliver any kind of weight, I took measures to do it away from my house. I never kept more than I could flush down the commode in the event of a raid. I also only moved dope up to a certain hour. I went to bed around midnight, and I was known for not doing anything after eleven at night They also knew better than to bang on my door before a decent hour in the morning.

As I will explain later, my neighbors assumed I was a hood, but I kept the neighborhood rid of thugs that had created a problem before I moved in, so they just minded their own business. Also, you could not be sure what I was doing because of the crowds we generated just with building our race cars.

In addition to "War Boots," I was working on a '32 Ford coupe, and some of my crew were building a '36 Chevy, a big block, but we had agreed to never run against each other. I had a two-car garage that housed the two coupes, and my race car was inside of my fenced backyard. At least one of these cars was always rolled out front, having some kind of work done, and people were always stopping off to look at them and see what we were doing or to get advice. So unless you knew who was whom, you could not swear to the traffic being drug related.

Of course, the authorities knew who was dealing, but if you were considered a nickel-and-dime dealer, you were listed with a thousand other dealers in the city, and you got a visit once a year or so. You just had to be on your toes and not get sloppy. I had a number of search warrants served on me but without any results. A couple of times, I had to flush dope, maybe as much as twelve or fifteen hundred dollars' worth, but that was just the risk of doing business. I never kept more than I could flush, and if that was my loss for the year, I probably gave away as much over the same period.

I also did not make any enemies, but I never showed any weakness in my operation either. The worst thing a dealer can do is beat down a customer who owes you money and starts avoiding you. If someone owed me, I brought him in and told him that I would work with him. You then continue to deal to him and let him pay off a little at a time and keep him coming to you. If you scare him away, he will just go to another dealer. You just have to make sure your customer understands that this is a kind gesture and not done out of weakness. That way, you build loyalty, not contempt. You just do not extend him credit like before; you keep him reeled in close. If you beat a guy down, he may set you up with the police and rat you out. So if it does come down to that, you better never do business with that guy again.

CHAPTER 14

The 1970s

Staying Alive

The decade of the seventies was a hell of a time for me. I got married for the first time, my son John was born, and I put together my own crew and made more money than I had ever thought possible. That's not to say it was not a time without its problems. I would be challenged on a number of fronts business wise, and there would be problems with women, but my arrest record alone would have driven most people over the edge. You add all that to the fact that when I was released from Terre Haute Federal Prison in the summer of 1972, I was on parole for six years with the state of Pennsylvania, so I had those guys looking over my shoulder.

The first time I got pinched was right after I got out on a driving-under-the-influence charge. I had been out partying all night and got popped on the way home driving a friend's car. This was about the time that I went to work for Tommy Monk, so Monk set me up with one of the top criminal lawyers in the city Bobby Simone. That was when I learned the importance of having a top-notch lawyer when you went to court. All the times that I went to court as a kid, I did not have a lawyer; and the three times I went to prison, I had pro bono lawyers, all young kids who had spent less time in court than I had.

When I told Monk about the DUI and that if I caught a conviction, I would be headed back to Holmesburg for four years for violating my parole, Monk took me to see Simone and explained my situation. I later learned that Monk kept Simone on retainer, but I was shocked when the court date rolled around and Bobby Simone showed up himself instead of sending one of his associates. I wasn't the only one who was surprised. When we walked in, everybody in the courtroom looked at him as if to say, "A DUI?" I guess they expected him to only handle homicides and other major crimes, not a mere traffic offense. After a short hearing, the verdict was "not guilty." We were in and out that fast. I learned that day the importance of having a top attorney beside you when you went to court. I would keep Bobby Simone busy for the rest of the decade and into the next.

My next arrest came on January 18, 1973, just a few months after beating the DUI. I was hanging out in the back driveway behind my house with a friend named Robert Romanoff and two neighbors Bobby and Richie Marks. We noticed the police driving up and down the neighborhood streets. When they came down the alley and saw us hanging out, they took us into custody, and we were loaded into a police van and accused of burglarizing the Paintarama Body Shop a few blocks away. We were driven over to the Paintarama and sat in the van listening as the police questioned the owner. Apparently, he had driven up and spooked the burglars, but he saw them as they fled the building. Although we had denied doing anything wrong, the police asked the victim to come over and identify us. When he looked as us, he said, "I don't think that's them." Well, needless to say, I wasn't much liked at the 12th Police District, and my buddies had had their own problems as well, so the cops delivered us to the detectives at Fifty-fifth and Pine, and we were charged with burglary of a business. That's the way the system worked in those days, and I would become familiar with it over the next few years.

We had a preliminary hearing on February 9, 1973, and the witness still insisted that he could not say for sure whether it was us he saw in his business that night. Even without the eyewitness being able to identify us, the judge held our case over for the grand jury. Despite being on parole, I was allowed to make bond, and I went straight to Bobby Simone. Finally, on May 22, without my even being present, the case was dismissed. It was the first time in my life that I got justice in a courtroom, and it took a reputed mob lawyer to get it for me.

But even with that not-guilty verdict, I was still not off the hook. Only a little over two weeks before my not-guilty verdict, I got popped for another DUI. This DUI would have been comical had it not been for the probation violation hanging over my head. I was on my way home from downtown and a night of social drinking with a bunch of that crowd. Naturally, I didn't think I was drunk—drunks usually don't. I was driving a '64 Nova with a beefed up 327-cubic-inch Chevy small block engine I was going to use for street racing. There was a police car sitting on the side of the road; so when I passed them, I popped it into high gear and opened her up. As I roared past the two cops and they lit their lights up, I thought, *Damn, guys, can't you take a joke?* It turned out the only thing they were taking was me to jail. It was time for my lawyer to work his magic one more time. Thank you, Bobby Simone.

After three arrests and three acquittals in less than a year, things got quiet for a while—with the cops, anyway. Word gets around on the street just like it does on the inside. I was juiced in with the right people. I had Bobby Simone keeping me on the street, and I was on my way.

During this time, my daughter Charlene was living with her mother and grandmother. When I was first out of Terre Haute, I did not get to see her much because I had no car. I would have to catch the "L train," then get on a bus, and finally switch to a trolley. The trip one way took longer than I was allowed to spend with Charlene. Getting my own car and beating the two DUIs allowed me to see her more often, despite her mother and grandmother's efforts.

Like I said before, most of the collections were run-of-the-mill affairs; but every now and then, you got one that got interesting. I was hanging out with Monk at one of the clubs when a guy named Pepi came in. Monk asked if he "got the money," and Pepi answered, "The guy claimed he didn't have it."

I knew that Pepi was just a "gopher," so it must not be too big of a deal, but it seemed to piss off Monk, who said, "Go get the $1,500, and take Bojack with you."

I have no idea who the guy was, but he lived in a second floor apartment a couple of neighborhoods over. Though the apartment was on the second floor, the door was at the ground level at the foot of a set of stairs. Pepi knocked on the door, and when the guy came down, he was moving like a speed freak. He started going off on Pepi, yelling, "What the fuck are you doing back here? I told you get the fuck out of here and don't come back!"

There were people across the street at a gas station and people walking down the sidewalk We were drawing too much attention in front of too many witnesses. I said to Pepi, "Let's go."

Then the guy says, "And that goes for you too, mother fucker." Now he was talking to me.

Later that night, after the street was deserted, I went back along with an eighteen-inch pipe. I pounded on the door, and the guy came running down the stairs, snatched it open, and started to go off on me. I caught him square on the collarbone, and he went down. He started crawling up the stairs with me kicking his ass all the way to the top. At the top of the landing, the guy's parents were there, and they were all three more than happy to tell me where his stash of money was.

By the summer of 1975, I was out on my own with my own crew, and the money was flowing. There was one point where I was going out to meet friends, and a guy met me out front of my house and gave me thirty thousand dollars that he owed me. This was such a frequent occurrence that I remember getting pissed off that I had to take the time to go back in the house and put the money in the safe. Another time I was having a Super Bowl party at my house as usual. Frank 'The Beard,' one of our associates whose last name I never knew, came early and brought a shopping bag with thirty-three thousand dollars that he owed me. I just set it on the floor by my chair, and it stayed there until the next day. I took it all for granted back then. I sure wish that I had that problem today.

By the summer of 1976, I was back on the cops' radar. I was in the shower, and my girlfriend Betty, who was two months pregnant with our son John, was in the living room and heard someone outside the front door. She went and looked out, but before she could open the door, the cops smashed out the glass and came barging into the house. I threw on a pair of shorts and came out of the bathroom to see what was going on. The cops accused me of dealing drugs based on all of the people coming in and out of our house.

I did not deny the foot traffic. It was summer, the height of racing season, and the motorheads I hung with were always in and out of the house. My garage was the hot spot; and at any given time, you could look down our back driveway and see two or three hot rods being worked on. There were no druggies or junkies in our group. There was an occasional weed user, but event that was minimal. Nevertheless, they turned the whole house over. The basement was full of weights and was loaded with health products and supplements. The head cop seemed like a decent guy, and he started questioning me on all of the vitamins and supplements and what each one did for you. When he found out what a health freak I was, I could tell that he did not think that I was a dealer because most of your dealers were using their own product. He thought for a minute as his men continued to ransack our house, then he yelled, "He's not dealing. Let's go."

Before I could breathe a sigh of relief, another detective came up from the basement and asked me, "What's this?" He was holding what looked to be a nickel or dime bag of weed.

Knowing that I had never had weed in the house, I answered, "Looks like whatever you brought with you to cover the damage you did here."

I could tell that pissed him off, and he said, "It was in your trash can out back."

I was not surprised by this statement because of all the young guys hanging out up and down the alley. I figured that one of them was holding the weed, and when they saw all of the cops, they thought the raid was for them. My trash can was the only one out on the alley, so they must have just dumped it there and ran. This should never have come down to me being arrested, but the cops had destroyed my front door, nearly cut my pregnant girlfriend with the flying glass, and accused me of being a drug dealer. They had to cover their own asses, so I was marched out in cuffs in front of my neighbors. Time to call Bobby Simone.

They brought me into an initial appearance that same day, and after a few questions from Bobby, the case was marked, "Charge Withdrawn," and I went home.

You would think that beating four arrests in court in less than four years while on parole for armed robbery and narrowly missing a hit from one of the top button men in the city would be enough excitement in anybody's life. But the cops and my old boss were not the only ones giving me shit in the seventies. On February 15, 1975, my son John was born. His mother Betty and I got married and moved to a bigger place on Elmwood Avenue. The house was a large two-story duplex with a driveway and garage. Across the street was a row of stone houses. They were all pretty much constructed the same. There were about five or six steps going up to the front door and forming a patio out front.

I noticed that most of the people were older and were home all day. I also noticed that none of them ever came out of their houses to socialize, preferring to stay indoors. At first, I wrote it off as their being apprehensive about me. I had a lot of traffic in and out of my house, and I am sure it did not take them long to figure out what was going down across the street. It did not take long to disguise what I was doing by building hot rods, either. All my crew were motorheads anyway, so it was easy to cover our business transactions. Besides, none of my guys did drugs to begin with. I would never have allowed it. I had learned that lesson by watching Tommy "Monk" Oteri, but it turned out that I was fortunate enough to have a drug-free crew by their own choice. We were very respectful of the old people; and other than opening a case of cold beer, things were quiet.

But despite our respectable appearance, the old people stayed inside; and other than a few stares and an occasional wave now and then, we had no contact. I soon learned that the old people had become comfortable with me, but there was another problem, one that kept them inside long before I moved in.

There was a bowling alley on the corner of the block down the street from me but on the same side of the avenue. This caused two problems, the least of which was that several nights a week, they had tournaments and several teams who would come for league play. One night, I came home to find a car parked in my driveway despite the fact that I had a "Private Drive" sign posted. I was out front in the street, and one of my neighbors came up. Seeing I was visibly upset, she took the opportunity to approach me. She pointed out to me that my side of the avenue was fortunate to have private driveways. The homes on the other side did not, and they depended on the space in front of their homes to park. The bowling alley had plenty of parking behind their building, but the bowlers liked parking on the lighted street despite the very limited parking. The neighbors had asked them not to park there many times, but they continued to do so, forcing the old people to park blocks from their homes. Some of the bowlers had even become verbally abusive to my neighbors.

It was time to put a stop to this crap. I told my neighbors to point out the bowlers' cars and not to be shy about it. I called my crew, and we waited until fifteen minutes before the leaguers came out to go home. This was just enough time to ice pick the tires, only the rear ones, and create slow leaks. We only did the rear tires, so there was never an issue of somebody losing control of their vehicle if they drove an extended amount of time, and they went flat in transit. The point of hitting both rear tires is so they had to call for help rather than just change one tire and go on to work. We made sure to put the ice pick in the side wall because we wanted them to know that it was no accident. Two nights later, when another league night rolled around, we were out front on the avenue in case anybody needed help finding another place to park. Problem solved.

It was this same week that my neighbors brought another problem to my attention. On league nights and throughout the entire weekend, a rowdy crowd of young thugs hung out at the bowling alley, controlled the environment, and terrorized the old folks indiscriminately. They shouted obscenities to the neighbors for no reason and made crude remarks and gestures to anyone walking by. If a woman walked by, she was at risk of verbal abuse at the very least. It was my neighborhood, so it was up to me to handle things.

My crew moved all of the product in Southwest Philly at this point, so these punks already knew who Bojack was. That weekend, I took a few of my guys and explained that I would no longer be tolerating any of their bullshit. I also explained that taking a ball bat to a situation is an art form, and one that I used regularly when making a point with someone, and if I had to visit this corner again, they would all get a very thorough demonstration. I then suggest that rather than risk any further bad experiences, "Why not make the park your new hangout?" The park was about two blocks away, and they eagerly complied.

We continued to keep the neighborhood safe in other aspects as well, and the locals were happy. They never minded the crowd coming in and out of my place because they understood that we were the enforcers of the peace. Every night, weather permitting, the old folks were sitting outside, enjoying their patios. They knew they had nothing to fear from us.

Jack with his mother, sister and step-grandmother.

Although he would later learn that Mrs. Conway
was not his biological grandmother, she would
provide love and support in his early life.

Jack, at what would be the end of his childhood at
age 8, when Jack Conway returned to their lives.

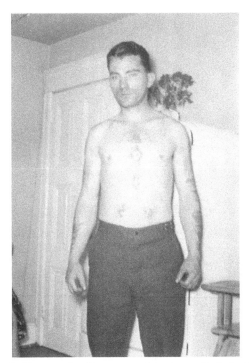

Jack Conway looking every bit the sadistic bully
he would prove to be to his family.

The menacing walls of Holmesburg Prison where
Jack would spend several years and rise up in
the boxing ranks as a middle weight.

The gates to the Navy Yard in Philadelphia.

The street where the Federal armed robbery took place.

The entrance to Terre Haute Federal Prison
where Jack's life would begin to change.

The farm at Terre Haute Prison.

Bojack in the 1970's.

Bojack posing with one of his prize street racers.

The duplex on the right where the home invasion took place.

One of the cook houses in the Endless
mountains of Pennsylvania.

Jack, far right, helping search for missing children
in Atlanta while on the run from the FBI.

Jack and one of his prize K-9's.

Jack and his attorney Fielding Wright, Jr., having
dinner at the Tiki Restaurant in Gautier, MS.

Jack on one of his wedding days with his
best man, Frank the Beard.

Jack with his FBI handlers, Clyde and
Judy, shortly before Clyde's death.

Jack returns to the Turnpike tollbooth
where the loyalties collided.

CHAPTER 15

A Swift Response to a Home Invasion

It was early spring 1976, a little after one in the morning. Only about thirty minutes earlier, the last of my outfit, Mike Corsetti, had left to go home for the night. This was a normal night for me. Anywhere from six to ten guys frequented my house during the course of the day; and as late evening drew near, the crowd would dissipate until everyone was gone. There were never any dopers or junkies around, just guys either working on street racers or picking up a pound or two of product to deliver to the street dealers.

I had the second story window raised and was lying across the bed, enjoying the cool evening air. My wife, Betty, was in the bath and our son John was asleep in his crib in the next room. Life was good. For the first time in my life, I had a real home and family and more money than I knew what to do with. Although Elmwood Avenue was a busy street during the day, this time of night, the silence was only broken by the occasional car passing by. I was so in tune with the quiet gentleness of the evening as well as my own sense of contentment that the voices I heard brought me to my feet and across the room in an instant. I listened for a second, but I could not see who was below me, so I eased the window up about another six inches, which caught the attention of two black males standing down below me near my front door. My first thought was that these two fools were about to try to steal my new car. Parked in the drive a few feet away was my brand-new 1976 Lincoln Continental, Bill Blass

Edition. It was only a couple of days old, just off the showroom floor, burgundy with a silver landau top and burgundy interior—what was not to steal? But all that faded with their next action.

Seeing me suddenly in the window above them, one shouted out, "Search warrant. Open the door." One of them did have a piece of paper in his hand, but I knew it was not a search warrant. I had seen more than a few over the years. Plus, I knew these two assholes were frauds who had picked the wrong house. I told them, "I'm going to lean back out of this window, and when I step back next time, I'll be armed. And if you sons of bitches are still under my window, I'm going to fucking shoot you where you stand." When I got my pistol from the dresser drawer and returned to the window, they were running down the street. I yelled, "You better run, you mother fuckers!"

No sooner than I got the words out than my back door came crashing in. I ran down the hall and dove on my chest, sliding to a stop at the top of the stairs. I had a gate up in the hall to keep my dog, a large Doberman named Satan, out of the kitchen garbage at night. Lucky for the intruder, Satan was not a jumper, or he would have eaten his ass up. Nevertheless, his snarling and growling in the darkness kept the guy at bay. Meanwhile, Betty was freaking out but ran to the bedroom phone and called the cops.

By now, the guy had come all the way to the gate, and I could see the barrel of his weapon sticking around the corner at the foot of the stairs. The weapon was a sawed-off single-barrel shotgun, which explained why he had not shot my dog and come the rest of the way in. Not knowing where I was, he did not want to take the chance of firing his one shot and having me on him before he could reload. I had a similar problem; the only weapon I had upstairs was a .22 pistol. The wall he was behind was thick plaster, and the .22 could not penetrate it. Downstairs, I had several rifles, a couple of .45s, as well as a .44 magnum Smith and Wesson with an eight-and-a-quarter-inch barrel. What I would have given for any one of them. I can remember feeling no fear at all, only rage and indignation that this piece of shit had invaded my home where my family lived.

The punk new his crew had left him by this point but continued to say he was the police and to come down and get my dog. My gun had a nine round clip, and when I found out my .22 would not penetrate the wall, I focused my vision on an old cast-iron radiator and fired three or four shots into it, hoping to create a ricochet effect and bounce some lead back into the intruder. I knew that I had the perfect vantage point at the top of the stairs, and if he would just step into the clearing and face me, it would easily be "good night" for our uninvited guest.

I guess one of my ricocheting shots must have come close to him because a few minutes later, when the police got there, he had escaped out the back way where he had come in. The cops scoured the neighborhood but found no sign of the three males. So after they wrote up the damage report, they left as well. Besides, the Sixty-Fifth and Woodland precinct, who responded to the call, knew me well, so I am sure they were not surprised, nor did they seem very interested. I knew that I was going to have to handle this myself.

As soon as the cops left, I immediately called Rick and Mike and told them what had happened and to come over right away. I wanted at least two of us there in case those punks returned. Both Mike and Rick were there in minutes, and we began to discuss what had taken place. Was this a hit on me? Was it guys trying to take over our operation? I never saw the guy in the kitchen, so I had no idea who he was. I did see the two men out front, but they were complete strangers. All I knew for sure was that I was going to find them.

CHAPTER 16

Message Time in Southwest Philly

As I stated about that night my home was invaded, I felt no fear. I did not have the luxury of reacting like a normal citizen and letting the police handle it. Instead, I was filled with rage and revenge, which in my mind was the key to our survival. All I thought about was my wife, the mother of my son, in the tub naked, my infant son in his crib asleep, and this trio of lowlifes coming into our home to do us harm. I was prepared to kill all three of them on the spot and would have if I could have gotten a clear shot.

There was no yelling to the man in the kitchen, "What do you want?" Never for a moment did I think of asking that stupid question. There would be no negotiation. If he had not run away, one or both of us would have had to die, and I had no intention of dying now that I finally had something to live for. I was just glad that I heard the voices and armed myself before the back door was breached. I was glad that it was Betty, not me, in the tub; otherwise, the whole ordeal might have turned out differently.

The first step to finding out who was behind the home invasion was to figure out why it had taken place. I had to figure out "hit" or "take over." Were they trying to scare me off and take over the area I had cultivated? Although this was a possibility, I did not think it was likely. For one thing, no one could touch my product for its purity or for the price. My customers knew that and would not deal with anyone with a lesser product, so just trying to run me off and take over my operation made no sense. This was especially true since these guys seemed to be such amateurs. It would have taken somebody with real muscle behind them to run me off and make a takeover.

Was it a hit? I had no enemies except for Tommy "Monk" Oteri, and he would never have the balls to try another hit on me after our last conversation. Besides, by this time, Monk had lost almost everything and was well on his way to becoming a street junky. He no longer had the resources or the trust to put something like this together. However, I was not taking any chances. I moved Betty and the baby into hiding until I solved the problem.

The first order of business was a reward. Even though these guys were not local to my area, somebody knew them or knew someone who did. Philly is a massive city, but the speed freaks got around. They followed the dope, and it was everywhere, and they all knew one another. Through one connection or another, I had countless happy customers. They were getting a solid product from me with no worries about getting ripped off, and that went a long way on the streets.

At the time of the incident, I had taken a short breather and was not dealing. I did that from time to time. It makes your regulars appreciate you because when you replenish and release your product again, they return to you after having learned where the grass is greenest. So I put out word to every dealer and junkie in Southwest Philly that until I found the culprits responsible, there would be no more dope. I was shutting it down. However, there was a reward of ten thousand dollars, as well as a package of top quality speed when I got rolling again. It only took about a week when the big break came.

I was at home with Rick and Eddie—there were always at least two guys at my house now, even when I was gone, in case anything else went down. I was in my backyard when I noticed a tall, thin black guy passing my driveway for the second time. He was walking back and forth like he was wanting to do something but was hesitant. I thought this dude was one of the guys from the other night, and by the third time he passed, I was sure. Where I was standing, my shoulder was halfway behind the back wall with my right arm hidden. I slid my .45 out of my belt and held it down by my side out of this guy's sight. I then told Eddie and Rick to go through the house, out the front door, and get behind this guy.

As the guy was about to pass the fourth time, he stopped and locked eyes with me. I raised my weapon and told him to start walking toward me. His first reaction was to put up his hands to show me he was clean. He looked like he was about to break and run, but before he could move, my boys were behind him, weapons in hand, and "invited" him into the house.

I sat him in a chair in the center of the living room. Satan, my Doberman, was right beside me, letting out a deep menacing growl. He sensed the man's fear and no doubt recalled his scent from the night of the invasion. At first, he denied being a part of the group, but a ball bat refreshed his memory along with a threat to let Satan loose on him.

I was right about their being from out of the area. He and the other black guy I had seen out front that night were from the Powelton Avenue section of West Philly. The guy who broke through the back door was a white guy from Center City called Kim. He and his partner had heard we were hunting them, and that there was a reward. I had put out word in the Powelton Avenue area through some of the guys I had done time with at both Camp Hill and Holmesburg, so I figured he was telling the truth. As soon as they got the word, his partner had taken his wife and daughter and left town. I asked him, "Why the hell are you here now?"

He said that he had no family and no money to leave town, so he had come to ask for mercy. I quickly told him, "The only way you're going to get anything from me besides two in the back of the head is with information." That was enough to start him talking.

The guy Kim, he didn't know a last name, had approached him and his partner about a home invasion and robbery, but they had no idea who they were going to rob. He assured me that he had heard of Bojack and would never have agreed to the robbery if he had known I was the target.

The way this Kim guy came to know about me was through a customer of mine Steve Mancini, a small-time dealer who was always trying to score big enough to get in with the "guys from downtown."

Mancini came into my house one day kind of by accident. Normally, Mike Corsetti would never have allowed a guy like that past the front door, but like I said, we were taking a break. And since we were clean, and the guy wanted to talk to me, Mike yelled, "You got a visitor." And I let him in.

Normally, the guy would have just asked when we would be up and running and try to get me to reserve some for him and left. The problem came from the fact that while we stood in the living room and talked, the guy looked over my shoulder and saw five thousand dollars lying on my dining room table. It probably looked like even more as about half of it was in twenties and the rest in hundreds. Mancini saw this and must have thought that I kept large sums of cash lying around the house. He was wrong; I never kept that kind of money in my home. With all of the search-and-seizure visits that I had from the law, I never had as much as a plastic bag in my house. Lots of cash was subject to seizure.

The money Mancini had seen that day was going to the Ford dealership to pay the balance on the new Lincoln I had just bought. I had traded in a fine 1974 Eldorado Cadillac blue-black custom, and they had allowed me to take my new Lincoln home and bring back the five thousand dollar balance the next day. The reason that I had to come back the next day was I had to get the cash from one of the stashes I had hidden around the city.

Mancini. knew me, so he could not do the job. So he recruited these guys; at least that is what he told me. I knew Mancini well enough to know that he did not have the balls to do a home invasion, especially at my home. He probably figured he could recruit these three screwups on the idea that three of them hitting me in the middle of the night would catch me off guard and outnumbered, and they would kill me and get the cash. In the event I killed them, there was nothing to link them to Mancini. What my tall talkative friend said next sent me off the deep end. "Mancini and Kim said to try to take you alive. Then all we would have to do was put that shotgun up to your baby's head, and you'd give up everything."

I went ape shit on the guy. To think that these pieces of shit would come into my home with this plan, putting a gun to my baby's head and threatening an innocent child, God knows what they would have done to my wife coming out of the bath. I backed off the guy and was about to turn my Doberman loose on him when I thought better of it. If I wanted the other guys, this was the quickest way to get them. I told him to start talking, and if he wanted to live, he had better talk fast, or I was giving Satan the word. And talk, he did.

The day after the invasion, Mancini had heard what happened and took off for New York. A couple of days later, word reached this guy and his partner in the hood as to whom they had tried to rob. His partner had left town with his family that same night, but this guy Kim was still running around the city. I told my new snitch that since he had never entered my home, I was going to let him off the hook. I could go to New York later and deal with Mancini, but I wanted Kim right now.

That is when he started telling me how crazy this guy Kim was. It seems that Kim had a plan to rob a bookie and his family. The guy's name was Harry, and I knew he made book and ran a numbers racket out of a corner bar. I also knew that he was a made guy in the Angelo Bruno family. This Kim guy had to be fricking crazy.

I sat there in amazement as my snitch detailed how they knew all of the family's names—his kids', his wife's, and even the dog's. He went into detail about how they were going to follow this man home on a Sunday night when he would have the cash from all of the weekend's betting with him, and then they would rob him with his family present so they could use his wife and kids to threaten him to give up everything he had. I could not let this slide and knew I needed to get word to Harry. Besides, I might need some of his friends in New York to help me find Mancini. This was all falling into place.

We stuffed our new friend in the middle of the back seat between Rick and Eddie, and I drove down to Harry's place. When I entered the joint, there were only a few patrons drinking at the bar. It was early afternoon, and I knew the crowd would not start coming in until after work. I did not know Harry. I had only heard of him, so I asked the bartender where he was. When he asked me why I wanted to know, I answered in a loud voice, "I have something important to tell him, and I drove over from Southwest Philly to alert him about something." I knew Harry would be one of the guys sitting at the bar, so I had thrown out the word "alert" to get his attention.

Sure enough, one of the guys slid off his bar stool and said, "I'm Harry." All the other guys were staring me down. I figured they were his crew. I told him to step over to the window with me, that I had something to show him. The window was small with a lighted beer sign, but I had parked right out front, and you could see the guys in the back of my car. I told him we needed to talk in private about the black guy, and he could do whatever he wanted after that; I was just making a courtesy call. He told me I could talk in front of the guys in the bar, proving my theory that they were all part of his crew.

I told him everything that this thug had told me. I could tell he was shocked when I told him his family's names. All he said was, "Bring him in here."

I motioned for the guys to bring him into the bar. That is when Harry told me, "This is Angelo's money. These guys will answer to him same as me." When the guys brought the snitch in, we hauled him in the back with some of Harry's crew, and I told them the whole story of what had gone down. I also told them that I needed to take this guy with me when I left because I needed him to catch Kim and deliver some justice. I could tell Harry was upset and was convinced that this was no joke. Harry looked at the guy and said, "I can see Bojack and his crew have gotten your attention. We can do this the easy way or the hard way. I'll start with the easy way. If I think you're bullshitting me, we'll go the hard way."

He started to milk this guy for more information than I had ever thought about. He wanted to know where Kim stayed, where he would go when hiding, the names and whereabouts of his friends and family, the girls he hung with, who supplied him with his dope. By the time he was done, we had Kim's life story. He also knew I had stopped what would have been a bad scene at his home, and he told me, "I owe you one."

Harry must have figured out what I did for a living. He asked me if I wrote book for anyone. I told him, "No, I just supply a product."

He nodded his head and said, "You gotta do what you gotta do. If you get this guy first, let me know."

We shook hands as I left with my crew and my informer. I felt good about warning Harry. It was the right thing to do. Besides, the money he was holding was Angelo Bruno's money, and I knew that if I did not catch this Kim guy, someone would. We were both on the hunt for him; it was going to come down to who got him first.

After leaving Harry's place, we headed to my snitch's home in Powelton Village. He had told us that after the invasion, Kim had broken down the shotgun and had dropped off the barrel at his place. He also told us that Kim might be there because Kim came and went as he pleased as though it were his own home. Although they were supposed to be partners in crime, it was plain he was scared of this crazy ass white boy. When we got there, Rick and I did a SWAT-style entrance, weapons raised. We swept the lower floor, then cautiously mounted the stairs where we cleared the second floor bedrooms. I led the way, hoping this piece of shit would pop out of somewhere now that I had my .45 in my hand and would end this once and for all. I remember feeling pissed off when I realized the house was clear. I knew this was not over.

The one thing we did get was the shotgun barrel. I took it with me and told our snitch if Kim came back for it, "Tell him you got paranoid and threw it in the sewer."

We hung out for a while, hoping that Kim would show up. We came up with a plan to get this scumbag. I told our snitch to tell Kim that he was working on a drug deal, and that he needed Kim as backup because there were no drugs. When the guy showed up with the money, they were going to beat him down and take it. This was right up Kim's alley.

The next night, our boy called up and said Kim had come by and wanted in on robbing the fictitious drug dealer. Kim also said when he got some money, he was going to get some dynamite and "throw it into Bojack's house when they are sleeping." No one knew that I had moved my family out, so when he said, "When they are sleeping," that's whom he was talking about. My blood started boiling all over again. I could not wait to meet this guy.

I planned the deal for three in the morning on a particular street in University City. University City is a residential area where a lot of the college students lived who went to Drexel College. It was risky because the cops patrolled the area regularly, but it was also ideal for what we were planning. The streets would be deserted that time of night, and any college kid out and about would be in no shape to give an accurate description, tag number, or coherent story to the cops.

I told our guy exactly what route to take and not to deviate from it. I told him the spot where we were going to take Kim down, but I anticipated that he might give it away with his apprehension when they got close. So I set up the attack one block sooner. In truth, I also knew my snitch was worried that we might do them both, or he might throw back in with his old partner at the last minute, so I needed the element of surprise. We would take them one block from Thirty-Fourth Street where the trolley left the street and went underground.

There were five of us, three from my crew, me, and a guy named Joe Cardone. Joe was what we called a weekend warrior. He worked hard all week at his job, but on the weekend, he would get a forty-dollar-bag from me to go to a motel with his honey and chill out for a few days. Joe was not a speed freak; he was an ironworker by trade and was very muscular and strong and had courage. He knew how to mix it up and was not afraid of anybody. Plus, he liked the one thousand dollars I was going to pay him.

When we got to our spot, Rick dropped us off and drove off to see if they were on their way. Joe and I settled into the entrance to an alley, Eddie crouched between two parked cars, and Mike got behind a huge hedge. Not long after, Rick pulled up, motioned that they were coming, parked the car, and slumped down. He did not even have time to get out and hide. I peeked from the alley and could see they were less than a block away with our guy walking on the outside along the curb, giving me a clear shot at whom I wanted.

We all five had aluminum bats, and I told Joe, "Fuck up the white guy. Leave the black guy alone." Joe went for a home run aiming for the knees, but his swing was high, and he caught Kim in the thighs. Our informant took off down the street, screaming like a little girl. That was the last time I saw him. Kim took about three good shots the whole time, screaming, "Police! Police!" of all things.

I have to hand it to Kim; he never went down. He made it between two parked cars and out into the street where Rick was idling in the car for a fast getaway. Rick stomped the gas and rammed him, knocking him several yards down the street. But, like a cat, he came up on his feet and started running. I can tell you after that night, I had a whole new respect for adrenaline.

During all of this, the neighbors started coming out of their houses, and I noticed some had gone back inside. I was sure this was not the type of neighborhood where people knew to mind their own business. And when two guys were out in the street yelling for the police, somebody would call them. We went down the street after Kim, but he was nowhere to be seen. In seconds, I heard police sirens coming our way, so I told my crew, "Let's get the hell outta here." We piled into the car and were gone before the cops got there.

Later that morning, I called Harry and told him what had happened. He said he would have his guys check the hospitals. Later on, Harry called me back and said his guys had found the hospital, but Kim had slipped out before they got there.

That afternoon, I got a last call from my informant who said Kim had just showed up at his house with one arm and one leg in casts and his head and ribs wrapped like a mummy. He was wired out of his mind and kept saying, "I need to call Bojack. I need to call Bojack."

As I said earlier, all speed freaks knew each other. I learned that Kim had contacted a whole lot of users in my area to get them to talk to me for him. I am proud to say, none of them did. Everyone he tried told him, "You fucked up, man."

He finally went to one guy Tommy Huran, who was a friend of mine and a good customer. Tommy told me up front that the only reason he was contacting me was that he figured I would want to try to get him to make a slip as to where he was laid up. He told me, "Bojack, he gave me this pay phone number and told me he would be there for fifteen minutes. I told him he did a bad thing, and he's insisting he didn't. It's all a mistake."

I told Tommy I appreciated it, and Tommy assured me he had no love for the guy, that he wanted to help me out.

When I hung up, I called Harry and gave him the number. He said, "It's probably near where he's hiding out," and hung up. When I called the pay phone, a guy answered and, without even saying hello, said, "Bojack, I swear I didn't try to break into your house." He was all excuses.

I let him ramble for a moment, and he incriminated himself several times. Then I shut him off with, "I thought you were dead, you son of a bitch."

More rambling and self-incrimination and then I let him know that I was not the only one looking for him. I did not say who, but he knew. That's when I told him, "You give me Steve Mancini, and I will try to call everybody off."

He said, "Hell, I don't know where he is."

With that, I hung up. I never heard from him again and neither did anyone else in the months and years that followed.

A few weeks after that phone conversation I was in a bar and ran into a guy from Harry's crew. I told him I was still looking for Kim. All he said was, "That's over with."

Steven Mancini did go to New York, where he got arrested on a mail fraud charge and went to federal prison. A friend of mine Bo Darby ended up in the same institution. Bo was a real badass with a lot of connections. He told me that the last thing Mancini heard before the lights went out were the names Harry and Bojack.

CHAPTER 17

Peaks and Valleys

Once I got this whole home invasion crap straightened out, 1976 continued to be a good year. I had gotten married, my son was born, and business was booming. Sure I had been challenged by this Mancini thing, but I had met the challenge. I knew if the name Bojack was going to mean anything on the mean streets of Philly, you needed to respond to a threat and send the proper message. There was treachery around every corner and rampant jealousy of what you had. I already had a reputation for not going around making enemies, but now I had made a reputation for taking care of business when I did, and I had made some valuable friends in the process.

The ironic thing was that not long after this, before the end of 1976, I was given an early release form parole. Thirteen months early for "good behavior." It seemed life was making up for all the bullshit of the first twenty-five years.

That is not to say I did not have problems. After all of the attention from the home invasion. the cops were at my door more than ever. However, they never found anything. I never kept more product around than I could easily flush down the toilet in a hurry, and I always kept it in one place where it was easy to grab on the way to the toilet. On more than one occasion, the cops busted through the door to find me sitting there with a wet sleeve. Sometimes they would still toss the house, but sometimes they would just say, "Shit, he flushed it," and leave.

The narcotics officers were around so much, not only could we recognize them on-site but so could my neighbors. They were still grateful for my cleaning up the Elmwood Avenue area, and I could always rely on a phone call whenever there were any cops around. One particular pain-in-the-ass cop was a 12th District cop we called "Pretty Boy." It seems that one of the guys in my crew had slept with his girlfriend, and he took it personally against all of us. Every time you turned around, this guy was down the street, spying on my house with a pair of binoculars. This had been going on for the better part of a year, and by the winter of 1977, he finally got his chance.

One of my customers was leaving my house, and they followed him out of the neighborhood. When he was clear from prying eye, they grabbed him. They had no probable cause to stop him and certainly not to search him. All he had to do was keep his mouth shut, and they would have had nothing. Even if they had searched him and found the dope, if he had just kept his mouth shut and called me, I would have put Bobby Simone on it, and the guy would have walked. But the minute they asked this guy if he had any dope, he started to squeal like a pig.

He told them that I never kept more in the house than I could easily get rid of in one flush, that the only way they could take me down was to get me when I was outside the house and then make a search.

On February 7, 1977, the Philadelphia narcotics squad laid out a plan to snatch me before I entered the house. That morning, I left to go eat breakfast, and they decided to grab me when I returned home. There was a trolley turn around beside my next-door neighbor's house. I would always pull into that turn around when I came home, reverse, and back into a parking space in front of my house. This meant that my car was out in the open; and if anybody tried to tamper with it, the whole neighborhood could see.

As I looked back to back up, there was a gun in my face. Suddenly, there were guns all around, and I was being pulled from the vehicle. It was so fast that I never saw them coming. All I recall was being manhandled, taken to my door, and told, "We have a search warrant for your house." The door was kicked in, and they proceeded to ransack my house and vehicle. In minutes, the narcotics guys were elated that they had finally caught Bojack "holding dope." Not only had they caught me holding, but they had caught me with a bag of bagged up pieces. That constituted manufacturing and delivered a much more serious charge than just possession.

I was already cuffed up, so they threw me in the back of a cruiser and took me to the "round house," which is what we called police headquarters. I made it clear that I was not talking to anybody, and that I wanted my lawyer. They threw me in a cell. A few hours later, they put me on the phone with a DEA agent that I knew from the neighborhood named Charlie Davis. Needless to say, he was thrilled that I had been caught red handed and proudly announced that my case was being taken over by the Feds. I just kept my cool and made my bail.

About this time, Bobby Simone was tied up in several high profile cases with some heavy hitters. I hired Joseph Santaguida, another heavyweight lawyer who could get things done. There had been something that felt wrong about this whole arrest, and the more Joe and I looked at the police reports, the more it came to light.

First off, they had a search warrant for my house, nothing else. There was no arrest warrant for me, and no search warrant for my car. The entire arrest and vehicle search were illegal. Then you look at the search warrant for the house. It had been obtained on the word of some guy the cops had stopped on the street without probable cause and then questioned. Even though the guy was not a reliable or proven informant, the search warrant had been obtained based solely on his statements—statements that were made while he was under the threat of arrest. Furthermore, my vehicle, where the dope was found, was not on the premises of the house listed on the search warrant. It was still in the trolley turn around when they searched it. In short, the Philly cops had screwed up.

A few days later, Charlie Davis approached me about my case, telling me that I belonged to him now, and that I had better cooperate. That's when I told him how everything had gone down, how the dope had been in the car and not the house. I could tell by the look on his face that I had his attention. One thing about the Feds, they do everything by the letter of the law. They even check with their "legal department" before they pull off something like this. Seeing his reaction made me feel better about my own case. One thing was for sure, the Feds had gotten pulled into a mess that they had not made, and they were not going to let it go easily. My every step was monitored. I had suits sitting on my front door, and I could not leave the house without an army of them on my tail.

At one point during this, one of our runners, a guy named Frank Palmer, showed up at the house unannounced to tell me he had a couple of pounds out in his car that he wanted to drop off from a fresh cook. I freaked out. I told him that the law was all over me and to get out right now. I said, "Get in your car, don't look around, don't look back at the house, and for God's sake, don't speed or give them any reason to pull you over. Do you understand?" Fortunately, the Feds had seen him walk in empty-handed and leave less than a minute later, still empty-handed, and calmly drive away. They did not bother to check him. God only knows what would have happened if he had walked into my house with two pounds of product under his arm.

Not long after this, sometime in March 1977, I went to the Mississippi Gulf Coast for the first time. One of my guys had family down in Gautier, Mississippi, and he suggested that we get out of the cold Philadelphia winter and head south. Betty and I had separated by this time; and with everything going down, I needed to get out of town for a while. Philly was having an ungodly cold winter that year, and we loaded up wearing peacoats and wool hats with the temperature below zero. Two days later, we were sitting outside on his cousin's patio in shorts, planning my first fishing trip in the Gulf of Mexico.

The next couple of months were what I needed. I found a local gym to work out, went fishing, helped his cousin remodel his house, and took it easy. We lived off fresh seafood and hit the bars and juke joints whenever we felt like it. I was not much on the country music in those days, but there was a rock and roll club in Pascagoula called Thunder's Tavern. It was owned by a guy named Thunder Thornton who had played on the offensive line for Ole Miss.

Some years later, I would get my start working for his dad, Mr. Walter Thornton, and his kid brother Waldo, who played offensive line for Southern Miss, as a bail enforcement agent. There were also several rock and roll clubs across the Back Bay in Biloxi, along with a few discos that were still holding on. The casinos and the tourists were still over a decade away; but on the weekends, there were a lot of people from New Orleans coming to hang out on the beach, fish, or play tennis and golf. There were plenty of women to take my mind off Betty and a lot of things to take me away from the streets of the Philly meth trade.

On June 7, I got a call from Joseph Santaguida. Not only had he beaten the charges against me, but he had gotten back the eight hundred dollars they had confiscated off of me as well as the guns that I had in the house. Technically, the guns were not mine. I was a convicted felon and could not own one. They were all registered in Betty's name. It was time to go home.

When I went down to the narcotics squad to collect my eight hundred bucks, I took Betty with me to pick up "her" guns. There was Pretty Boy staring me down with a pissed-off look. A few years later, when I was working for the FBI, Pretty Boy would go down for bribery and shaking down dealers and pimps for a "street tax" to work in his area. That was part of his beef with me. Not only had two of my guys done his old lady, but I had let it be known early on that I was not going to be some crooked cop's punk. If you could take me down, do it; if not, get out of my damn face. I was not paying any street tax.

During our stay in Mississippi, we spent a lot of time at the King's Inn on Highway 90. It was the place to go in Pascagoula. They had a large bar that was packed with all of the nice ladies, and anyone who was someone in Jackson County hung out there. It was here that I met a guy named Maurice Gregory. He loved to party and was great to hang out with. It was Maurice who introduced me to a guy named John Coggins, who owned a gas station across the street from the King's Inn. I had heard of Southern hospitality and was taken by the friendliness of everyone we met. So it did not take long for me to start seeing the Mississippi Gulf Coast as a place to escape to and leave the drug trade behind.

No sooner than I mentioned moving South than everything started moving. Maurice said he knew of several houses where the owners had very little equity, and we could probably just assume the notes and not have to go through credit checks. About this same time, Coggins and his wife were taking over management of the King's Inn and were looking to get out of their lease on the gas station. This really piqued our interest.

Coggins explained that he had eight months left on his lease, and if we came in on it with him and did well, when renewal time came up, the owner of the franchise would probably okay us and allow us to renew it in our names. This seemed like the perfect setup. I had been to the station several times and knew they were not maximizing its potential. All they had been interested in was selling gas and a few snacks and sodas. Meanwhile, two bays sat idle. Mike Corsetti and I were top mechanics and could keep those garage bays full. In addition to our work, we would begin selling oil, filters, and other accessories at a reasonable markup, and we could easily double the income this place was producing in no time. I had plenty of cash to fill the tanks and stock whatever inventory we would need to turn the place into a real garage as well as a gas station and a store.

This was about the time that I got word from my lawyer that everything had been taken care of back in Philly. We decided to go over to New Orleans for a few days and see the sights. We ended up in some little bar in the French Quarter. It was set up with a bar along the right wall when you walked in and a walkway that went behind the people seated at the bar that led to a larger area in the back with several tables as well as pool tables.

We were seated at the bar when a couple of young hotshots came in and said we were in their seats. As quick as that, it was on. Mike and another friend of ours Obie were mixing it up with these guys, so I checked over my shoulder. Sure enough, these two clowns had three buddies in the back coming up fast. Fortunately, the bar was so narrow, they had to come single file. I rolled off my bar stool, and a short left hook stopped the first guy, and a right uppercut to the heart turned his lights out. I started mixing it up with the second guy, and when he went down; the third guy had backed off. By this time, Mike and Obie had cleared a path to the door with the owner yelling that the cops were on their way; we got the hell out of there.

We all decided we'd had enough of New Orleans and that we should go back to Philly by way of Daytona Beach and Disney World. On the way, we stopped off in Pascagoula to see Obie's family one last time. While we were there, I called Coggins and told him it was a go on the gas station and that I would be back in a couple of weeks to finalize everything. I also told Maurice to locate homes for Mike and me. We headed down to Florida for about ten days where we even hit Miami for a few days of hard partying before heading north.

During this time, I had gotten in touch with Betty, and we were getting back together. She was excited to be moving to a new place and getting a new start, and we both agreed that if things did not work out, we could always go back home to Philly. However, once I got back to Philly, I knew moving to the Mississippi Gulf Coast was my best option. The heat was on, and cops were following my every move.

Mike and I flew back to Mississippi a few weeks later where Maurice had lined up a couple of houses for us. I bought a house not far from the station for $3,500 in equity and took over the note. The house was less than three years old and still looked like new. Mike found a house across the river in Gautier about fifteen minutes from the station for $1,200 move-in equity. The only thing left now was to move our furniture and other belongings south and become Mississippi residents.

We returned to Philly apprehensive about the move. Other than my time in the joint, I had never lived outside of the Philly area, and what little traveling I had done was to New York and Atlantic City. So the Mississippi Gulf Coast was a whole new world to me. It was a serious undertaking, but we now had houses and a gas station waiting on us. All we had to do was take hold of our dream of working on cars in our own business; fishing the warm waters of the gulf; and leaving the insane world of drugs, gangs, and the Philly streets behind us for good.

CHAPTER 18

It Bes that Way Sometime

The Spring of '77 was supposed to be the start of everything I wanted. Mike Corsetti and I, along with our families, were brand-new residents of Mississippi with big plans for our new business. We were going to take that gas station and make a real moneymaker out of it. Gas stations neglected their bays and pumped gas only. Mike and I, being good mechanics, were going to put our bays to use and make some real money. We figured the regional office would be glad to have us selling and using their products instead of just gas, chips, and soda.

We had not been on the Gulf Coast a week when John Coggins told us that Chevron was not going to lease to us. Despite the fact that Coggins had eight months left on his lease, they were shutting him out due to his being shut down more than the allowed time. My hopes were still kept alive when I found out that I could get an interview with the regional boss to lease the property in my own right. There was also a younger guy up for consideration; however, I found out he was asking to be credited the gasoline and other supplies up front. We had the cash for everything to start up.

I knew as soon as I met with the regional boss that he did not like me. He looked at my tattoos, heard my Philly accent, and turned his nose up, acting like a jerk and a snob. Needless to say, he went with the younger guy who never made a go of it. Within a few months the station, was sitting vacant again. This kid did not know the difference between a socket set and a monkey wrench and had tried to make it by just selling gas. I was left insulted and with a bad taste in my mouth.

Here we were uprooted to a strange place with no business, no jobs, and no contacts or prospects. We had put everything into our dream of opening our own business. To make matters worse, Mike had no savings. He had put everything he had into the down payment on his house, thinking we would be up and rolling very shortly. He found work at the local Dodge dealership. They were glad to get someone of his skill; they just did not want to pay him what he was worth. He quickly became disillusioned and went back to Philly, leaving me on my own in Pascagoula. I was easily able to live off of my savings for the next year and was even able to pick up a little side money training dogs for Bullock's Kennels, but that was lean income with no future. Let me tell you, a guy with no contacts in the area, no formal job training, and only a GED, along with an extensive criminal record—well, jobs were not exactly falling off trees. That is when I made the biggest mistake of my life.

I had made friends with a couple of my neighbors. They were young guys who like to party and ran their mouths a lot, two things I normally would have avoided back home. One day, they got to talking about speed and how much they liked to party on it. For some reason, I opened my big mouth and told them about the quality stuff I used to be around in Philly. They knew I was headed home for a visit in a few weeks; and after several days of badgering me, I gave in against my better judgment. So when I came back to the Gulf Coast, I brought them a forty-dollar bag of some good stuff, thinking they would keep it for personal use. They cut it and sold it, and even I could not believe the money they made. They had not had anything like that, and they started driving me crazy to get them some more. So I started getting them small amounts and eventually ounces. The product basically sold itself, and it was not long before they started drawing heat from the narcotics squad. They got busted in early July 1978; and two days later, they ratted me out. That is when my Mississippi nightmare began.

Robert O'Brian, a good buddy of mine who had first brought me down to the Gulf Coast, was staying with me for a while. O'Brian had flown up to Philly and was coming back with two ounces. He was up there when these dudes got busted, and they alerted two narcs that he was flying into the airport in Mobile, Alabama, and even the date and time. When I drove over to Mobile to pick him up, the cops were on my tail. As soon as we were back across the line in Mississippi they pulled us over.

After a long night of interrogation, it became evident that neither one of us was going to talk. So they threw us in a cell on the fourth floor of the courthouse. That night, O'Brian whispered to me that he would take the blame and admit to the two ounces that were in his suitcase. I told him, "No, we are in this together. We'll both keep our mouths shut and ride it out together."

That's when he told me he had thrown a small bag of dope on the floor of the car. When the cops pulled us over, he said he had freaked out and thought the window was down and tried to toss it out of the car. It had bounced off the closed window and landed on the floor by his feet in plain view. I never saw it because I was too busy watching the carloads of cops approaching our vehicle and surrounding us. I had no idea there was a second bag of dope in the car. He admitted to me that this second bag was a small helping that he was stealing from me for his own use. Like everybody else around me, O'Brian knew that my two main rules were no using and no stealing from me. Plus, if there were dope around, I was to know where it was and exactly how much. Many times over the next few years, I thought I should have let him take the heat and walked away, but I always stood by my people.

We bonded out of jail, and I hired a top local criminal defense attorney Fielding Wright Jr. His father had been governor, and Fielding knew his way around. Fielding did an excellent job. He attacked the admissibility of the evidence based on an unlawful stop and search as well as the agents following me across state lines—all valid legal arguments, none of which worked. The DA made us out to be East Coast mobsters trying to take over the Gulf Coast as well as Damn Yankees selling dope to kids. It did not matter that the only people we had sold to were our two neighbors who were well into their twenties. The jury came back with a guilty verdict. It was "let's make everybody happy" time. The judge gave us twenty years like he was throwing out Mardi Gras beads. My lawyer filed an immediate appeal and convinced the judge to let me out on an appeal bond. Meanwhile, the neighbors I had provided product to had kept talking, and I had additional charges filed against me. Attorney fees and bail bonding costs were piling up with a total of four pending charges. Finally, my lawyer, my bondsman, and I all agreed that I should move back to Philly until all of this could be settled.

It was at this time that my attorney explained to me that the judge had given me twenty years, the maximum for sales, but I had been convicted of possession with intent, which only carried fifteen. Therefore, no matter what else happened on the appeal, it would at least be sent back for resentencing. By that time, all of the publicity about "East Coast Mobsters" would have calmed down, and Fielding would be able to negotiate a five-year deal on all charges. As I said, his dad had been governor, and Fielding had political contacts all over the state. If he could not win your case in the courtroom, he could manipulate it in other ways.

CHAPTER 19

Return to Philly

City Streets Ain't Got Much Pity

I returned to the city and was only back about a week when a good friend of mine Don Laken came to me. Don and I had worked search and rescue dogs together as well as guard dogs, and I considered him to be a good friend. Don had a swollen and bruised eye as well as a cut down the side of his face.

Don had a sister who was mentally challenged, and he often looked out for her and went by her house to check on her. She also had a son who was a little lowlife punk. It seemed that he and his thug crew, all guys in their early twenties, had taken over her house and were terrorizing her and her neighbors. She had asked Don to talk to him.

When Don came over, his punk nephew took off his belt and struck Don across the face with the buckle. Don was no slouch. He had been in the marines, but he was getting older, and there were five of them. He said, "Bojack, this is still your neighborhood. Why don't you visit these punks and teach them something about Philly paybacks?" Don was my friend. I could not turn him down.

A few days later, accompanied by Stash Palmer, a tough ass member of my crew who had just gotten out of Holmesburg, I paid them a visit. Stash carried the handle from a pickax, and I had a pipe. As we started up the front steps, we were met by two of the nephew's friends who asked us if we were lost. We started there. We left them piled up at the door and went on in. The screams of panic and pain had alerted everyone inside, and I found Don's nephew in the front room trying to bow up at me. That lasted until the first swipe of my lead pipe introduced him to reality. I beat his cowardly ass all over that house while Stash dealt with the others. They were climbing out of windows, doors, wherever they could find a way out.

I pummeled this punk out the back door into the yard and halfway down the alley. That's when I looked up, and who the hell was standing there but Charlie Davis from the DEA. He lived behind this guy's house, and their yards apparently backed up to one another. Charlie was just standing there like, "What the hell?"

I could not say much because I did not want Stash to get the wrong idea or to drag Charlie into this. So I just said, "I'll call you later. We're just doing a little housecleaning."

By this time, the nephew was crawling down the alley begging for mercy. I told him, "That's all for today, but I'll be back unless your uncle tells me not to."

The boy called Don the next day and begged his forgiveness. He also promised to give up his gang and to start taking care of his mother.

Later I also called Charlie Davis. He told me that he had heard screaming and came out the back door to see me beating the shit out of his worst neighbor. He also made it clear that he was in support of my housecleaning deal as this dude was a problem in the neighborhood. He added, "I know you entertain the occasional enforcement venture. If I hear of any other problems out of this guy, I'll let you know."

This whole eviction was not just a favor for a friend, sending a message to a punk kid, and protecting a helpless woman. It sent a message to all of Southwest Philly. Bojack was back in town.

CHAPTER 20

Taking Back My Empire

Moving back to Philly brought home to me what my move had meant. Instead of going straight for the first time in my life and giving my son the chances that I had never had, it simply brought everything home to roost. I knew that I was probably facing anywhere from five to fifteen years in prison and was pretty well broke. Not only would I need more money for attorney fees, but when I went away, my family would need money to live on while I was gone. The first thing I had to do was locate all of my old customers who never really understood what the hell had happened to me and where I had disappeared to. I also had to establish a decent connection for quality product. I had several sources that I could go to, but like before, I only wanted the best that the streets had to offer.

Mike Corsetti had been back for quite a while and was on top of his own action; and very soon, he was hooking me up with decent meth. Despite how close we were, he was not ready to tell me everything he was into. I did know that he was new to an organization and was sworn to secrecy. However, he was getting me a good product, and that was all that mattered. My street action started to pick up fast, and I was making great money with Don. I was still mailing money back to Mississippi to my lawyer and bail bondsman, but at least I was not racking up new cases down south. I was safe back in my own turf and stashing away money for when I had to go away.

I was also living pretty well, and I even had the money to put my son in Good Shepherd Catholic School to start his education. Since it was a Catholic school, I was given the "once over" as to why I was not married to his mother after eight years together. I was told, "You are living in sin, and it is not healthy for your child."

I agreed, knowing they were right, and said I would look into it. However, my old crew was going to see to it that I had no excuse. Don, with whom I worked canines, arranged through a family doctor to do the blood work for free. My best friend Mike Corsetti actually bought the wedding rings, a really nice set, and Don arranged for a judge he knew to perform the ceremony. All I had to do was show up. So Betty and I became husband and wife; and thus, the slow decline began. We had gone together for eight years; but once we were married, it only lasted two more.

In addition to moving all of the product that Mike could get me, I had a legitimate "day job" working a security and canine service. Part of our work took us to Delaware City, Delaware, to take over the security for the Getty Oil Refinery there.

Getty was experiencing a major strike, and things were starting to get nasty. Their refinery covered acres and acres of property, so we brought in twenty-five protection dogs to assist with security. The job lasted for thirteen weeks, and I was being paid one thousand dollars a week as chief of operations. It was the height of winter, and the conditions were brutal. Tempers were short, and it was not long before the union thugs came in with their dirty tricks, violating all of the injunctions that had been put into place by the courts. Things soon got ugly.

The union thugs attacked state trooper vehicles and refused to break up when confronted by the limited number of troopers. That's when we were set loose with our crowd-control dogs.

I handled Butu, one huge crazy ass rottweiler. I started to approach the mob of strikers who were jeering and threatening to kick my dog's ass. I held a thirty-foot-long lead; and as I began to let it out a foot at a time, Butu would increase his fanning motion. Swinging wider and wider with each foot of lead I gave him. Anyone with any sense would know if you did not disperse, you would get your ass eaten up. We were flanked on either side by a number of other canines, and we covered the entire width of the main entrance. We had the strikers cleared out, and the gates secured within minutes. We then went across the acres of property, posting canine crews at all of the pumping stations. We employed crews to drive the terrain and check on the dogs to make sure their shelters were okay, and there was hot food.

Getty was well prepared for the strike. They had brought in key personnel from all around the country. They could not risk driving their cars through the groups of angry workers every day, so arrangements were made for them to sleep on the premises. Food and hygiene products were stockpiled along with cigarettes and whatever else they could think of. Cots were set up for my men and me, and we were even provided hot showers. I ate like a king and lived like one in the fields overseeing my men. Motor homes were later provided and stationed around the fields with the security canines. Getty even rented an empty trailer for my weights so that I would not have to drive into town to the gym and be off-site.

Despite a few punch ups here and there, we did not have too much of a problem. I even went into town with a couple of my men to the union hall where the strikers had set up headquarters and kicked in fifty bucks to their coffee fund. We spelled it out for the head honcho that we were not there to deny them anything, just to guarantee everyone's safety. The strike was not personal to us, just our job.

Despite our reaching out, we still had a few issues. One incident involved boxes of roofing nails being thrown in our driveway. I personally gathered them up and in the early morning hours scattered them all over the parking lot of the union hall. That was the last of the trouble for a while, but it got uglier when the union, finding out that Getty had prepared for the strike and was not about to buckle, sent for their real goons. There was conflict and fighting for the rest of the strike.

The union workers were prepared to miss a couple of weeks of work at the most However, even with the kind of money they had been making, once the strike went into the fifth week, car payments were due, and mortgages and other bills had to be met. These folks had mouths to feed, but they kept it up for another eight weeks. Eventually, Getty won the strike, and everybody went back to work.

Everything was going smoothly, and I had almost stopped thinking about the situation in Mississippi, having been assured that the appeal would take several years. Therefore, I never expected to answer the telephone one day and have my attorney tell me I had to come back to Mississippi for the decision on my case. The way it works is you show up at the sheriff's office with your attorney and your bail bondsman, and the sheriff would call the clerk of the state supreme court. You are then told if your case is affirmed or overturned. If affirmed, you are taken to jail. If reversed, you walk away. I was affirmed and taken to the county jail.

My lawyer was prepared to take the appeal to the next level, the US Supreme Court. The procedure for the second phase of the appeal is you must file a motion for rehearing with the state court; and once that is denied, you proceed to file for a writ of cert to the US Supreme Court. The state supreme court had six weeks to respond to our motion to reconsider, and they took all six weeks, so I sat in the Jackson County Jail for the next month and a half.

During that time, my attorney offered to pay a fine of twenty-five thousand dollars and for me to be banished from the state of Mississippi. My lawyer told me that this was often done. However, a new DA had been elected and was not having any of it. His name was Mike Moore, and damn he was stubborn. He made it clear to my lawyer that he "had it in for that Yankee" and was going to make an example of me. We proceeded with the appeal; and after about sixty more days, my lawyer walked me out of the county jail on a fifty-thousand-dollar bond. Believe me, I did not hang out in Jackson County; I was Philly bound that very day.

I spent the summer working with Don and started hustling meth on the side, preparing for the day that I might have to go away for twenty years. I was on a roll again, and I put the Gulf Coast behind me. I figured the US Supreme Court had to get it right. The whole thing was surreal. Don and I worked with law enforcement on most of our jobs with the canines; and at the same time, I was dealing meth in my old turf; and the whole time, I had a twenty-year sentence hanging over my head plus three other pending charges in Mississippi and a writ of cert filed with the US Supreme Court. Just when I thought things could not get any stranger, they did.

In November of 1980, we received a request from the city council of Atlanta, Georgia, to come down and assist in the search for the missing children of that city. The request had come from Arthur Langford, and we were going to assist the Georgia Bureau of Investigation in their search for missing children or in the location of their remains. Atlanta and the surrounding areas were horribly overgrown with kudzu, a plant that grows along the ground as well as up trees and embankments and makes it impossible to determine what is underneath, so tracking dogs were badly needed.

A few days later, Don and I, along with the rest of our team, drove to Atlanta where we were introduced to the sheriff and sworn in as special deputies. We set up our headquarters at the Stadium Hotel across from where the Atlanta Falcons played. This case would become known as the Wayne Williams case. He would be sentenced to life in prison where he remains until this day.

On December 23, 1980, my attorney called me and told me that the US Supreme Court had denied my appeal, and that I had to come back to Mississippi and turn myself in. *It's two days until Christmas. You have to be kidding me,* I thought—how cruel is that? Fielding told me that he would talk to the judge and call me back. When he called back, he said that the judge had agreed to let me stay out on bond until January 2, 1981. He also explained that even though my conviction had been upheld, the court had remanded me for resentencing since I had been sentenced in excess of the maximum. Therefore, I would go back before a circuit judge in Jackson County. My bondsman kept saying I would only get five years, but I knew that the new DA was telling everyone, including my lawyer, that he was going to bury me. That is when I made up my mind that I was not going back to Mississippi.

I told Don what had happened with the appeal. He asked me what my plans were. I said, "I am going back to Atlanta and look for whatever pieces of shit were murdering those kids." So I went back to Georgia like nothing had ever happened in Mississippi. So here I was, a fugitive from Mississippi hunting for bad guys in Georgia. My heart was in the right place.

This is a good time to explain how I came to finally use my birth name. I had never told anyone about what my mother had told me. I was embarrassed at first, so I just stored it away with all of the other sordid secrets of my life.

When I posted bail after sixty days in the Jackson County Jail and had returned to Philly, I decided to send for my birth certificate. I had never seen it and was not sure what it really said. When the birth certificate arrived, I was ecstatic. First, I finally was somebody with a true name, the one given to me at birth. But I also had an awesome new identity if my appeal did not work out The best part was that no one outside of my mother knew this secret, and even she would never suspect that I would use this name.

I took my birth certificate to the social security office prepared for the questions I would get about why, in my thirties, I had never had a social security number. I knew there would be people in a number of lines. I needed that special somebody behind the counter to single out. I saw a young black agent and waited until the right moment to catch his eye. I motioned that I needed to speak to him. He came over to the side as I had hoped, and I asked him if I could speak to him about an embarrassing matter. He replied, "Certainly," and I wasted no time telling him how humiliated I was making this request. I said that I had just completed fifteen years in prison and had gotten a great job. My boss needed my social security number, so I would have to get a rushed card, or I would lose my job. The man was more than helpful and took me back to his desk where he checked my birth certificate and filled out the standard paperwork.

I received my card in less than two weeks, and I immediately filed for a learner's permit with the OMV. Once I got that, I took the driver's test and got my license. These are the three most important IDs required. I made up an entire second wallet with a gym membership card; and by the time I got the bad news from Mississippi, I even had a credit card listed under John Saltarelli. The beautiful thing about this was that everything about my identity was the same;

I just had to memorize a new social security number. I was now John Michael Saltarelli with no connection to John Michael Conway. For the first time in my life, I used my true identity.

This would prove to be one of the best things I did.

A short while later, I returned to Georgia to continue the search for missing children. One night, I was in my room working out with dumbbells and doing sit-ups, when the door burst open and three guys claiming to be law enforcement officers came bounding in with guns drawn.

They told me they had a fugitive warrant from Mississippi on Jack Conway, and they were taking me down. I managed to keep my cool, and told them they had the wrong guy. Of course, their response was, "Yeah, right." Still sitting on the floor with my hands behind my head, I said, "My wallets on the desk; see for yourself." Sure enough, everything, including a couple of photo IDs, said I was Jack Saitereili. After a while, they said "Sorry to bother you. We were just responding to a tip," and left.

As soon as they were gone, I stood at the door and listened; when I heard the ding of the elevator, I grabbed a bag that I kept packed for a quick getaway, and ran for the stairs. I was out the back door and in my car in under two minutes, leaving the state of Georgia for good.

CHAPTER 21

When Loyalties Collide

As soon as I got back to Philly, I arranged a meeting with Corsetti. He told me that there were now three guys running their organization: him, John Drum, and a guy named Ronnie Pierce. The fourth member, a guy named Leo, had been murdered. Due to the heat from this, they were not going to take anyone else into the crew. They still wanted me to handle distribution to my network throughout the city, but I would have to keep it on an even lower profile than before due to the extra heat on me personally. Mike also told me that he wanted me to get into the production side of the business as well. I had helped with cooks before, so I said no problem.

Most of their production at that time, or at least the part I was involved with, took place in a house over in New Jersey. The family who lived there was sent away on the weekends, all expenses paid by our outfit, and we cooked down in their cellar. I was fine with this in that it enabled me to have direct access to all of the product I needed as soon as it was completed and not have to wait around for them to get it to me. It also gave me an extra place to hide out from Friday afternoon to Sunday night outside of Philly. During this time, I extended my distribution area in New Jersey and met a new contact in rural Pennsylvania who would help me move into that area as well as Western New York.

Eventually, John Drum and company found a place nestled on the side of a mountain in the Endless Mountains area of Pennsylvania.

It was perfect for what we were doing and an ideal place for me to stay where I could both keep an eye on it and stay out of Philly. So I put a couple of trusted friends in place to handle my city action, and I stayed up in the mountains.

During this time I found out that Walter Thornton, my bail bondsman back in Pascagoula, had to pay out the fifty-thousand-dollar bond because I ran. I contacted Walter and told him that I would make it good, and then I explained to him that he should not send anyone for me because it would be dangerous for any bounty hunter. I was not only facing a twenty-year sentence, but there were other charges pending as well. I had no intention of being brought back.

Not only did I guarantee him his money, I explained that it would be sent in five-thousand-dollar increments. The next day, I drove all the way to Binghampton, New York, to a bank and purchased a five-thousand-dollar cashier's check and sent it express mail. A few days later, I spoke with one of my contacts back in Philly, who told me that the Feds had been by looking for me and mentioned that I had sent money to my bail bondsman. I called him up and told him not to be telling anyone that I sent him money. He agreed and begged me to turn myself in.

The next week, I drove to Wildwood, New Jersey, and once again sent Walter a five-thousand-dollar cashier's check. Now, if ten grand in two weeks didn't show him that he wasn't going to get burned, I didn't know what would. The reason I was sending the amount of five grand was to stay below the radar and not make the banks suspicious. You can't just walk into a bank and ask for a fifty-thousand-dollar cashier's check and hand them the cash without bringing a world of attention on yourself. Besides, buying and mailing them from different states would make them think I was either on the run or still hanging out in Philly, proving to the Feds that I could be anywhere.

A few days later, I contacted my people back home on business, and they mentioned that the Feds had been around and knew that I had sent a second payment to my bondsman. I immediately called him up and explained that I was disappointed but not angry. He was obviously over a barrel, and the Feds expected him to report all contact with me. Nevertheless, he would not be getting any more payments from me. I told him I had his forty grand and would put it away so not to fret about taking a loss. When the time came for me to go back to Mississippi, I made sure he was taken care of. We later became good friends, and he even gave me my start in bail enforcement because he knew I was a man of my word.

During this time, I was making trips back to Philly to meet with the three bosses of our crew. Leo's execution-style murder was eating at me. I was expecting Drum, Pierce, and Mike to feel the same way and wanted to avenge Leo's death. Whenever I brought this up and would get really pissed off and rant and rave about how we needed to find the fucks who did this, they would tell me to settle down and dismiss the subject. At one point, they even told me that they suspected a Muslim guy that Leo knew from jail. I offered to move on the Muslim guy because we had to send a message, or we would lose all respect on the street. They told me to sit tight and take care of my end of our business and not to do anything. That's when I became suspicious.

I went back up into the mountains and continued to go out on the road and tend to business as well as overseeing the cooks. But the wheels in my head were turning. and I kept my eyes open. The next year would prove my suspicions right.

CHAPTER 22

Missing My Children

Being a fugitive was by no means an adventure. I lived every moment of every day missing my children. Even though Charlene was not with me, I carried an awful guilt knowing that just at the height of getting to know my daughter and having her spend time with me in my home, I had to vacate without any explanation and run to Mississippi. My son was still in diapers and with me, but I did not have paramount custody of my daughter where I could have taken her with me. She was eleven when I rolled out to the south of Mississippi, and how do you tell your eleven-year-old that you are being smothered by DEA agents and the local narcotics team? You don't. Not when you want to be her hero. I couldn't tell her mother because she was the type of woman who would have it all over the neighborhood, something I wanted to avoid.

Charlene was spending weekends with me, and we were getting close. We would go to the park on Cobbs Creek Parkway and walk our Doberman. I wanted to make up for the years that I was away while she was in her infancy and later, her early adolescence years. The visits I did make to see her back in those earlier days were hardly comfortable for me. Without revisiting those days, I'll just say I was never comfortable around her grandmother, who always seemed to be standing guard. The greatest ache I suffer today, and I always will, is that I missed out on those "daddy's little girl" moments when she jumps on your lap and tells you she loves you, knowing you will never ever let anyone hurt her—a real hero.

John had all that I had: enough love for the two of them. Had her mother ever come to me and asked if I wanted to raise her, I would have jumped at the opportunity. Thinking back now and the money I had available, and knowing her mom's greed, I would have offered her money. But I say that in retrospect. The life I entertained, I always kept John safe, and I would have managed fine with both of my children.

During my days as a fugitive, I often thought of Charlene. It was a major project that had to be in place to manage seeing my son. I know it would have been difficult trying to see the both of them. Yet though I did not know the road I would eventually pursue in the months to come, I spent many a lonely night in the mountains or in hotel rooms or wherever business took me thinking how wonderful it would be if I could turn everything around and walk into my daughter's life and begin to make up for my stupidity and the hurt I caused her. How cruel it must have been for her to go through life being cared for by uncles and her mom's friends when I could have given her a good life.

Charlene once told me that when she would spend weekends with me and her brother, John's mom, Betty, was not nice to her. I didn't see it, but I would have sent Betty packing if she did something distasteful or mean, and I caught it. It must have been a jealousy thing. I do know that in her drunken stupors, she acted mean to John. This was later, after we got back from Mississippi, and I was about to get the bad news about my appeal. I worried terribly knowing John was with her, and I could not come into the city to check on him.

Betty was clubbing every chance she got, and babysitters were a regular thing at the house. She was also running around on me, so I pretty much felt like John was doomed. All that time, I kept getting messages sent to me from the Feds through a contact of mine who, though he insisted he didn't know where I was, knew better. "Tell him he doesn't have to do that twenty years. Maybe we can help him with that sentence." I heard that for over a year and never once thought about turning. In my heart and mind, I believed I would be shot down trying to escape. I know I did not want to go back to Mississippi because, aside from the twenty-year sentence, I had other charges, and the new DA was gunning for me to make an example out of me.

At the time I was pining for my children and an end to the running, one of the outfit's heads started moving some of the product, a little bit at first. One of the workers said that Ronnie wanted a small amount—I want to say an ounce. No big deal; hell, he's one of the bosses. Well, I thought he was giving it to someone, perhaps to barter for something or whatever. Had I known he was grooming a customer, I would have raised the issue early on how that would eventually create a problem.

I always understood that nobody carried dope back to the city after a cook. So when we cooked another time or two, the subject came up that Ronnie wanted larger amounts. I saw the writing on the wall. Give someone half an ounce of our product and in a week, they'll want a pound. All through my writing, I insist that my biggest problem was not getting enough speed, and that I was moving just about most of what was out there in the streets. Ours, and product from anyone else who was cooking, was given to me untouched. I was paying ten thousand dollars a pound, so I was insistent when Ronnie asked for more and said, "No way. I need all of it because it's promised out already."

I know Ronnie was upset with me and probably thinking, *Who does he think he is?*

Ronnie had other issues with me, like my weaponry. No one was to have guns in the lab. Even though I discovered a small caliber automatic stashed on an upper ledge of the kitchen closet at the lab, Ronnie claimed it to be a rule that no guns were allowed. But he wasn't wanted by the law. A point to ponder is that Leo was murdered with a small caliber weapon. Too bad it was removed later and wasn't there when the lab was taken down.

Regardless, Ronnie thought I was a problem. He wasn't getting the dope he requested; I blocked that. Then there's me with the guns. He couldn't raise an open vote on what to do with me because

Mike would've had my back, leaving it a two-man vote and not a clear three man vote. Plus, I'm not sure Mike knew he was sending for dope when they all agreed no dealing on the streets. They had workers doing everything, and I kept the money flowing and the dope moving. Why risk the heat? I also heard from the workers that Ronnie was saying that because the Feds were after me, there was heat everywhere, so he was certainly building a case against me. The thing is, it wasn't including Mike. And if I'm right about how Leo was killed, with what, and by whom, Mike would never have voted on that either. Mike was all business, but he was made of a different fabric than John and Ronnie. John and Ronnie were brothers-in-law and pretty cunning. Ronnie was ruthless, and John was the politician, always looking for a swift and silent solution. I guess I knew I was pushing things, but what was about to take place cemented my beliefs about this team. It would start the downfall of this outfit and the reason all loyalties would collide.

CHAPTER 23

When Loyalties Collide, Part 2

Despite missing my children and the regrets about how all this affected their lives, it was time for me to move and shake. It takes money to be on the run for nineteen months, to get more money to your kids to take care of them, to put money away for them in case you get taken down, and to try to take care of your bail bondsman. It all takes planning and hard work while keeping one eye trained over your shoulder to make sure the people after you don't get too close, and it seemed like everybody was after me.

As soon as the FBI got their fugitive warrant on me, it was turned over to Clyde Witson III, a really sharp agent whom I would later come to consider a true friend and confidante. His partner was Judy Tyler, who was new to that office. The two of them were both under the supervision of George Sherwood, who headed up squad number 2 of the Organized Crime and RICO Unit of Eastern Pennsylvania. I was later told that when my file was delivered to them, Judy said, "I'll have him in ninety days." It would be nineteen months before I turned myself in.

In addition to this new advisory, I had the local Philly drug task force boys who had been after me for years, looking to take me down for a trip to Mississippi and out of their hair.

Then on one of my runs to Philly, I stopped by a local bar to do some business when an old friend pulls me aside to tell me that some guy claiming to be a cop from Mississippi had been in, showing my picture around, flashing his badge, and talking about there being a ten-thousand-dollar bounty on my head down there. Then my friend said, "We started to take him to the salvage yard but figured you didn't need any more heat on you from some dead cop. So we just let him go."

I told him he did the right thing but thanked him for the thought and made it clear that if anybody else came up from the Gulf Coast to tell them no one had seen me and let them go. So now I have a bunch of half-ass wannabe bounty hunters on my trail, looking for a fast ten Gs from the state of Mississippi—as if I needed any more complications in my life.

So here I am on the run, seeing my son only one or two week-ends a month, completely alienated from my daughter, my wife running wild, and a pack of hellhounds on my trail wanting to take me back to Mississippi for what I figured would turn into a life sentence by the time they racked and stacked the new charges onto the twenty I was already facing. That's when I knew I would never be taken alive. If I only had a few more years, I was going to spend them as best I could, leave as much money for my kids as possible, and go out like a warrior.

During the summer months, I traveled to the Jersey shore to visit my sister Lillian, who was staying there with her kids. We were close, and she had room for me, so I would just show up at any time during my travels. My contact in the mountains had some of the best weed on the market and would always give me a generous gift out of respect. Since I didn't smoke or do any kind of dope, I gave it away.

I had developed my own groupies down on the shore, and my unannounced visits were welcomed by them. Believe me, a quarter of an ounce of great weed could get me a whole lot of loving from this little bikini crowd. The shore was a summer hangout, and the doll babies all flocked to the boardwalk to live their dream for the brief summer season before heading back to the city.

On occasion, I would hook with a beauty and take her with me for a week. Now I only did that on a few occasions because I was not going to ride off into the sunset with just anybody. These were girls that my sister either knew or checked out and would tell me who was cool and who wasn't. It was an adventure for these girls. They were secretaries, nurses, and school teachers living a quiet little life, taking off for a week with a muscled-up fugitive drug dealer running dope across three state lines. It was the adventure of their life, and I always treated them like queens. We ate great meals in the best restaurants, I took them shopping in the best stores, and I never initiated the sex—that was their idea. We were always good to each other. I was generous with them, and they were the same with me.

This filled out some of the lonely times. I knew my marriage was over. I heard stories about my wife and her partying, and I knew that if I ever got myself squared away, the first thing I was going to do was get divorced. So I found loving wherever it presented itself.

During this time, I developed a strong friendship with John Nystrand, the biggest mover in the Pennsylvania mountains. John had a great setup. He was the owner of an old rustic and historic hotel and bar in a small mountain town. All the locals went there, and a lot of our crew from the city—everyone hung out, drank, and played pool. The town had only one police officer, and he hung out with us. There was no crime there, and John never did any business there, keeping it far away from where he lived.

I knew John's supplier was Stash Palmer, my partner on the enforcement end of things. When John approached me about supplying him with product, I was hesitant. I valued Stash's friendship and could not afford for things to sour between us. John explained that he only saw Stash about once a month; and by the time he got out of the city and up here, he never had any real weight left. He promised to keep buying whatever Stash brought and could move plus anything that I could provide. So I began loading John up.

He continued buying whatever Stash brought him; and soon, he was doubling his orders from me. I rarely got to see Stash once I went on the run other than when we had to do enforcement work down in the city. He would occasionally come up to the mountains on a run and hang around for the weekend. During one of these times, I told him about mine and John's arrangement, and he said, "That's cool. I get nervous driving that shit all the way up here from

Philly anyway." Stash was a great guy and a great friend. But like a lot of the people I got close to in those days, it didn't last long.

Another friend of mind, Joe from Southwest Philly, lived near Stash. He walked his dog every morning between five and six o'clock in a small park about a block from their houses. One morning, he found Stash slumped over on a park bench, shot in the head. I heard about it a few days later and would have thought it was a hit, but the gun in his hand was a revolver that his late father had left him, and the wound was self-inflicted. The investigation showed that the gun had misfired the first time, which would have stopped the average person from committing suicide, but not Stash. He was as committed in death as he was in life; he was all man. Once he made up his mind, nothing could sway him. He had told me he was having serious issues with his wife and kids and thought the was going to lose his family. The collapse of his family weakened him to the point of calling it quits and took his will to live.

Meanwhile, Nystrand got an apartment out of town and started living with a gorgeous young lady that he met through his business with me. John had so much money, he never knew what to do with it or where to keep it. John started using, and that was a problem with me. I worried about his bringing attention to himself. He bought a new Corvette with cash and drove it home. I came by the next day to see it, and he had taken all of the wiring out from under the dash and piled it up on the floor. He had to have it towed back to the dealership and put back together. He would go and buy a complete five-sectional stereo set with speakers for several thousand dollars and the next day go out and buy the exact set in a different color and never remove the first one from the box.

I never knew exactly where John was moving his product from, but I knew he was all over the map. I had a key to his place, so I started telling him to put his money in the freezer, and I would just go around when he was away, take what he owed me, and leave new product.

He really loved that new girl of his. I think he took her to every mall in New York state and bought her anything she wanted. I always liked her; I just hope she stood by him when he went to prison.

It was the latter part of the summer of 1981 when life and death reared its formidable head, and I was put in a serious circumstance that would change my life forever. At this point in time, I was spending a lot of time hanging out at the cookhouse, or the lab as we called it. It was a two-bedroom, one-bathroom trailer with a cookroom and a garage built on. After each cooking we would carefully clean and stack all of the equipment and close the door leading into the trailer, giving it the appearance of a normal storage area. The lab was very secluded and safe for what we bought it for. Neighbors were few, and the nearest one was about a mile away.

I spent a lot of time up there and only left the safety of the lab to either pick up money or deliver product. I always dressed neatly; drove the speed limit; and drove a nice, dependable vehicle, but nothing flashy. When on the road, I kept moving, never staying more than a couple of nights in the same place. I was running from the lab to Philly to Jersey and back into upstate New York and back to the Endless Mountains in Pennsylvania. I had been on the run for over sixteen months, and I had not had any incidents since Atlanta. That's when trouble came from a place it had been brewing for a while.

Tension had been building between me and Ronnie. Ronnie had been considered to be the muscle until I came on board. From that time on, Stash and I handled any problems that came up. Ronnie was not a tough guy, but he was devious and cruel. Our type of work could not afford the publicity of people blowing up or Ronnie wielding a chainsaw in front of people. Business had to be taken care of by professionals and quietly, so I always felt like there was some resentment from Ronnie that the other three heads of our family trusted and respected me more than they did him.

In the late spring of 1981, during one of our cooks, Jerry Cohen, a "chemist" for our crew, told me Ronnie wanted him to bring some product back with him, only a small amount, about an ounce or so. I did not think anything about Ronnie wanting the dope. If you know a dealer who doesn't use you, you can give him an ounce of the good stuff, and he'll soon be wanting more from you and leaving his old source behind.

What I did have a problem with was that one of our rules was that no one left a cook, especially one of the workers, with any drugs. If they got stopped, and the drugs were found, that would lead the cops straight to the lab. In fact, our workers would bring an extra set of clothes with them; and once everything was cleaned and stored away, everyone would shower and put on fresh clothes and wash the clothes they had cooked in. Then they would leave at different intervals in separate direction. No one wanted some random state trooper with a drug dog stumbling on them by accident in a random traffic stop.

At our next cook, Cohen told me Ronnie wanted him to bring back a pound. My response was, "What? Fuck that shit No way. I got it all promised and sold already. Besides, if you get popped leaving here with a pound, we're all going down." When Cohen reported back, Ronnie got pissed, and it really ate his ass that I said no to him.

Also, ever since Leo was killed, I had still been pushing for us to find out who was behind the hit and take care of the matter. Every time I brought this up, they tried to feed me the story about the Muslims, claiming they had kidnapped Leo, forced him to teach them to cook meth, and killed him. This made no sense. The night he disappeared, Leo had gotten a call and left, telling his wife and daughter he was going to a meeting. Why would Leo meet with a bunch of Muslims without backup, let alone without bringing a piece? The person who called had to have been someone Leo trusted. Besides, if it was the Muslims, why had we not hit them back?

It was midafternoon. I was relaxing at the lab when I heard a vehicle roaring up the drive from the bottom of the hill. The driveway was steep and narrow, and I looked out to see a large yellow rental truck straining to climb the hill. When I saw who was driving, I relaxed. It was Dennis DeLuca, one of our crew from Philly who helped out with the cooks. However, when he got out of the truck he was nervous and in a hurry. He told me that Ronnie was not far behind him and was bringing an electrician to look over our wiring. He said that Ronnie wanted the lab equipment and anything related loaded up and driven away so that the electrician would not see anything suspicious. We had blown a lot of fuses during our last cook due to excess usage of electricity, so bringing up an electrician was not out of the question. But something in my gut told me things just weren't right.

Then, DeLuca said something that reinforced my gut reaction: "Ronnie wants you to pull your van around back out of sight and sit tight until he gets here."

I asked DeLuca why he was taking the rental all the way back to Philly, why not just go somewhere and hang out a few hours and bring it all back. He couldn't give me an answer; he just said he was in a hurry. Hell, I now knew something wasn't right. We loaded everything up except my household goods into the truck, even the trash. The whole time, my mind was going a mile a minute. DeLuca mentioned that Ronnie and the electrician would be in a brown Cougar, and then he took off.

I pulled my van out of sight from the road as requested, then went to the rear of it and dug out a long-sleeved flannel shirt. It was warm out, but I needed something long and loose to conceal a weapon. Ronnie knew that I had two weapons, a Smith and Wesson .44 magnum with an eight-and-quarter-inch inch barrel. It was nickel-plated and referred to as a Clint Eastwood gun. It had been a gift to me from Bobby Marconi, a good friend and loyal customer of mine who was a heavyweight with the Pagan's Motorcycle Gang. The other weapon was a Dan Wesson .357 magnum that I had picked up on a trip to Wichita, Kansas.

What Ronnie didn't know was just a few days before, John Nystrand had given me a .45 nickel-plated automatic, so I had a third gun that Ronnie didn't know about. I hadn't yet fired the new gun and didn't want to risk an untried weapon in combat, so I decided on the Don Wesson and hid it under the front of my shirt. I went back into the house and prepared for their arrival, still hoping that the visitor really was an electrician.

It wasn't long before the brown Cougar arrived. I walked out on the deck of the house to greet them as they got out of the car. We said hello, and Ronnie began to walk his friend through the house. They talked about the electrical system and the blown fuses, and I started to hold out hope that this was all legit, and everything would be okay. Then I heard Ronnie telling this dude in a low voice, "This is where we set up our plates for cooking."

The lab equipment was moved so that the house would look normal should anyone respond to the scene, and the equipment would not be lost. The house was under a bogus name and not traceable to anyone. Dennis was nervous and in a hurry to get out of there, and this guy was being schooled on how our operation was set up.

Like I said before, Ronnie had a lot of connections with the roofer's union and was one of their goons whenever they would strike a nonunion worksite. I had heard all of the stories about him. He would come after an unarmed man with a chainsaw or throw dynamite into someone's business, but he wasn't a fighter. He wouldn't come at anyone face-to-face unless the numbers were on his side; and here we were up in the mountains, and it was two on one.

I also noticed that Ronnie had taken the smaller caliber handgun off the closet shelf and put it in his pants pocket. This was the same type of weapon Leo had been killed with. I had closely observed them both when they came in and could not see any bulges under shirts or anywhere else where a weapon could be hidden.

I knew that if Ronnie wanted to use that small caliber weapon on me, he would move in close. They had finished their business and should soon be leaving. How were they going to do this? Was his partner going to jump me, pin me down, so Ronnie could put one behind my left ear?

I have had many fights both with weapons and without, and that readiness that comes over you had embraced me for this telling moment. If Ronnie did not pick up on my readiness, then he really didn't know me. The goon with him wouldn't be expected to sense my resolve and had no inclination that he was about to enter his darkest hour.

Then, as if on cue, Ronnie blurts out that his friend is a gun lover, and that he had been telling him about my weapons on their way up. "Bojack, show him that big one," he said. "You know, the silver one. You got two, right?"

This is it, I thought, and I had played it just like I wanted. I had kept a table between us, and on it was a large brown leather travel bag. I reached in, never taking my eyes off Ronnie, whose hand was near the pocket with the gun. By process of elimination, I had to give priority to the only weapon I knew they had. I pulled out the .44 Smith and Wesson and placed it in the middle of the table within his partner's reach. The gun was empty.

The guy eyed the gun nervously. "That's one bad motherfucker," he said, moving a little closer.

Still watching Ronnie, I reached in the bag and pulled out the .45, setting it on the table closer to me. At that moment, they exchanged a look between them. That's when I pulled my .357 from under my shirt and said, "This one never leaves my hand because you just never know."

Ronnie took a step back. "You have three now," was all he could say. I could see the fear in his partner's eyes. Their count was off, and the tables had turned. In my mind, I was already loading them in the trunk of the Cougar, driving it back to Philly, and leaving it at the same intersection where Leo had been found.

Suddenly, Ronnie had to go. He kept his hands in sight and away from his pocket, and they hit the door and headed for their car. The equipment was gone, and so was my livelihood. Still, in all, I did not want to be around if DeLuca did come back, not knowing who or how many might come out of the back of that yellow rental truck. I had to contact Mike Corsetti and tell the only guy I could trust after what had just gone down.

CHAPTER 24

Testing the Waters

What with my "family" looking to whack me, I had to lay even lower than before; but more importantly, I had to figure out who I could trust. The only guy I had trusted one hundred percent was Mike Corsetti; I had to make sure that trust was not misplaced. This was way before cell phones, and with me on the move and Mike taking care of business in the city, it was about a week before we could arrange a meeting.

When I finally got Mike on the phone, we agreed to meet at Fisher's, a high-end restaurant in Bensalem just outside of Philly in Bucks County. I told Mike we needed to stay out of Philly because I was too well-known, and there was so much heat from the Feds. Truth was, I wanted a place where we could talk without being overheard, where Mike could relax and I could get a good read on whether or not he was still on my side.

I got there early and scouted the place out, then got a table where I could see all of the doors. I had not told Mike anything about what had gone down at the lab. I wanted to do that in person so that I could watch his reaction. I did tell him he should come alone so that we could catch up, and that I had money for him.

Nevertheless, I did not know if Ronnie might have overheard him say he was coming and show up for whatever reason, either to act shocked and deny everything or maybe take Mike and me out at the same time. There was also the outside chance that the FBI had a tail on Mike. If any of these possibilities did go down, I wanted to have every door in sight and was prepared to shoot my way out.

Mike showed up alone, and we ate and put down a few drinks and caught up with what was going on in the city since I had to abandon it for the mountains. After the small talk and we both relaxed, I laid my concerns right on Mike's lap. I carefully studied his face and movements as I told him every detail of what went down at the lab. All I saw was awe and disbelief. Mike was the best friend I ever had, and I knew right away he wasn't involved. A wave of relief hit me. There was one person in the world I could still trust.

When I finished, he acknowledged knowing about the plan to move the lab. They had been discussing it for a while. However, there had been no talk about fixing the electric problems, and he sure would've been told if anyone was going to bring an electrician to work on it. The only talk had been about taking a break, putting the stuff in storage, and then finding a bigger and better place to reopen. There was never any talk about fixing anything. In fact, once they moved out, they were going to torch the place to get rid of any evidence that might get left behind on accident. Besides, Mike would never have okayed a stranger going there and being told what went on. This enforced the theory that this so-called electrician was really someone Ronnie trusted, more than likely an enforcer from the roofer's union.

Now that I knew Mike was still with me, I let him know how freaking mad I was. I also told him they probably wouldn't even tell me where the new lab was, how worried I was about getting the product I needed to finance my life on the run as well as needing a new place to hold up. Mike attempted to talk me down, assuring me that I would get what I needed and promised to keep me in on all of the cooks as soon as they got set back up. He said, "Let me talk to these guys."

I made it clear he needed to say nothing. I didn't want to alert Ronnie that I knew what he was up to that day and wanted to play it like everything was cool. Ronnie had missed his shot, and all we had to do was keep an eye on him. I never saw him, and he wouldn't do anything to Mike without taking me out first. He knew if something happened to Mike that I would kill him and John Drum first thing. There was no sense in starting a war now over something Ronnie could just deny.

Mike gave me assurances that I would be cooking again as soon as they had another lab up and running. I felt a lot better after this meeting and walked out to the car with Mike to give him the ten thousand dollars I had brought. We shook hands and said goodbye. That was the last time I talked to Mike as a friend. The next time I saw him was in the hallway of the federal courthouse when he was about to plead guilty.

During this time, Betty became an even bigger problem. I was getting reports from my contacts in the neighborhood about her serious drinking as well as several affairs she was having. It didn't have to be that way because despite the Feds monitoring her every move, we managed to be together on holidays and a lot of weekends. At one point, she bitched so much about our hotel-room meetings and having to travel to see me that I got an apartment in Bensalem, in the Shaminy Brook Apartments. I even gave her several thousand dollars to furnish the place so she would feel at home.

Throughout all of this time, there was a guy named Rick who was handling my financial affairs. Rick was a product mover of mine and a very loyal friend, second only to Corsetti. He was holding a lot of my money for me, and I made arrangements for Betty to go by his garage twice a month to get paid. I also arranged for Rick to pay all of her living expense, and I bought her a new Camaro titled in Rick's name so that if the Feds tried to seize it, she could claim it was a loaner. I controlled the amount of money that Rick gave her; but since all her bills were paid and whenever she and John spent the weekend with me, they shopped for whatever they needed, she always had plenty of dough. Despite this, she went and got on welfare to have more money to spend on booze and whatever else.

I had been in the meth trade for a while and had contacts everywhere, so I was moving weight from other sources to my contacts in Philly, Jersey, upstate New York, and the Pennsylvania mountains. This junk was not near the quality of ours, and everybody was complaining. I told them that we had run out of oil and were waiting to get in a supply of P2P. I kept them on the hook by promising them some of Bojack's good stuff soon.

The Feds knew Rick was a friend of mine and came by to give him a telephone number for me to call when I decided to come in. They reminded him of it every time they dropped in.

It was early Christmas season, and I had convinced Betty to meet me at the apartment, just the two of us. We were going to have a weekend to ourselves and plan Christmas for our son. I had gotten to the apartment earlier that week and had spent most of the time decorating for Christmas. The place looked great—warm and bright and festive. I stocked up on food, champagne, and flowers.

Betty arrived in the new Camaro that I had bought her, and I could tell she had been drinking—a lot. Like so many times before, she started her crap the moment she arrived. At first, I tried to calm her down, but nothing I said could calm her down. I asked her, "So who is it tonight? You don't want to be with me, so tell me who."

Betty had a temper, and when she was on the booze, she could be a maniac. She was standing between me and the door, and she stopped cold, looked down at the coffee table, and zeroed in on a large Christmas candle. Before I could get across the room, she seized it and hurled it through the large picture window in the front of the apartment. She raced to her car, threw me the bird, and yelled, "Fuck you! What good are you to me?" and sped off to whatever or whoever was waiting for her.

The one thing I had been trying to do for months was keep a low profile, and she pulled this drama in public. I jumped in my car and left as well. If the neighbors called the police, I didn't want to be anywhere around. After over a year on the run, I wasn't going to get busted over a bullshit domestic violence call. I made the block and parked down the street for several hours to see if the cops showed up. When it became obvious that no one had called the police, I returned to the apartment, put a sheet of plastic over the window, and cleaned up the broken glass. The next day, I reported it to the manager, saying I had broken the window by leaning on it while putting up Christmas decorations. They replaced it without question.

Not knowing what Betty might do, I stayed on the move the next couple of days.

During this time, my despair grew. These were the bad times. I no longer had a way of making the big money that I had previously. I could no longer trust anyone in our crew but Mike and never knew when one of them would try to take me out. My mountain hideout was gone and now, so was my apartment in Bensalem because I had no idea if Betty would call the cops and tell them about it. I was already worried about my son's living conditions and knew I didn't have enough money to take care of him until he was grown if I got whacked or if I got caught and sent back to Mississippi for twenty years. In the back of my mind, I knew that I had one option I would never have even considered before the attempted hit.

Every time the Feds would visit Rick, they would always leave a number for him to give me to call them. Rick was my only real confidante, and whenever I would call him in one of my "what am I gonna do" moods, he would always suggest that I call Clyde Wilson and Judy Tyler. My life was a mess on all fronts, and my future was to keep running until I was killed or captured. I did a lot of soul searching.

A few days later, I called Rick and told him I wanted the number. He said, "Really?"

I told him, "Yeah, I just want to have it with me as an option."

Even after getting the number from Rick, I did a lot more soul searching, hiding out in cheap hotel rooms, staying on the move with no one to talk to. The one thing that kept going through my head was Rick's words: "They said you didn't have to do the twenty back in Mississippi. They could make all that shit down south go away."

I knew that I would be taking a chance calling that number. The whole thing might be a setup, but I had few options, and the clock was ticking. Taking every precaution, I drove a couple of hours from where I was staying and found a pay phone. I knew to make the call brief, so it couldn't be traced. It was a New Jersey number, and I stood there for a long time getting the nerve to do it.

I finally made the call. On the second ring, Agent Judy Tyler picked up. Before I said a word, she said, "Hi, Jack."

CHAPTER 25

Taking the Last Viable Option

The number was a special line that the bureau had set up for me. I asked, "Is this Agent Tyler?" She assured me it was, and that she was glad that I had called her after so long. Her voice was soft and her demeanor calm, both of which I found disarming. I told her that I had heard a rumor that there might be a way that I didn't have to do that Mississippi time. She said something could be worked out and told me they were looking into Leo's death and the drug world. She then started naming off everyone I had been in contact with for the last eighteen months.

We talked for a while, then she gave me her direct number at work and told me to call her the next morning, and she would have Clyde and their boss George Sherwood on standby so we could start setting things up for me to come in. I felt like I could trust Tyler, but I got my ass out of there and as far away from that pay phone as I could the minute I hung up.

Driving away, the only thing on my mind was my kids, and what was going to happen to them. Charlene was with her mom; and although I had been sending them money, she had not let me see Charlene for almost a year. Despite our differences, I knew she would take care of my daughter. On the other hand, John's mother was a drunk and had no morals. I had a lot to worry about with him. I swore to myself that night that if I ever got out of this mess, I would become the bad guy's worst nightmare. I would make my children proud of me.

Over the next few days, I spoke to the Feds several times. Agent Tyler told me that they had to get the federal fugitive warrant lifted before they could meet with me. That's when I started to learn that the FBI does everything by the book. Everything has a certain process, and they always run everything past what they call "legal." That explains why their conviction rate is ninety-eight percent, with ninety-five percent being guilty pleas. When the FBI comes for you, they have everything locked in place.

Our first meeting was at the Sheridan Inn, located on the boulevard where Philly ends and Buck County begins. I met Judy Tyler and Clyde Wilson for the first time. They were accompanied by two US Marshals and a female assistant US Attorney.

The marshals were there to explain how the witness protection program worked. When I explained that I had no interest in the program, they excused themselves and stood watch outside the door. In the next few years, I would turn down this offer two more times; and to this day, I have no regret about having done it.

My first impression of the FBI was a good one. Clyde was all professional and got me to relax and open up in minutes. Judy had already won my trust in our telephone conversations. She built on that and played off of it.

We talked for most of the day about my knowledge of the drug trade not only in Philly but in the mountains of Pennsylvania as well as upstate New York and the Jersey Shore. I realized how serious the Feds were when they informed me that they had already talked to Mike Moore, the DA back in Jackson County, Mississippi, and they had worked out an arrangement on my charges there based on how well I performed for the Feds.

After hours of conversations, the US Attorney adjourned everyone to the hallway to talk. I couldn't hear what was being said, but I could tell there was a very heated discussion going on. About a half an hour later, Clyde and Judy came back into the room alone.

Clyde later told me that the US Attorney wanted to take me into custody and had ordered the marshals to arrest me on the

Mississippi warrant. Clyde knew that once that happened, I would be of no use to them and tried to reason with her to no avail. He had to call Louis Rusch, the US Attorney for that district, who had authorized the whole deal to begin with. Rusch was livid and ordered her and the marshals to leave the hotel, informing them that Clyde and Judy were in charge. I later heard that she got fired for going against orders.

The next move was to slip me back into Mississippi and quietly have my bond reinstated and effectively put everything on hold. I would still be listed as a fugitive on NCIC, in case anybody in the association were able to run a check on me. With the DA and the trial judge acknowledging the deal by court order and sealing my file, I was now legal to work for the Feds without possibly tainting the evidence. It also protected me from a double cross, or so I thought. I knew that driving would be safer than flying back down south, so I literally snuck back into Mississippi.

I spoke with my attorney Fielding Wright back in Mississippi. He told me that the Feds had already informed him of everything that was going on. In fact, they had been dropping in on him to check on my whereabouts from time to time. Fielding had told them nothing because he knew nothing. He told me he knew that I would be back because, like he told the FBI, "Is that boy of his still around Philly? Because if he's here, Bojack is here. He ain't going nowhere without that boy."

Fielding had already spoken to DA Mike Moore and Judge Darwin Maples and had engineered the reinstatement of my bond. All I had to do was come in on an arranged date and time so that we could all get together on the paperwork, and then I could check back out of town.

Before I got on the road, I called John Drum to see if he knew when we were going back to work. I also mentioned that I was holding ten grand for him to let him know that I was serious and to act like I suspected nothing on the attempted hit. To my surprise, he told me that the cook crew was going up to the lab that weekend to move the equipment back in and run a batch. He figured Mike had told me. Truth was, I had tried to stay as far away from Mike as I could after talking to the Feds. I wanted to keep him out of it, if at all possible. Meanwhile, I had to get back to Mississippi and get legal in order to start my FBI deal.

I made up a bullshit story that I had met this great chick, and that we were going to go to Virginia Beach for the weekend. Still wanting to keep John on the hook, I made arrangements to meet him at a bar on the river in Philly to deliver the ten grand. It was a public place, and I was friends with the guy who owned it, so it was a safe place to meet. I went heavy anyway. Now that I had the cops off my back and on my side, all I had to do was stay alive long enough to complete the deal, wipe my slate clean with the law, and get payback form John and Ronnie at the same time.

When we met, John did not seem suspicious or ill at ease, just happy that I was handing him the money. But he did let me know under no uncertain terms that I was not getting any of this cook. It was all coming back to Philly. In other words, it was going back to him and Ronnie. Also, in the future, they would decide how much I got, not the other way around. I just smiled and agreed.

The trip to Mississippi went smoothly. My vehicle was in good shape and all legal. I drove from daylight to dark, staying off the road at night and careful not to speed. I spent the night in Biloxi across the Bay in Harrison County and slipped into Pascagoula the next morning and got legal.

Fielding had everything ready, and we were good to go. The DA expressed his reservations and made it clear if I welched on the deal, he was going to come after me with everything he had. Judge Maples was a stern but fair man who congratulated me on wanting to turn my life around and wished me good luck.

The entire trip home, all I could think about was turning my life around and not having to be away from my son for twenty years. I was out on bond and was about to start a new life of "giving back." After thirty-six years, my life was finally going right. I felt truly blessed.

CHAPTER 26

It's Showtime

As soon as I got back to the city, I checked in with the Feds. The first thing I mentioned was that we should visit the lab and check for evidence of the cook that had taken place while I was gone. Without me there to supervise, I figured they might have gotten sloppy. This would show the Feds my good faith and let them get a look at the layout for a future takedown. Now that I was on legal release and no longer a fugitive, they could travel with me.

We scouted the place out to make sure it was unoccupied and then drove up the hill and parked in the flat parking area in front of the porch. Since I was living there with the permission of the owners, I went in while the Feds held back and got a lay of the land outside.

The minute I opened the door, the smell hit me. They hadn't even bothered to air the place out before they left. The place was a mess. All of the utensils were filthy with dope evidence as well as used glassware lying all over the place. After every cook, I washed up everything to get rid of any evidence from chemical residue and put everything away in the storage area. While I was doing this, I would open the doors and windows to air out any smell from the cooking process. I always sacked up the trash and took it to a dumpster in town. Within an hour of finishing, there wouldn't have been a trace of evidence as to what had taken place during any one of my cooks. I also kept all of the cooking utensils in the cookroom out of sight. I had the place nicely furnished and had sheer curtains on the windows for a reason. If anyone looked, all they would see was what looked like a normal household.

But on that day, I did not one thing. I picked up a Corning glass plate form the table and walked outside. The Feds could testify that I had walked in empty-handed and walked out a few seconds later with the plate. The plate later tested positive for drug residue and was a great piece of probable cause evidence for warrants.

The agents had gotten what information they needed form outside, and we drove back to the city. Cleaning up the lab by myself would take hours, so I rode back with them and returned on my own. When I got back, I called John Drum and bitched about how I had found the lab and how dangerous it was to leave it that way. He was pissed that the cook crew had left things that way and told me I would be back in charge the next time things went down. I hung up the phone with a sense of relief. Things were finally falling into place.

A few weeks went by before I got word from Drum that there was to be a cook the following weekend, and I was to have everything ready to go. I immediately called Clyde and Judy, and they put their plan into play.

The FBI had set a meeting spot and base of operations at the Ramada Inn in Clarks Summit. Located several miles from the lab, Clarks Summit was the last exit of the Pennsylvania Turnpike that delivered you through the Pocono Mountains and into the Scranton area. I would go there to meet with them. I had never spent much time there as it was too close to the lab, but there was a popular restaurant and nightclub on the first floor. I would go in there and hang out for a while, then slip upstairs to the Feds' rooms and meet privately. Even if anybody I knew did show up, I could claim that I was there to have a few drinks and was going upstairs to meet a woman.

Clyde and Judy explained everything to me in detail. I would be wired with a small transmitter with a small cloth antenna. It was powered by a small camera-type battery. The whole thing was placed in a cloth sleeve that went around my lower chest with the transmitter nestled in the small of my back. The problem with this was that the battery had to be charged every three hours. This sent me a hell of a shock. How could I pull that off? This would have never worked if Drum, Pierce, or Corsetti had been there. My leaving would have aroused their suspicions.

Knowing that none of the three remaining bosses would be there gave me some comfort. Everyone present would be there to work, and none of them had any authority over me. Jerry Cohen was the senior guy over all of the workers, calling the shots for the bosses back home. Everybody respected him, but he had no control over me. I was not only a cook and a worker, but I was also a mover of the product with my own business in the mountains. So I had a certain level of independence. If I sensed something was going wrong, I could leave under the pretense of going to collect money, and no none could stop me.

The only problem that continued to bother me was having to swap out the batteries every three hours. I practiced this maneuver over and over, and it took only seconds. But in those few seconds, my life would be hanging by a thread.

The FBI's plan was to have a group at the Ramada Inn in Clarks Summit as well as a group set up in a vehicle about a half a mile from the cookhouse, receiving my transmission and recording everything that went down. In addition to the FBI, there were several other jurisdictions brought in. The DEA and Pennsylvania State Police were also involved. However, I was strictly dealing with the FBI and no one other than Clyde and Judy. They relayed what was going on to everyone else. I had to completely trust the two of them and was totally at their mercy.

The plan was to take the lab down "start to finish." In other words, the Feds wanted the chemicals cooking as well as a finished batch already bagged and weighed on the table. That way there, was no doubt in proving manufacturing. This was to be the first joint operation between the FBI and the DEA, and they also wanted it to be the first time that a meth lab was taken down in process. This would not be difficult as we always cooked multiple batches. The only problem was my making sure I knew when to come in and not get caught giving the go ahead.

When all of the workers showed up that night, Cohen told me that Drum was talking to a new potential supplier in the city. They had brought along a sample that we were to cook first to see if it was legit before cooking from our proven sources. I didn't care. A cook was a cook, so I didn't waste time arguing. This would prove to be a mistake.

We began to have trouble with the unproven source. It wouldn't cooperate with the other chemicals as the temperature started to rise. We continued to battle with the liquid, and I instantly knew something wasn't right. We even broke it into small batches and tried to cook it on hot plates, and it became clear that this was not P2P, and thus, not meth. That meant we had to scrub every single piece of equipment so that it would not contaminate our next batches. The pressures had to be thoroughly flushed and the stainless steel vats and glassware sterilized. When we should have been well into cooking our second batch and making the lab ready for takedown, we had just finished cleaning up and starting from scratch. It was a freaking nightmare, and everyone was exhausted. They all decided to take a nap before we started a batch from our proven source. I took the opportunity to steal away and go into town to the Ramada Inn. I wanted to explain to the Feds in detail what had happened, so they wouldn't think I was playing games with them. I told the crew that I needed to meet a connection of mine who handled the product in the mountains.

As soon as I got to the Ramada Inn and met with Clyde and Judy, I began to feel a little better. The bad batch had thrown me off of our plan, and now I was worried about the transmitter not working. I certainly didn't want the FBI to think I was sabotaging things and renege on our deal. I told Clyde what had gone down, and he assured me everything was fine, and the wire was working perfectly. He even named everyone there: Jerry Cohen, Short Sullivan, Jimmy Robinson, and Kenny Smith. Kenny had only assisted on one cook before, and this was Robinson's first time; he took Dennis DeLuca's place. DeLuca had gone out on his own and was trying to launch his own operation. We later took him down, selling me a pound of product while I was wired up.

Feeling a lot better after the agents assured me everything was good to go, I headed back to the cookhouse. The cook went off just as it was supposed to. The temperature came up like expected, and I knew it wouldn't be long. I had told Judy and Clyde that I would signal them when there was at least a pound of finished crystal on the table and another vat brewing. Even though we wore masks, at this point we would be experiencing contact highs. That means everybody's talking ninety to nothing, and everyone is at least a little bit paranoid. That's why we always had a rule of no guns in the cookroom.

When I excused myself for the last time, I quietly changed out my battery and let the Feds know it was time. I also told them I had on a blue sweatshirt and white painters pants, and I would be standing in the door to the cookroom so that no one could turn over the vat of cooking product. I wanted to make damn sure they knew where I was and what I was wearing in case someone did have a gun and all hell broke loose.

The next seconds passed like hours as I stood there, praying everything was still a go. That's when the doors came down, and I heard the words I had been waiting for all night: "FBI. Down on the floor!"

The next few seconds were total chaos as they secured the place. The agent who grabbed me patted me down and then began to pull up my shirt, almost exposing my wire. I yelled, "What the fuck are you doing?" and several guys turned my way.

That's when Clyde grabbed me and said, "I got him. He's wanted in Mississippi." Making everything look legit, he hauled me out in cuffs and loaded me into his car. However, my night was not over yet.

I was driven back to the Ramada Inn and taken up to Clyde's room where I placed a call to Drum. I called his house and didn't have to fake anything. My heart was still pounding. All I said was, "John, we have a problem. Go to a pay phone and call me back immediately," and I gave him my number there at the hotel. Feeling this was serious, he called me back in minutes from an outside line.

When I answered, he said, "What's wrong?"

"The FBI hit the lab and everyone's gone down," I said. I knew that I had to extract information from Drum to show he was a boss, so I mentioned the bad P2P he had sent up and told him that had delayed our cook and not to buy from that guy anymore. I also told him that after the first cook, I had gone to collect money from a contact, and when I had come back, the FBI was all over, and I had just kept driving. I told him he should warn Pierce since they were the ones in charge, and without question, he said he would. He also said he would arrange for attorneys for everyone, once again portraying himself as the boss.

Once this call was complete, I called John Nystrand and told him to meet me at the Ramada Inn. I had a supply of product for him. When he showed, the Feds took him down. He even had a MAC-10 in his possession, adding a firearms charge to his problems. As all this went down, I sat in the hotel room as the agents congratulated themselves. I felt sick about having brought John into this and even sicker knowing Mike Corsetti was next.

A short time later, Clyde came back into the room and informed me that his boss George Sherwood was going head-to-head with some rogue state narcotics agent who was trying to take me into custody. He had run me on NCIC and found the old Mississippi warrant we left out there. He also found out about the reward. He had put our whole operation at risk by calling down there, thinking he could get a bounty. George had to threaten him with obstruction of justice to get him to back off. Apparently, it got really crazy at one point, and Clyde and Judy now stayed right with me until they got me out of there.

I laid low for a while, being hidden out by the FBI until June 1982. At that time, I headed back down to Mississippi to get everything finalized down there. It was a whole lot different feeling than the last time I had snuck down. With me this trip was Judy along with my wife Betty and my son John. Judy came along for two reasons. First, my undercover work had resulted in nine arrests, but they still needed to keep me alive to testify, so my safety and that of my family were necessary. Second, I had cases pending in Mississippi, and they wanted to finalize those so I could continue to work for the bureau. In the end, the judge asked how long I had been in jail in Jackson County before I jumped bond. I told him two months. He gave me sixty days, removing the previous twenty-year sentence. Then he dismissed the other pending charges with prejudice. I was a free man.

My next order of business was to get a divorce from Betty. After we got back down to the coast, she started talking about letting bygones be bygones. No way in hell. As soon as we had been down there long enough to establish residency, we obtained an uncontested divorce, and I put her on a plane to Kansas where her family lived.

Once I had my life back in full, I was just waiting on a call from the FBI. In the early spring of 1983, it came. I received a call from Clyde and Judy, who had something in the works that I could help with. They wanted to know if I was interested. I jumped at the chance.

They were in the process of assembling a multijurisdictional task force between the FBI and several New Jersey counties along the Atlantic Seaboard. They had a biker-turned-snitch by the name of Champ that was engaged with a major drug operation along the Jersey Shore. Champ had told them that the crew had lost their chemist and were looking to replace him. They needed someone who was street smart and had walked the walk and was also proven reliable. That was me; plus, I was a chemist.

The crew was run by a biker known as Whale, who had a reputation for cutting people. He was a huge guy, crude, a drunk, and a barroom brawler. Whale worked the commercial fishing boats and carried a razor-sharp knife in a scabbard on his belt. It served as both a work tool on the boats and an enforcement tool on shore.

The rest of his outfit were a bunch of equally unsavory bikers and fishermen who frequented a club in Cape May. It was not a club you would wander into on accident, and you sure as hell wouldn't take your lady there for a night out on the town.

CHAPTER 27

Joining the New Jersey Task Force

I drove from Mississippi to New Jersey in my personal vehicle. I met with Clyde and Judy, who removed my Mississippi tag and inspection sticker and replaced them with Pennsylvania ones. It had taken two days of driving, and I considered the time alone as part of the preparation phase for what I was about to do.

This job would be very different than the takedown of the lab in Pennsylvania. That took place in a building that I was not only familiar with, but I had actually called home for much of the previous nineteen months. Even more importantly, I knew the guys I was working with. I had a long-standing working relationship with those guys and knew how to read them. If any of them had suspected anything, I would have read it in a minute. Besides, they all knew me very well and had complete trust in me.

This situation, however, was the polar opposite. I would be going to a different state, meeting with total strangers, and trying to build their trust. Even the cops were different. Judy and Clyde would not be there for the FBI. Instead, there would be guys from the Wildwood, New Jersey, office as well as state and county guys from New Jersey.

I had no worry about being able to pull off my end of the job. Hell, all I had to do was be me. I had been living the life on the other side of the law for most of my life. All I had to do was be myself or at least the guy that I used to be. My main worry was that these new guys might harbor a distrust or even dislike for me because of who I used to be. As far as I was concerned, Jack "Bojack" Conway was gone. I was now Jack Saltarelli, law enforcement.

CHAPTER 28

Setting Things Right

We had arranged to meet at Rexy's Bar and Restaurant a short distance over the bridge from Philly just inside of New Jersey. I parked in the back and went inside. That's when a team of guys switched out the plates and stickers on my car. Judy and Clyde were there to make the introductions, and they were not happy.

It seemed that two federal agents from Lynwood got spunky and busted one of the key players in the outfit I was to infiltrate. So rather than let a couple of pounds get by, they arrested the carrier and blew the chance of taking down the entire operation. The carrier was the guy who was closest to Champ and was interested in a cook, which was supposed to be my intro into the group. Once this guy was busted, the Feds tried to make him out as a major player, and the judge gave him an insanely high bond that he couldn't make. Needless to say, this was a great disappointment, but what came next was a total shock. Clyde said that the New Jersey task force wanted me to join them on a state venture to take down this outfit without federal assistance. I had come this far, and I wasn't about to let the Cape May County guys down.

We met at a house on a small out-of-the-way street. It was the first time that I had seen any of them; and coming from different parts of the state, they were new to each other as well. Three members of the team would turn out to be constant companions and close friends: Jack Trombetta, Billy Miller, and Frank Dailey. We all discussed ways to launch our own operation now that the Feds had pulled out.

If the carrier that Champ had planned on using would have asked for a bond reduction, we could have brought the judge into the loop and gotten him to set a reasonable bond. But the guy was just sitting in jail, not even trying to get out. So if we got the judge to reduce the bond on his own, it would have looked suspicious.

Champ came up with the idea that I had been sent by some of the heavies in Philly to see what had happened and where the twelve grand had gone that had either been seized or disappeared. The idea made sense to me, and since I was the one putting his neck on the block, the rest of the team came on board. The head man Whale was out on a boat; and since everything had to be okayed by him, we would have to wait.

About a week later, Champ took me to their hangout in the Cape. We had been there once before when we knew he was out on the boat so that I could get the feel of the place. When we arrived for the meeting, Whale was on the other side of the bar. He was a huge ogre-looking man, drunk, loud, and very obnoxious.

He noticed Champ and me at the bar and called Champ over to where he was seated. In a loud drunken voice, I heard him ask, "Who the fuck is that guy?" I knew that I was in their bar, uninvited by any of the major players, so I had come ready for a confrontation if necessary. I was not looking for one, but I could tell this guy was a nutjob, and anything could go wrong for any reason. I had known hundreds of guys like this, both on the street and in the joint, so I would handle anything that might go down.

They talked for a while, and Champ explained that I had been sent to the city to find out what had happened to their money. He also explained that I was a chemist, and they could use me. Then I heard Champ tell him where we were staying, which pissed me off. The task force had rented us an apartment in another part of town, and I wanted to keep our whereabouts quiet. I especially didn't want this guy to know where we were staying. Whale told him to go home, and he would see Champ later.

When we left, I got on Champ's ass and told him not to tell anyone where we were staying. When we got back to the apartment, I called Jack Trombetta and set up a meeting. When we got together, I told him what had gone down. He must have thought I was afraid because he said, "If you want to go and call it a deal, we'll understand. No one will be upset with you."

I gave Jack a hard look. "I hope you don't think I'm afraid of this piece of shit. That's not what I'm unsure about. What if this motherfucking drunk tries to cut me and I have to shoot him? I just beat a twenty-year wrap down in Mississippi. I don't want to end up looking at life here in Jersey."

Trombetta's response was simple: "Shoot the prick. You're one of us now, and he's the bad guy. Do what you have to do, and we'll handle it."

With that, I said good night and went back to the apartment.

It soon came to light that after their carrier went down, their whole organization was going dormant for a while. I don't know if it was paranoia or just being careful, but they all went under until the smoke cleared. Despite this, the task force asked me to hang around. During the season, Wildwood became a drug-riddled town, and they needed someone who knew the ins and outs of the drug world to help train them. We finally went fishing the nightspots and local bars to make drug buys. I taught the guys to relax, leave the trained law enforcement guise at the club parking lot, and blend in and talk dope. You can't sell drugs undercover, but you can make people think you have sources to get your foot in the door to find out what their sources are and what is available. They were all young guys and eager to learn the drug world. Everyone was professional and a good cop.

Frank and I got involved with a dealer who was moving weight in the Wildwood area. Playing the role of two drug dealers from Philly, the guy told us he wanted an ounce. Our plan was to tell the guy our source had ripped us off and get him to take us to his. He had advanced us five hundred dollars. I didn't know much about this guy, and I sure didn't expect his reaction to the bad news.

Frank arrived at the scene right before I pulled up, and the dealer was already there. When Frank told him what happened, the guy went off accusing Frank of ripping him off and went for his gun. It was a good thing Frank was well trained and wrestled the guy's gunhand down just as he fired a shot into the ground. Frank had him subdued as I got out of the car, and he motioned for me to leave. I made sure Frank was all right and left before the cops got there.

I returned to my apartment and called Jack and Billy, who took care of everything. Both Frank and the dealer were arrested. The dealer was charged with discharging a firearm, and Frank was snuck out of the back of the police station. Later, after the task force took everybody down and the organization was disbanded, the dealer was charged with attempted murder of a police officer.

During this time, one of the agreements I entered into with the task force as well as the prosecutor was that since we were going after drug buys in this area, there was one person I didn't want hurt, my sister Lillian. She was a user and would often frequent the area we were targeting. She had been a user for many years, and I knew she sometimes moved a little product to support her habit. I was afraid for her. She would always trust me never to hurt her, and I wanted their assurance that no one would do a buy from her. This was not a free pass to break the law, just an agreement not to set her up. Her associates were the worst of the worst and, as far as I was concerned, good hunting ground.

Frank and I went by to see her. She had grown weak and pathetic from her drug use and had caused herself and her children so much misery. Frank became good friends with her, and I knew he had her back when I wasn't around. Later on, after I had returned to the Gulf Coast, I learned that one of the new guys on the crew had made a buy form her after I had left. I contacted the prosecutor and reminded him of our deal. He was awesome, said it was a small deal, and agreed to take care of it.

We continued to work all of the hot spots, and the guys got to be damn good at infiltrating the drug world. Nothing ever developed with the Whale crew, so after a while, I wasn't needed anymore. The task force even threw me a going-away party before I left. I told them I would be glad to come back if they ever needed me.

A good thing about my time in Wildwood was that I got to reconnect with my daughter Charlene, whom I hadn't seen in a long time. She was seventeen and getting ready to go off to college. I was afraid she would be cold and unfeeling to me; but more than anything, she seemed amused that I was visiting. I couldn't tell her that I was a good guy now and what all I was doing, but I was able to let her know that I had truly missed her and wanted to make up for having been gone all of those years. It turned out to be the best move of my life. She eventually moved in with her brother and me when I moved back up east and rented a place in Bensalem.

CHAPTER 29

Assignment Jimmy Kennedy

After leaving Wildwood, I met up with Clyde and Judy again. My next assignment was a guy named Jimmy Kennedy who was known as Skinny Jim. Jimmy had grown up with all of the heavyweight burglars in the Kensington and North Philly areas and knew a lot of people on the streets.

Burglary had gotten to be a dangerous business and too much work. Most of the guys with any organization were going into the chemical procurement side of the drug trade. The Feds had their eyes on certain heavy hitters, and Jimmy had done burglaries with these guys in the old days. Jimmy was already working with the Feds, but I never knew on what; I figured it was none of my business. They needed someone to teach him to cook so that he could convince his old buddies to sell him chemicals. The FBI couldn't do that, so they wanted to bring me in.

The main ingredient in meth is benzyl methyl ketone, known on the street as P2P or oil. It was, and still is, a controlled substance on its own in the United States. However, in those days, it was legal in Canada and Europe. If you were caught with it in this country, it was worse than being caught with meth because it would be used to prove a charge of manufacturing or at least conspiracy to manufacture, both of which carry more time than possession. In order to get a supply of oil, you had to have a Canadian or European connection. At that time, most of the European oil was coming out of Germany.

Needless to say, this was only one of a number of chemicals needed, although the others were mostly legal but were closely monitored by law enforcement. So when you started buying them in large amounts, it threw up red flags.

The dealers that Jimmy was being groomed to set up were well schooled and were suspicious of everyone. That's why he couldn't just walk up to someone and ask to buy oil. Even though they knew him from the neighborhood bars, and many had done burglaries with him in the old days, the moment he inquired about oil, he would be under serious scrutiny. I was going to school Jimmy in the meth business—how to make it, how to sell it. Although Jimmy had never done drugs or even hung out with dealers, he was a street guy who had been in the life since he was a kid, so this should have been easy. The problem was, Jimmy was an alcoholic.

Clyde gave me a few pieces of equipment form an old drug bust, and I went to purchase the rest. I taught Jimmy how to approach someone about buying oil, and we selected a guy he had done a lot of jobs with in the old days who trusted him. Despite their history together, the request was met with skepticism, and Jimmy was sent to see someone lower down in the ranks. The big man had insulated himself by saying, "I don't mess with that shit, but go ask so and so. Maybe he knows someone who does." The problem with dealing with underlings is you often get ripped off, and Jimmy did.

Jimmy was not proven in the drug world, so the guy diluted the oil with isopropyl alcohol after pouring off some of the pure stuff for himself. If the guy does this enough, he can end up with a quart of oil for himself, enough to cook his batch. This type of alcohol is used in the cooking stage, so it doesn't hurt the oil; it just decreases the end yield. Instead of three and a half pounds of meth from a quart, you will only get about two and a quarter, depending on how much oil was skimmed off. At that time, a gallon of oil ran about twenty-five thousand dollars, and this guy charged us fifteen thousand dollars for the one quart of diluted oil. So Jimmy got ripped off twice, but we had our foot in the door.

During this time, I was staying with my good friend Don Laken. Don was the owner of Safe Pet Kennels, and I had worked for him in the Getty Oil strike as well as search and rescue in the Atlanta child murders. He had trained and sold dogs to law enforcement agencies all over the country and provided security for many celebrities as well as selling them dogs for their personal use. I had worked on a lot of details over the years with Don and had gotten to meet a lot of famous people like Stevie Wonder, Jermaine Jackson, and Rosey Grier. Don's kennel would usually number around one hundred dogs at any given time. They were trained as guard and attack dogs as well as bomb and drug dogs and search and rescue tracking dogs. He also had a high-end pet supply business that did grooming, boarding, and trained pets not to chew up furniture.

Don lived with his wife, Lenore, in Bala Cynwyd, a high-end suburb of Philly. They had a three-story stone house for just the two of them. I had moved in with them in the late summer of 1983 and went back to work at the kennel. Don and Lenore knew all about my background and knew I was working with the Feds. The ironic thing about all of this is that Don had a DEA drug permit, which allowed him to lawfully keep small amounts of controlled substances at the kennel for the purpose of training drug dogs. This would prove to show me what a treacherous son of a bitch he was, not the trusted friend I believed him to be.

Don knew what I was up to with Skinny Jim, and he told me I could use his attic to cook. I didn't like cooking in such a confined area, especially in the city, but I took precautions. I put plastic sheets up in the stairwell and sealed off the door to the attic. There were windows on either end of the attic, so I set fans up in both. One on intake, the other on exhaust. We were up on the third floor, and I knew the smell would rise once it exited the window. It would be a short cook with just one quart. We started around one in the morning when no one would be out walking their dog and finished just before dawn.

I was cooking with isopropyl alcohol, which has a flash point of one hundred degrees. You have to cook it at 168 degrees, which is what makes it so dangerous. This was the most important part of my lesson to Jimmy. Although he wouldn't be cooking with these guys, he had to know what chemicals to mix and how to mix them. You especially had to know what chemicals to mix when the temperature reached 168 degrees. Once the raw chemicals are cooked, you begin the filtering process. At that point, you can remove your gas mask and go to a painter's breather cup. The cooking solution will suffocate you in an instant by shutting down your lungs. The main problem I had that night was that Jimmy showed up drunk.

While we were filtering, Jimmy lit a cigarette. Why we didn't explode into oblivion, I still don't know. I snatched the smoke out of his mouth and threw it into a nearby toilet. I knew he was drunk to begin with, but the alcohol fumes from the cook had made the situation worse. As soon as I knew the cigarette was completely out, I dragged his drunken ass down to the first floor. I made him lie down on a couch and sleep it off. I knew teaching him to cook would be a waste of time, and we would have to go about things differently.

Jimmy really didn't need to be able to cook, just to know enough to convince the Feds' targets that he knew the business and had a top quality product. So since he couldn't stay sober long enough to remember the process, let alone not blow himself up, I finished the batch. Once we got him sober, all he would have to do was to return to the crew and try to get them to bid on his product.

When they saw what a high-grade product he had and that it was pure and uncut, they knew he either had to have made it or was very close to a great source. Jimmy told them his partner did most of the cooking and didn't want to be known. He also bitched about the oil being diluted and not getting the yield he should have. Jimmy bitched so much about getting screwed on the purchasing end that the source agreed to buy the whole cook, thus proving that they were on the sales end as well. Skinny Jim had built his credibility among what we started calling "the oil dynasty of ex-burglars," and that's what we needed to do.

The money we made went to buying larger amounts of P2P form whomever the Feds put us on to. Meanwhile, I was still working with Don at Safe Pet and had moved into my own place out in Bensalem. By this time, all of my old crew from the lab takedown had pled guilty and were doing time in federal prison. This gave me a little more freedom out on the streets. For the first time in over two years, nobody was actively hunting me.

As we made money, I put it back into our operation, getting more equipment and making sure we had backup tools in case something broke in the middle of a cook. The most important thing you had was the pH meter. The meter is a very sensitive glass probe that lets you know when you have reached a safe level while adding hydrochloric acid to the meth. This is usually from 6.8 to 7.2, but I always set my meters for 7.0. I would also keep three meters on hand as a fail-safe method. That means that the substance is no longer poisonous, and you can switch from the gas mask to a painter's mask.

During these times, I would hit the gym every morning, then head down to the kennels where we would work the dogs. This was supposedly how I earned my living. However, after this, I would go run errands for the kennel. This included unannounced visits to local nuclear power plants where we ran K-9s through the locker rooms and parking lots looking for drugs. All the while, we were getting oil from people and furnishing finished product while helping the FBI to make their cases.

Several years earlier, when I was working with Don on the Getty Oil strike and on the Atlanta child murders, Don had introduced me to longtime Mafioso Harry "The Hunchback" Riccobene. Harry was an old-time mob guy and one of the top captains in the Bruno family. In those days, Don had a gorgeous diamond watch; and whenever he needed a few grand, he would borrow it from Riccobene and leave the watch as collateral. I think by putting up the watch, he could avoid paying the weekly vig; and when he had the money, he would go to Riccobene and pay off everything at once and get his watch back.

Nevertheless, a month or two later, the watch would go back to Riccobene on another loan. I knew the Hunchback was the most powerful mob guy in the city after Angelo Bruno. Bruno had long been a Philadelphia godfather, and he and the Hunchback were close friends. Don also had a running contract with the Hunchback's right-hand man Frank "Frankie Flowers" D'Alfonso, who always had a Doberman he kept around. Don would train Frankie's dogs and come by and work with them on a regular basis.

I had tried to do a deal with the Hunchback when I was on the run. Don had mentioned to me that Riccobene had twelve thousand dollars' worth of quaaludes that he wanted to get rid of. For years, the Mafia guys in Philly never touched drugs, under orders of Angelo Bruno, who was completely old-school. But the Hunchback always went against the grain and got away with it because one, he was so close to Angelo, and two, he was such a huge earner.

I didn't mess with pills, but I knew some buys who did. Butch Mingone and Carmen Grecco dealt in everything and had taken care of me when I needed something in a hurry. So as a favor to them, I had passed the word along. Butch thought it was a good price and gave me the money to buy the pills from Riccobene. Don and I set it up to meet him outside of the Oregon Street Diner to do the deal. I held the money and went over to the car where the Hunchback and another guy were waiting. When Don returned, he said, "Harry wants another $50 a pill." I went off. Here I am doing each of these guys a favor, and one of them ups the price in the middle of the exchange. Either way, I didn't need this crap, especially at this time in my life.

Not only was I on the run, but Riccobene was one of the hottest mob guys in the city, subject to being filmed everywhere he went. Not only was all of law enforcement after him, but during this time, he had at least three attempts on his life. In March of 1980, Angelo was murdered, setting off a full-scale war among the Italians. This war would rage on for several years, resulting in dozens of deaths and even dragging some of New York's Five Families into it before it was over.

By the time it ended, the "Young Turks," who took over, would represent everything that Angelo had been against. The Quiet Don, as he was known, had ruled behind the scenes, preferring negotiation over bloodshed. And when violence was called for, there were no bodies left in the street. Everything was low profile, and nothing interfered with business. The guys who took over, Nicodemo "Little Nickie" Scarfo and the rest, all wanted to be celebrity gangsters and ended up dead or in prison for life within the next ten or so years, leaving the Philly Mafia a mere shadow of what it had been during Angelo's reign of almost three decades.

During these days, Frankie Flowers was beaten within an inch of his life with ball bats and left for dead. When he recovered, he wisely skipped town and would have been left alone had he not returned in the mid-1980s. He was murdered not long after he got back.

Although I met with both the Hunchback and Frankie Flowers during my time with Don, not much materialized. I still had a bad taste in my mouth from the quaalude deal, and they were under so much pressure from the mob, as well as a brewing war with the Pagan's Motorcycle Gang over a double cross on a gold deal, that nothing ever got off the ground. But that didn't mean that our other targets weren't paying off.

Despite his failure as a cooker, Skinny Jim and I were still doing deals. I made several cooks in Don's attic, but this was a real pain to do. All of the equipment was stored in the cellar, so you had to haul it up four flights of stairs to the third floor. I was giving Don one thousand dollars every time I cooked but was still rolling in the cash.

Clyde suggested that I should go back up into the mountains and buy a piece of property about three and a half acres with a house and two sheds on the side of a mountain. The place was well off the main road, very secluded, and not the type of place someone would wander upon by chance. The price was thirty thousand dollars. I worked a deal with the owner to give him ten thousand dollars down and two more ten-thousand-dollar payments within the year. I told him I was going to use it for a weekend getaway, which I often did, but that I would also be bringing canines up from the city to train, which I also did. He never knew it would be the front for an undercover FBI operation.

CHAPTER 30

Shades of Greed

It was common knowledge among everyone in the meth trade that P2P was not a controlled substance in Canada. However, it was carefully monitored, especially in regard to sales to Americans. I was convinced that if we could establish a source of this major ingredient from Canada not only would it help us get in with the major dealers in this country but it would help the FBI in stopping a major ingredient from coming into this country. Although a lot of the P2P, or oil as we called it, came from Canada, the other main source was Europe, especially Germany, and the real players were bringing it in in fifty-five gallon barrels. A barrel being smuggled into the U.S. woud run about ten thousand dollars in expenses, but the raw oil would have a street vaue of about one million three hundred thousand dollars. You can only imagine the pforit margin if you cooked it into a finished product.

When I laid out this plan to Clyde, I suggested we use a guy named Frank Zappacosta, better known as "Frank The Beard". The Beard and I went way back and I had gotten to kow him when I came back from Mississippi and went on the run. I knew he had connections for the oil but did not cook or even have a lab. Frank and I just hung out in the same bars and I knew he often supplied oil to my old crew before they went down. When I presented this to Clyde he was all for it. As it turned out, the Beard had been working for the Feds for years.

The Beard was a legend from the old days among the home invasion and burglary crews and he had more than a few bodies under his belt. He later told me himself how he became a street op for the Feds. He had gone on a home invasion of a jeweler who refused to open his safe. While the other guys stood around trying to figure out what to do, Frank the Beard just grabbed they guy and hung him off the sixth floor balcony until he saw things their way. One of the guys in the crew got popped on an unrelated charge and ratted them all out. Even with one of the best Philly lawyers representing him, Frank would up doing a five year stretch in Huntington State Penitentiary in upstate Pennsylvania.

The FBI made contact with Frank through his wife and Frank took the deal. It was arranged to lok like he had filed an appeal and ws released on appeal bond. Frank walked out of prison knowing his case would get 'lost' somewhere along the way in exchange for giving the Feds intel on a variety of things.

Frank and I first met at a Denny's restaurant in Bensalem just outside of the city. Since we both knew the other's full story, we relaxed and got down to business. I told him about working with Jimmy Kennedy. The Beard knew Jimmy was a drunk and agreed he could not be worked with. I explained to Frank that all I needed was someone to get the oil from and I would do the rest. Clyde had already filled him in on the fact that I had my own lab and Frank and I agreed that he would supply the oil. I would process and cook, and we would both handle distribution. We would split all expenses and profits equally.

During this time I was working for Don at the kennels. It was located in a working class section of Philly on an old railroad yard and at any given time housed over a hundred dogs of every type. Don had tracking dogs that he had flown in from Germany that were used for law enforcement related jobs, such a s missing persons, hunting fugitives, as well as drug searches. Most importantly, we were DEA licensed for drug research and training. Our drug dogs had to be worked regularly on the premises to keep them sharp so we always kept a certain amount of drugs on site. We were also allowed to travel with a modest amount of drugs when going on assignment.

We were regularly traveling to nuclear power plants in New Jersey and Pennsylvania doing unannounced drug searches of employee's lockers and desks. This DEA Research License was going to be the tool I planned to use to start a Canadian connection.

Don knew full well that I was working for the Feds and I explained that I wanted to see if I could get a Canadian company to sell me P2P and that the FBI was fully on board. He even knew I was ordering drums of 99% isopropyl alcohol and having it delivered to the kennels. I would then wait until Sunday when no one was around and take it to my place in the mountains.

Don never passed up an opportunity to make money and was all in on the deal; provided he got a taste. He then explained that he wanted to buy the old railroad property that the kennel was on and if we gave him the money, not only would he allow me to use the business to purchase the oil, but we could brin it across the border in a company vehicle labeled DEA licensed.

I went straight to Frank with the offer. When I told him the price for the land was twenty-two thousand dollars, he was interested. "Christ, Frank, that's not shit when you think about what we will make if we pull this off." As usual, Frank sat emotionless, as I continued.

"Frank, we each throw in twelve grand. Thats pennies, dude. Twenty-two for the property and another two for the trip expense. If any other expenses come up, I'll pay them.

Finally, Frank said, "Okay, but if this mother fucker doesn't come through, I am going to kill him."

Now with Frank, Don, and Clyde on board, I began to put a plan together. I made arrangements to purchase six liters, which was more than I had planned on. This would make it more difficult to bring across the border. Don came up with the idea of using a canine company in St. John's, Canada. I would explain to everyone involved that we were going to attempt to use the oil by getting the dogs to hit off of the main chemical. The fact that we were licensed to do this type of research, and by assuring them that the oil would not leave Canada, we were good to go.

Don and I traveled to Toronto and got rooms at the Sheraton Inn on Lake Huron. We had located a small chemical company there and showed up in our uniforms with law enforcement insignia. We met with the owner and I did all of the talking. I explained that you cannot handle meth solution without masks and face gear, so we wanted to train our dogs off rags doused in P2P. The guy was a chemist and full of questions, all of which I was happy to answer. He then explained that he could make the oil right there; the cost would be four thousand dollars, and we could pay him when we picked it up.

Not long after we got back to Philly, I got a call from the Royal Canadian Mounted Police. They had plenty of questions but I answered them all to their satisfaction. In the end he said, Good luck with your research", and hung up. It was a little bit different when the U.S. Embassy called. They asked the same questions, but were also very interested in the amount we ordered and where it was to be kept. I explained it was our first order and not being sure how long the solution would last on a rag, we had a lot of trial and error ahead of us. In any case, there was nothing illegal up to this point and they let it go.

When we drove back to Toronto for the oil, we were a bit paranoid to say the least. We decided to pick it up, take it to a storage facility, then check into a hotel and wait to see what went down.

I knew the minute we went to the chemical company that something was wrong. The chemist pointed to several cases of smaller bottles and said, "I poured them into one container to make it easier to carry." Right then I knew the six liter container was wired. They knew my intent was to dampen rags to scent a canine, and that would be much easier with pint bottles than a six liter metal container. I figured the can had a tracking device in it so they could nail us if we tried to cross the border.

As planned, we took the oil to a storage facility, locked it up and checked into a hotel. I wanted to wait for one more trip to bring any oil back, but Don wanted his money and was insistent. Before daylight we slipped back into the storage facility and poured off a quart of oil into a mason jar. I could see instantly that this was the real deal.

I called Clyde and filled him in on everything before we crossed the border and headed for home.

Don was already hollering for his money, so I went straight to the mountains and did a cook. As I expected, the quality was 99.9% and the yield was awesome. I got almost four pounds of pure product from this quart as opposed to three pounds from the supplies in Philly.

I knew things were taking a bad turn with Don when i paid him his twenty-two thousand and he demanded another ten. When I told Frank the Beard about this, his response was "Fuck him. He can be happy with the twenty-two, or I can put a bullet in his head."

During this time, Don had gotten close to Michael Jackson and Jermaine Jackson. He had sold dogs to several members of the Jackson family, and was now talking about going on tour with them as part of their security detail. I wanted to get the oil into the country before he left, as we would need his credentials to cross the border.

Don took off for California, or so he said, and I was left with the task of consoling the Beard. I told him that Don would only be gone a week; and as soon as he got back, he would bring the oil home.

By that time, Don was well into his second week in California, and there was no calming Frank. I got in touch with Don and told him we needed to get the oil back to the States now. He went ballistic, shouting, "Don't go up there." I knew instantly this creep was up to something. The deal had always been to bring it back, not leave it up there. I suspected that now that we had paid him, he was going to slip up there and get the oil himself. Don knew what a gallon of oil could bring, and he also knew Harry "the Hunchback" Riccobene and a lot of other mob players that he had gotten loans from over the years who dealt in the drug world.

About this time, I mentioned to Don's wife, Lenore, that I might need to go up and get the stuff myself. Her reaction confirmed my suspicions. "Oh, no, don't do that. Don said to wait. He'll be back in a few weeks."

I thought, *A few weeks.* That was not what he was telling me. I sure as hell wasn't going to tell Frank the Beard that. They might both wind up dead.

The more I thought about it, the more I realized Don might not even be in California, and the whole Jackson thing might not even be true. He might have already gone and gotten the oil and be selling to someone outside of Philly.

Not knowing how far Frank would go, I made up my own plan. I would ease up there and take my chances as a civilian crossing the border. This was the mid-80s, before terrorism was a concern. Besides, the Canadian border wasn't like the Mexican border with all of the checkpoints. They were just interested in citizenship. You showed your ID, but your car was rarely searched. I also decided to take my girlfriend with me. We would cross at Niagara Falls, just two lovers doing the couple thing. We were a nice-looking couple, well dressed, and I was driving a new Cadillac. I called Clyde, explained it all to him, and got permission to go ahead. Everything was legit.

We once again stayed at the Sheraton on the lake; and the next morning, we visited the storage unit. My heart was in my throat the whole time we entered the building, knowing there was a strong chance that the can would be gone or empty. I opened the door and started to breathe a little easier when I saw the can but didn't get excited until I picked it up and found it full. I breathed a sigh of relief and thought, *Amen.* We had brought a six-gallon heavy gauge gasoline container with us, and I emptied the contents into it. I took my lock and threw the old container into the dumpster. If there was a sensor in the can, it would show up as still on the premises. I would just stop paying the rent, and they would take it back over.

As I had hoped, the border crossing was uneventful. I just put down my window, declared my citizenship, and was waved through. Now that we were across the border safely, I had no intention of taking our cargo back to Philly. I went straight to the cookhouse in the mountains. We kept all of the chemicals in a dark hall closet away from any light. Most of it came in brown bottles anyway, but I was always extra careful about maintaining quality control.

Once there, I poured the oil into quart-sized jars so that we would be ready to go at our next cooks. When that was taken care of, we headed into town and had a hearty dinner. It was the first time I had been able to breathe easy and unwind in weeks. We went back to the house and made love under the stars.

The next day, we drove back to Philly, and I paid Frank a visit. I told him what I had done, and we were good to go from here. I also told him to chill out and knock off the talk about walking in on Don one morning and putting him out of his misery.

I might not have been so protective of Don if I had known the whole story. Several years later when I went to work for Thornton Bonding on the Gulf Coast, Waldo Thornton told me that it was Don who had turned me in to the cops when I was in Atlanta. It had been a close call, and I could have ended up spending the rest of my life in prison so Don could get a lousy five-grand reward. A rat bastard like that deserved whatever the Beard would have done to him.

The next weekend, I returned to the mountains for the first cook. I was moving most of the product as well as doing all of the cooking, but I still honored my deal with Frank, so he had it made.

I waited to tell Don that I had been to Canada until he got back. I actually told Lenore first, and her reaction was a dead giveaway. She ranted and raved about how pissed Don was going to be. She got Don on the speaker phone, and he started screaming, "I told you…"

Who the fuck was he to tell me anything? We didn't talk for a while; and when I told Frank about what had happened, he not only wanted to do Don but now added Lenore to the list. Once again, I went to Don's defense. It was over; we had everything at the cookhouse and were ready to roll. Why bring a bunch of heat down on us now with a double homicide? If Don had ripped us off, I would have let him go, but now it was over.

After a few weeks, Don broke the silent treatment and asked me to join him in New Orleans for the Jermaine Jackson Tour. Don had to fire one of his security guards and needed a replacement. I thought, *What the hell. I need a change of scenery.*

It turned out great. Jermaine was a really decent guy, and we all gathered in his suite after the concert to party. I would work a number of shows with Don after that. We worked Stevie Wonder and Patti Labelle in Valley Forge and put canines on Teddy Pendergrass's property as well as a lot of other entertainers and football players. Don never knew how close he came to getting whacked. I really liked Frank the Beard; but in the end, he was a killer.

Other than these security jobs, I saw less and less of Don, purposefully distancing him from Frank and me. I told him we had sold the oil off in bulk, and that we were not cooking anymore. It was obvious that he was so greedy that if he knew we were cooking and making that kind of money, he would toss and turn at night, trying to figure out a way to extort money from us. I knew there was no way I could call the Beard off again if that happened.

I knew that Frank had amassed a considerable amount of cash over the years, but I never knew how much. Now that we were up and rolling on our own, I found out how much.

One night, I brought Frank thirty-three thousand dollars. Most of it was in small bills, so it was quite a wad of money. I brought it to Frank in a grocery bag, not expecting him to carry it around like that. With my own money, I separated the bills by denomination and packaged them in manila envelopes to look like documents. This didn't draw attention if I put them in safety deposit boxes or other places I stashed them. Frank asked me to take a ride with him, so we went to one of the twenty-four-hour depositories where he had safe-deposit boxes. He cleared me through to the vault area with the young woman who was in charge. She stepped out to give us privacy, and Frank told her to stay close by; we wouldn't be long.

When Frank opened the box, which was the largest size they had, about the size of a mailbox, it was packed with cash. Frank just poured the grocery bag contents on top, and it spilled out onto the floor. He spent the next few minutes pushing down on it, trying to force the lid to close. Then to my shock, he calls the young lady back in and tells her he needs another box. She just stood there stunned, looking at all of that cash. Finally, she stuttered, "Y-Y-Yes, sir."

She came back with a card for Frank to fill out and another key. She left again as Frank began tossing wads of bills into the new box. I asked, "Are you crazy, Frank?"

He just laughed and said that the bank employees aren't allowed to tell what they see.

I told him, "That girl is in her early twenties, and she's never seen that much cash in her life, let alone stuffed into metal boxes."

Frank had several more of these boxes, not just the two that I had seen. He was a millionaire several times over. He owned a beautiful home and drove a new Jaguar. In all his years of hustling, he had made so much money, he didn't know what to do with it and couldn't launder it fast enough.

Luckily, the girl from the bank did keep her mouth shut; and when Frank went down, she had nothing to do with it.

CHAPTER 31

The Writing on the Wall

These were the good times. Business was consistent. Not having to work the streets through Frank's contacts to purchase oil, we only reached out to people when the Feds told us to. I would pick up the forty percent from a chemical outfit in Valley Forge just outside of Philly. I only ordered what I would need in the short terms so as to not set off any red flags.

My son John was into sports and played soccer and football for his school. I enjoyed being involved in all of his activities and being able to be a real dad. He and I would occasionally go up to the house in the mountains. The cookroom was locked off, and there was nothing drug related going on. All he saw was a comfortable house with nice furniture. He had two dirt bikes and would zoom around the three and a half acres having a blast. Now and then, I would let him drive the big Sears mower and help me with chores. We would even go into Clarks Summit to go out to eat, and I let him swim in the pool at the Nichols Village Inn.

Other than John, the only person who ever went up there was my girlfriend. Even Frank didn't know where it was. On weekends when we cooked, my mother would keep John at my house in Trenton. I told them that my girlfriend and I just wanted some downtime together, and we would head to the mountains.

We normally cooked a quart at a time; but when we felt energetic or had a big order, we would do two parts while all of the vats and glassware were unpacked. Cleaning after each cook was time-consuming, and it was necessary to wash and restore everything to mint condition before it was put away. That way, there was no residue to be found, and you also avoided any unnecessary odor. The cookroom was sealed off from the rest of the house and the only one exposed to the fumes. Once all of the tools were cleaned and put away, we would open all of the windows, and it wouldn't take long for the clean country air to mask what had taken place.

The only furniture in that room was a large tool table with drawers and a flattop. I had covered the top with a sheet of heat resistant glass that we used to spread the crystal for cooling and hardening. We kept all of our cooking tools in the drawers, and all of the glassware and chemicals and hot plates were either in a closet or the basement. Nothing was ever left out. When we cooked, we spread canvas painters cloth on the floor to catch any drippings. When we were done, I would spread new cloths and put out paint cans so it would look like we were renovating the room to anyone who might peer in the windows while we were away.

As I said, whenever we felt the desire for a second cook, we didn't have to clean everything, thus avoiding a lot of work. You just had to do two quarts of P2P; and even if you just crystallized a few pounds, the remainder was already filtered and ready to pH when you returned to crystal off the rest. There was no additional cooking, filtering, and cleaning. Just set up your eight or ten hot plates and start cooking off the isopropyl alcohol.

With a six-gallon supply of oil, we were set for a while. I had gotten our names out on the street as having the top product going, but nothing was happening. I wasn't getting any bites from any of the major kingpins looking for a chemist. Nevertheless, I did everything that the Feds told me to do, and I stayed in touch with Clyde and Judy. They okayed my every move.

As far as Jimmy Kennedy was concerned, I'm not sure what he was providing the Feds, if anything. One day, he came to meet me outside of the gym where I was working out. He got out of his car, drunk off his ass and stinking of urine. He had tried to piss in a cup while sitting there, waiting on me and had spilled it all over himself.

Think I shook his hand? I always worked out late morning, so it wasn't even noon yet. I had already had a meeting with Clyde and Judy about why I was avoiding Jimmy. I told them about his almost blowing us up, and that I couldn't ever rely on him to be sober. I had agreed to give him some product to display to his targets, but I wouldn't have him around a cook again. They understood. I cannot tell you all of the times an agent had to go and get him out of a DUI charge.

When I had left Mississippi to join the Feds on the Skinny Jim endeavor, I had no idea where it would lead. I figured it would be a pay-as-you-go deal and be over in a few months. I learned quickly that they expected my climb in the drug business to take shape as it normally does. Everything had to look authentic. They wanted me putting the best product out on the streets and plenty of it since they can't make or sell drugs. The FBI learns from ops like me, putting their lives on the line. Sure there are large amounts of cash flowing, but that's just part of the role you have to play. Being a chemist prior to throwing in with the FBI meant that I came self-taught with my own set of balls and loaded with self-earned street savvy. I always knew Clyde had my back. He proved it more than once.

I was moving from my apartment in Bensalem to Trenton, Pennsylvania, about fifteen minutes away. I changed addresses like I changed vehicles. My girlfriend and I were coming from breakfast at the local Denny's when I noticed a couple of manned cars situated around our end of the apartment. I had already parked when I noticed them, and I figured them to be local narcotics guys. We went on into the apartment. The entrance to the apartment wasn't visible to the cars, so I started turning things over in my head, trying to figure out why no one was beating on the door. I could see both cars from my rear window, and no one was stirring.

I had about three pounds of meth, several guns, and twelve grand in cash in my safe. I put it all in a bag and told my girlfriend that I was going to leave and head out a way not visible to the cars. If they raided the apartment, she would be okay because there was nothing else incriminating in there. If they did pop me, I would just call Clyde. As soon as I was out of the area, I would call her. I made my way out of the apartment complex up to Street Road and walked to my mother's house. I hid the bag and called the apartment. Back then, we didn't have cell phones, just landlines. There was no answer; it just kept ringing.

Then something else occurred to me. Even though all of my old crew was off doing federal time, my name was out there in the streets. Word might have gotten back to them. What if this was a hit, not a raid?

I called Clyde and told him what was going down. I told him that if this was a hit, I would storm the place and do what I do best when confronted with a threat. But if it was not, I didn't want to run in on a bunch of narcotics agents aiming a .45. Clyde said, "I'm on my way."

Clyde picked me up, and we went to the apartment. By this time, a few hours had gone by. We entered at the street level and eased up the stairs to the second floor apartment. Clyde brandished his Federal ID and pulled his weapon. I drew mine as well. There were no sounds coming from inside the apartment. He pounded on the door and announced, "FBI!" The door swung open, and there was my lady, glaring and calling me every name in the book.

Apparently, the telephone company had turned the phone off a day early, so all I was getting was ringing on my end, and she couldn't call out. She said the cars had left not long after I had, so they must have been looking for somebody else. Nevertheless, Clyde had come through as soon as I had called. He had come ready for anything and proved he had my back. He was a true and trusted friend.

In early 1986, I met Clyde at Fisher's Restaurant for lunch. It was a classy place and provided some privacy for our meeting. I often met with both him and Judy there. We met for about two hours and then walked to our vehicles. Clyde suddenly stopped and hesitated, looking like he was wrestling with a thought. He suddenly said, "Come in Monday, and I'll sign you out." I had no idea what that meant. He just got in his car and drove away. That was our last conversation.

Not long after he left, Clyde went up to Darby to spend the weekend with a lady friend. The next morning, he was burning up with fever, and she couldn't wake him up. They got him to a hospital and removed a tumor the size of a small orange from his brain. He didn't last long after that. I went to visit him in the hospital, but he just stared into space, looking lost. It broke my heart to see this giant of a man diminished in a weekend. This is a cutthroat business, and you had better know your ass is covered. When I was a fugitive back in the day, Clyde had saved me. Now he was gone. I began to feel a fear in this void. Judy was damn good, but she was no Clyde.

The past couple of years had been good. Not only had I gotten to spend time with my son and be a real father, but my daughter Charlene had moved in with us. I bought her a car, and she began to look at me through her own eyes, not her mother's. She soon got married, and I paid for her a first-class wedding. Those had been the good times. Clyde's death began to change things.

Actually, Clyde's death was part of a series of losses. My brother Frank died of an accidental overdose of pills. He was not a junkie, just a twenty-three-year-old kid trying to impress his new girlfriend. Apparently, she had a tolerance to the pills, and he did not. He passed out and drowned on his own saliva. My sister Lillian was then diagnosed with cancer and died a short time later at the age of thirty-eight. I visited her every day at the cancer center in Philadelphia. Not long after her death, her son Gary hung himself. I was surrounded by death and grief and started to go into depression.

About this time, I made a regular visit to my family doctor, who picked up on my signs of depression. He sent me to a psychologist; he knew I needed to talk to a professional. The doctor's office was located in Southampton. He was an elderly gentleman with an easygoing smile and a soft voice. We sat in large leather chairs. Between them was a huge carved tree stump that served as a table for his pipes and ashtray. I hated to leave when our sessions were done. I felt a measure of security in that room and knew when I left, I would come face-to-face once again with the demons that were ripping away my strength. It was as if they were waiting outside his office for me.

He gave me a barrage of tests, all of which I passed with flying colors. I told him everything about my life and held nothing back. He told me that my work with the FBI was a good thing. However, part of my problem was that I was living the part of someone made-up. I had no real roots and was living a lie in a dangerous world. That, compiled with all of the deaths around me, was taking its toll. He told me to put everything in its proper perspective: "You are a good person. You are one of the good guys now." Before long, I was doing better. He saved my life.

CHAPTER 32

The Finale at Hand

This is when the world got insane. I'm about to cover a number of theories that are the possible causes for the unnecessary conclusion of my assignment with the FBI. After thirty years of rolling these events over and over in my mind, I'm still not sure exactly what went down or why. I truly believed in Clyde and Judy and the FBI. I always believed, and still do, that I was a moving part of the system that targeted the drug lords and their counterparts. I risked my life more than once and never walked away form an undertaking because there was a chance I wouldn't come back. I'll always believed that if not for Clyde's sudden death, this book would have had a different ending.

Not long after Clyde's death, I got a tip that the DEA was making inquiries about me around the city. I called Judy, and her response was, "I'll handle it. Don't worry. You're with us."

Let me point out that when I needed help with product movement, I often used my girlfriend's son Tony. Again, this was with the FBI's full knowledge and blessing. Tony got busted in Bristol Township, which is the area where the DEA had been asking about me. Tony had no police record, so I reminded the Feds that he was one of mine and figured they would square it with the locals. But Tony wasn't very bright and soon got picked up on a second case that didn't involve me. You have to remember that Tony was delivering pure product for me—that alone is going to catch the eyes of the big boys. I asked him if he needed any help from me, and he responded, "I got it covered."

The next thing I knew, he had gone to Mississippi to work for his mom's ex-boyfriend driving 18-wheelers. The fact that he walked away from two arrests and never went back to Philly is something to put on the shelf.

Then there was my Uncle Bill, my mom's brother. He had gotten into trouble in his younger days and done some time. When he got out, he went straight and became a very successful businessman. He had bought and sold property as well as several businesses and made a lot of money. At the time, he had a thriving electrical business that he later sold. This happened to be around the corner from the kennels, and we often grabbed breakfast together in the neighborhood.

He knew I wanted to go completely legit and had the money to do so. We often kicked around ideas about my future. I had even mentioned this to Judy, who had not given me an assignment for a while. I knew at some point the crew that I had sent to federal prison would be getting out and, with all of my high profile work I was doing for the Feds, would know that I was still in the area. None of them had been hit with hard time and, as a result of a handful of Philly's top lawyers, negotiated guilty pleas that would mean they were hitting the pavement soon. My plan was to wrap up my work for the FBI and go back to the Gulf Coast. The FBI was fully aware of this.

Now, even though Uncle Bill was a legitimate businessman, he was still no angel. He had been involved with manufacturing meth a few years before and had gotten screwed by his outfit. He didn't make or sell dope, but he allowed some guys he had met through some of his friends from the old days to order chemicals through one of his company names and be delivered to a warehouse he owned. It had all gone smoothly for quite a while until one day, a couple of FBI guys walked into his office and started asking questions. He always kept his small dog at his office with him; and when the FBI guys came in, it got out and ran down the street. Uncle Bill took off after it, went around the corner to a pay phone, and called the outfit he was working with. He told me his intention was to warn them and then go back and tell the FBI he had nothing to say and not to come back unless his lawyer was there. But when he made the call, they hung up on him and left him holding the bag. Bill went back and cut a sweet deal with the Feds. It turned out they knew very little about what was going on, and Bill had just been the first stop in their inquiry stage. He walked away untouched. Even though I trusted Uncle Bill, you can put him on the shelf with Tony.

I will also say that Tony had never been to my place in the mountains. All he knew was that I had a house up there about two or three hours from the city where I did my work. Bill, on the other hand, had been up there. I had confided in him about my lab because he was an electrician, and I needed some wiring done. The house had a two-hundred-amp capability but was only set up for one hundred amps. So Bill ran the proper gauge cable and fixed it up.

We had gone up there twice, once to see what was needed and once to do the work. I saw a car stop at the end of my road at the bottom of the hill. I tried to make out the vehicle, but it was too far away, and there were too many trees. I mentioned to Bill that it was weird since no one ever came around. He just said, "Relax. Forget about it."

Around this same time, my girlfriend and I had gone up to the house for a weekend away. We weren't cooking, just checking on the property and taking some time to ourselves. Suddenly, we heard a *whoop, whoop* sound overhead, and a helicopter appeared out of nowhere. It was flying at treetop level and close enough for me to read the writing on the tires. The helicopter was unmarked and moving low and slow. It made me suspicious, but I knew that I was an FBI op, and I hadn't done anything that they hadn't approved in advance. I dismissed it.

Then there's Frank the Beard who comes in as the third leg of the trifecta of shelved mysteries. By October 1986, all of the Canadian oil was gone. As far as I was concerned, I was finished with my part of the operation. On top of that, I was burned out and never wanted to see another gallon of P2P again. I was financially well off and just wanted to move back down south and start a legit business.

I told both Frank and Judy that I was done and asked her what she wanted me to do with the equipment. What happened next started me worrying.

Before we had gotten the Canadian oil, Frank and I got it a gallon at a time from his contacts in Philly. We always talked about it first and made sure Clyde and Judy knew all about it. In October '86, Frank called me and told me I needed to get something out of his car. I asked him what, and he said, "You'll see. I can't talk now." In earlier days, when Frank scoured a jug of oil, he would call me, and it would be in a brown paper bag on the rear passenger floorboard of his car. I would pull up, remove the bag, and either take it to the mountains or to our storage facility in the city. So Frank's phone call got me angry and worried. Everybody knew that I wanted out and was done with the operation. Why was Frank insistent on another major cook, and where had this gallon of oil come from?

About this same time, I knew Frank was having a problem with one of the newer agents. He had learned that Frank was the god-father to a child of a target that this guy wanted to take down. He called Frank in for a meeting and told him he needed his help. Frank went off and said no way; his arrangement was no testifying in open court or hosting a bust that he would be exposed to. Had Clyde been around, this never would have happened, but he was gone.

I learned about all of this from Frank's constantly calling me and bitching about how this was not part of the deal and "fuck that dude." There, I'd be just sitting on the phone, letting Frank vent. I'd never met this agent, but I knew all about Frank's original deal; and apparently, Judy either could not or would not call this guy off. I never asked Frank where he was calling from, figuring he had the good sense not to call from his own phone that this agent might have bugged. You should never assume anything. I suppose the agent heard me consoling Frank and said, "Who's this guy?" Now I was on his radar too.

This was the type of pressure that Frank was under when he called me to remove something from his car. I pulled up to the bar where we always made the exchange and looked around. I had a bad feeling already. When I saw there was a gallon of oil in the bag, I almost drove away and left it there. I always regret not going with my gut instinct. I should have gone inside the bar and told him to jam the bag up his ass. He and Judy both knew that my next trip to the mountains was to remove all of the equipment, take it to the dump, and retire.

Going against all my best instincts, I took the bag out of Frank's Jag and drove to my house in Trenton. I would normally have taken it to my storage unit, but had they been following me, they would have learned about its existence. When I got Frank on the phone, I told him I was finished with the operation, and even Judy knew that I was getting out. Frank said he had ordered the jug a while back, and the guy had just shown up with it, so he had to take it. I called my girlfriend and said, "We have one last cook." I had yet to learn whom that gallon of oil really belonged to.

CHAPTER 33

And the Walls Come Tumbling Down

I told Frank the next week that I was going up to the mountains to cook that weekend. We had never felt the need or the desire to process an entire gallon on one trip, but this time, we were going to. We were going to do four cooks and complete all of the filtering, which would have been exhausting, then go into town, unwind, and return to crystal all of the liquid. My mom came to my house to babysit John for the weekend. All she knew was that we were going up for a weekend getaway, and she was spending time with her grandson. It gave her and her new husband, George, a getaway from their small apartment.

We were driving my brand-new Chevy Suburban outfitted with a professional body lift kit. Its height, along with four massive knobby tires, could handle any weather those mountains might throw at us. We were headed out feeling upbeat and positive, hell-bent on getting this last cook over with and starting a new life down south. If this oil was worth its weight, we should get at least thirteen pounds. This would not be as pure as our Canadian supply, but most gallons Frank got his hands on were good stuff. The most we had ever done was two procedures in a weekend, which takes about twenty to twenty-four hours. The Feds knew this because I had told them, just like I had told them all of the other details of the operations.

I didn't think there was any need to be looking over my shoulder. I had been doing this for several years with the full knowledge and cooperation of the FBI. The jug that Frank had given me had been sitting at my house all week, so if something had been up, they could have raided me at any time. If I had known the Feds wanted to bury me alive, I would have gone to Frank's house, put the jug back in his car, and told the cops where to find it. Frank knew I was going to the mountains that day. I always kept him abreast as to what I was doing. It was business.

When we got to the mountains, we stopped off at the grocery store and then went to the house. Whenever we got there, I would always do a security check of the doors and windows to see if anything had been disturbed. Everything looked all right, so we started to unload our gear and groceries. I happened to turn toward the road, which was a good distance from the house, and noticed a car that had pulled up and was sitting at my entrance. I knew all of my neighbors' vehicles, and I had never seen this car. When they noticed me looking their way, they slowly drove off.

My girlfriend had been inside getting everything ready and came out to see what was wrong. When I told her what had happened, we saw the car come back down the road. I told her, "Something's not right. I think we're being set up." She wasn't so sure.

We stood outside by the Suburban, and in a few minutes, I heard a motorcycle coming up our street. It slowed down and looked up the driveway. He then proceeded a short distance up the road and turned around. He came back and stopped at the house below my property. There was a heavy tree line between us, and I couldn't see him. But the bike was loud, and I could monitor the sound.

We stood there in shock. I kept listening and could hear men talking. There was apparently a large gathering down there. Living in the quiet of the county, I knew my neighbors by sound. I could tell you who had kids or dogs or even what they drove. Nothing like this had ever happened in the years that I had been coming here.

"We need to go. Put what's serious in the Suburban and ride out. If there's something going on, then it's not going to matter. I'm not sitting here waiting." We grabbed all of the chemicals, making positive that nothing criminal was left, and we pulled out. As I came down the hill, I passed the road leading to the house below mine, and

I kept looking in my rearview mirror. When I got to the main road, I turned right, which would put me on the road to Clarks Summit and in the opposite direction of the house where they were gathering.

I knew I would be easy to tail as my Suburban was unique, dark-blue with a silver streak down the side, and jacked up. I had bought it with the intent of attracting drug dealers, not avoiding cops. I made it to the Pennsylvania Turnpike and started to feel better as I could see that no one had followed me on to the extension. We were alone on the road for miles. The whole two and a half hours back to Philly, I was thinking all they had to do was put out an APB on the high profile Suburban along the only way home. I had some serious chemicals on board, a gun, and a couple of grand in cash, enough to send me away for a long time. When I got to the city, I figured they must have thought I was cooking and settled into the house to wait.

We went straight to the storage facility and unloaded all of the chemicals and left the gun. I felt better driving a clean car, but I wasn't about to test the waters by going home. I got us a room at the Sheraton on The Boulevard in the Trevose area. I needed time to think. I was shocked, pissed off, and in danger of not making rational decisions. I needed to be fresh and in control when I confronted Frank.

Early the next morning, I called Frank at home and told him to meet me at Denny's for breakfast. He didn't seem surprised that I was in the city. Frank was so stone-faced that he never really showed any emotion. It was going to be a challenge to read him, but I was going to try.

When I tell you that Frank the Beard never showed emotion, it's true. I've handed him bags of cash with tens of thousands of dollars inside, and he never smiled; his face never changed. Frank could be mad, concerned, or happy, but you never knew until he told you. Even when he was talking about whacking Don, he didn't appear angry. He just talked about it like he was talking about where to eat lunch. That's why I knew he was serious about it. With guys like Frank, even murder was just another day of doing business.

Frank and I had several breakfast stops, but I chose this particular one because it had a large dining area, and I could get a booth away from anyone. We were well-known everywhere we went as the top tippers, so requesting a booth away from the crowd wouldn't be a problem. We usually had our own waitress who knew us and knew we liked our privacy. If we needed a refill or something more, we would just wave to her. Conversations like ours weren't tolerant to continued interruptions like, "Can I get you anything? Are you sure?" We were known at our regular spots as private people. Their tip was guaranteed.

When Frank arrived, I told him everything that had happened except what I did with the chemicals. Frank had never visited the lab or the storage facility and had no idea about the latter. We went over everything in detail, trying to figure out if I was just being paranoid. I told Frank I was thinking about going back but only to load up the gear and take it to the dump. Normally, he would've said, "Call Judy and see if she's hearing anything," but he said nothing. I left that meeting not knowing a damn thing more than when I went.

CHAPTER 34

Here I Go Again

The more I chewed on what had happened, the more I decided to go with my instincts. There would be no more cooks. We would return to the mountains, clean out the house, and it all ended right here. I wasn't apprehensive about the trip back to the lab. There wasn't anything in the house that was truly incriminating. The equipment included items that you would find in any household, just a lot more of them. I scrubbed them each thoroughly after very cook, so there wouldn't be any residue to worry about. The only unusual items were the three fruit pressers, but I did have thirteen apple trees, a huge grape orchard, and other fruit trees, so even they could be explained. Besides, Clyde had given me one of the pressers, so there was probably a serial number or something in the FBI files to verify it. I kept telling myself if there was a problem, I could call Judy.

When we arrived at the house, I checked everything out, and there were no signs of any suspicious activity. We started to do what we had come to do. We packed up everything to do with the lab, placing it in plastic garbage bags ready for the dump. Somewhere during this time, we discovered that the water had been cut off or the well pump had quit. That seriously aroused my concerns. If we had been in the middle of a cook, we would've been in trouble. Though you don't use water in the manufacturing process, there's a lot of cleanup afterward. Once we were home safe, I would call the well guy. But for now, we could drain what little water we needed from the tank.

We pulled out of the drive and down the road. I'd be lying if I said I wasn't looking over my shoulder the entire time. I drove through Clarks Summit and turned onto the entrance ramp to the Northeast Extension of the Turnpike. That's when I saw we had a problem.

From out of nowhere, a car full of guys cut me off and jumped in from of me just as I pulled up to the ticket booth. Another car zoomed in behind me, blocking me in, and federal agents were suddenly all around me. I recognized one agent staring in through the front windshield with a gun aimed at my face, telling me, "Don't fucking move and show me your hands."

The last time I saw this agent, who was from the Scranton office, was when we took down my old crew in 1982. All I thought was, *Here I go again.*

The difference between then and today was that I had orchestrated that buy by working inside and wasn't marked for arrest. This time, I was the target and was getting some serious fucking commands to follow. We were removed from our vehicle and placed in separate cars. I might have expected this from the state or local guys, but this was the FBI. I had been working with them for almost four years, getting their approval on every move I made. Hell, I was happily retiring to the Mississippi Gulf Coast when they came and recruited me.

They proceeded to pull everything out of the Suburban and had garbage bags and equipment strewn all over the highway. After about a half hour, the agent I was familiar with stuck his head in my window and demanded, "Where are the fucking drugs?"

I answered," There are no fucking drugs."

Traffic was backed up, and people were rubbernecking as they passed. In exasperation, he said, "I'm taking you and all of your stuff to our garage in downtown Scranton, and I'll finish searching your vehicle there. I'll find them. They're there." I had packed the vehicle tight like a puzzle, and they couldn't get the bags all back in.

They were placing bags in the trunks of their cars, all taking off for Scranton.

When we got to the federal building, we were placed in a room with several agents. They made us empty our pockets, and they made copies of everything we were carrying, including credit cards and photographs. This is standard procedure for an arrest, though we hadn't been charged with anything or told we were under arrest. They continued to ask me where the drugs were, and I continued to answer there were none. Then they asked me what the items in my vehicle were for. I answered, "I role-play for you guys as a chemist. You know that."

I invoked my right to a telephone call, and they asked me whom I wanted to call. When I answered, "Agent Judy Tyler," they told me I wasn't permitted to dial the number. The call was made from another room, and an agent came into the room I was in, picked up the phone, and told me to go ahead. That told me she was somewhere in the building and was a part of this. I told her where I was, and they had picked me up with the equipment I had been using all these years, some of which had been given to me by her and Clyde. I also told her I didn't have any drugs.

Her reply was, "Well, just tell the truth."

Considering everybody knows that lying to the FBI is a criminal act, that wasn't much advice. I knew she was hanging me out to twist. I was left alone in the room.

Several hours later, my favorite agent with the attitude came back into the room finally convinced that there were no drugs in the Suburban. He started off, "I know you cooked yesterday, and you were there all night."

I stopped him right there. "No we weren't. We came up to get this equipment and take it to the dump. We would've spent the night, but there was a problem with the well, so we went back home to regroup. We stayed at the Sheraton Inn on The Boulevard. If you don't believe me, the receipt is in my wallet charged on my American Express."

He checked out the receipt; and by this time, he as fuming. "Then will you submit to our search of your house?"

I was surprised he hadn't already obtained a warrant for the search but was grateful for the opportunity to show that I had nothing to hide. I told him, "No problem."

When we drove up to my property, I was surprised to see at least fifteen vehicles parked everywhere. Everyone was there, Feds, state, local, all of them. I unlocked the door, and they began to search the house from top to bottom. Of course, all they found was a neat, well-furnished weekend getaway. I did point out that the well had quit working and asked if they did anything to it. They neither admitted nor denied it.

We were there for quite some time. I could see that the lead agent, whom I didn't know, was calling all of the shots. The agent that I was familiar with was getting more pissed off by the minute.

Finally, I was allowed to lock up and was taken back to the Scranton office. I was informed that I would be indicted for the contents of the Suburban, not that the case would be presented to the grand jury, just that I would be indicted. They seemed awfully sure. I was also informed that I was free to go for now, but the house would be off limits, and they were seizing the Suburban. After working closely with the Feds—at their request—for almost four years, I was suddenly the perp. What really devastated me was the bare fact that they tried to set me up to be busted with twelve or more pounds of pure meth, which would have sent me away for the rest of my life. I kept asking myself why.

They dropped us off at a hotel in Scranton where I booked a room for the night. Sleep was an impossibility, so I ended up booking a rental car for a one-way trip to Philly. Without alerting anyone in the hotel, we caught a cab to the rental lot and headed home. The ride was uneventful, but my mind was working the whole way.

I knew I would be under surveillance, but I also knew the most important thing I could do right now was to get all of the chemicals out of the storage unit. No one but me knew where it was, and Frank and Judy knew nothing about it. However, I knew it would be a matter of time before the Feds found it. It was under my name and always had been. Why use a bogus name, I was working for the FBI?

I then met with a contact of mine whom I trusted. I gave him the keys, gate code, and location of the unit. I explained to him how to handle and store all of the items, and I paid him two grand—it was worth every penny.

CHAPTER 35

The Sit-Down

The following weeks were unbearable. I told my girlfriend that I was being followed, and she dismissed it as paranoia. One night, during the early morning hours, we were restless and couldn't sleep, so we went out driving. After several miles, I noticed two or three vehicles that seemed to be behind me at different times, turning off and then later ending up behind me again, rotating turns with one another. We were riding the back roads and smaller streets of Bucks County. My girlfriend told me I was starting to worry her with this shit, and I could tell she was skeptical, so I said, "Okay, let's see what happens."

I remembered a nearby street that was a dead end I had taken once by accident. As you approached it, there was a slight hill, so you couldn't see that it was a dead end. I sped over the hill and turned around at the end just in time to see two sets of headlights coming over the hill. It was two of the cars I thought had been tailing us. As I drove past them, I just smiled and waved.

Not long after this, I got a call from the bureau to come pick up some personal items that were in the Suburban. They handed me a couple of large trash bags that they said contained clothing, toiletries, etcetera. I didn't bother to look through them; I just tossed them in the car and returned home.

When I got home and started digging though the bag of clothes, I found a gas mask. I knew this was supposed to be part of their evidence to try to prove a manufacturing case against me. I also knew that the FBI didn't return evidence to you by mistake. I figured they were hoping I'd take the mask to wherever I had the chemicals hidden or try to pop me with it later to claim I was still cooking. I then called the case agent and told him I had found the mask and thrown it in the dumpster and to come get it if he wanted it.

About two weeks of this fun and games went by before I got a call from Judy Tyler. She told me that we were going to have to meet at the federal building in downtown Philly, and I would be wise to get a lawyer. I hired Jeffrey Miller, a prominent Philly lawyer and former US Attorney. I chose him based on his reputation and his knowledge of the type of games the Feds play. Most of their cases are formulated by informants and street ops, so I had a better chance of his believing me and not thinking I was delusional.

When we arrived at the meeting, it was just us, Judy, and her boss Jim Sweeney, the supervisor over squad 2. We sat at opposite ends of a huge conference table, not anticipating just how threatening the situation could get. Sweeney told me this could go one of two ways. He assured me that an indictment would come down; and when I went to trial, a DEA chemist would testify about each item found in my vehicle and explain how each was used in the process of making meth. Once I was convicted they would request a forty-year sentence at Marion federal prison in Illinois, one of the toughest prisons in the country. Then he let the cat out of the bag: "Or you can return something that belongs to the bureau, and we will agree to let you plea to an information, not recommend any jail time, and not object to probation." He added, "The additional terms are the forfeiture of your house in the mountains and the Suburban."

An information plea is when the government and the defendant agree to forego the grand jury process, and the defendant pleads guilty to terms of a written agreement.

Jeff requested that we step outside for a moment and talk about the proposal. Once we were away from the agents in a secured area, Jeff asked me what they were talking about when they said I had something that belonged to them. I told him about the deal with Frank's calling me to pick up with oil after I told Judy that I wanted out. I told him I suspected that the oil was theirs, and I was right.

They had failed to catch me with a shitload of meth made from the oil as they had planned, and they now had to answer for what had happened to the oil. The FBI keeps a close tab on anything like that, and losing a gallon of P2P with a street value of at least twenty-five thousand dollars can destroy an agent's career. Jeff and I had a long discussion about the deal they had put on the table.

This all explained why they had let me go that day in Scranton. They were hoping I would go to my chemical stash, and they could arrest me for possession of the P2P and have a whole other separate case. I was glad I had waited them out. I may have been quietly coming undone from the stress, but I hadn't done anything stupid. We walked back into the sit-down. I looked right into Judy's eyes and said, "Okay, I'll work with you. You could have asked me for the oil all along."

Everything now made sense. When you're an op like I was, and the FBI designates your operation for termination, you aren't told to go home; you're put out to pasture by way of prison. They set you up and send you to prison to die. The whole deal was designed to catch me dirty with pounds of dope and an ongoing illicit lab then put me under the jail. They were using the Scranton office to make it look like they were the culprits. Since that didn't work out, the shots were now being called by the Philly office where all of this had been put together. Obviously, it was their P2P, not Scranton's.

I often regret not telling the Philly office to go to hell and taking my chances with a jury of American citizens. A lot of people knew about my deal with the Feds and how long it had gone on. I had stayed in touch with the guys from the Cape May task force in New Jersey and even had dinner with them as well as the head prosecutor. Even my lawyer back in Mississippi Fielding Wright and Circuit Judge Darwin Maples knew how and when the Feds had recruited me. But I had a son to think about and couldn't risk going away forever.

A few days later, Judy called me and wanted me to come down to her office for debriefing. I pictured meeting with a couple of agents for a long recorded interview, covering everything that had gone on over the last four years. It turned out to be just Judy and me, no witnesses, no recording devices, just a note pad and a pencil. She never bothered to write down a word. Before she started, she leaned over and whispered to me, asking if I had taped any of her conversations. Taping her would have meant I was suspicious. Why should I be suspicious of Feds that I was working with and trying to help.

CHAPTER 36

The Beard

Frank and I continued to talk over the next few weeks from the meeting at Denny's right up through my plea on the information. However, we never really discussed too much what had happened and what was going to be the next step. The only thing he did ask me was whether I had the oil and if it was in a secure place. This was proof that he was involved. If he hadn't been involved, he wouldn't have fronted the money for the oil and would be screaming about getting his twenty-five grand back, or he would've gotten it on credit and would be bitching about their being on his ass for the money.

When it came time to deliver the chemicals to the Feds, I took no chances. Without any prior notice, I called Judy at the federal building at Sixth and Arch Street from the parking lot. I told her I was loading a dolly full of boxed and carefully secured chemicals, and I needed to know where she wanted it delivered. It took the agency by complete surprise. There was no way I was going to alert anyone that I had them in my possession and was moving them in my vehicle. The last thing I needed was another agency like the DEA being sent to stop me and saying I was fair game for arrest with new charges. Judy told me to go to the tenth floor where she met me at the elevator. This was where the DEA was housed, and I didn't breathe easily until I was out of the building and driving off.

When everything was set up and Frank and I were both just waiting around to go to court, we met one more time. He had hired

Jeff Miller to represent him as had I. Since neither of us were going to trial, Frank was pleading to an information as well—there was no conflict. Frank was told he might have to do a little time, and it still looked like I was headed for probation. Neither of us accused the other of anything. We had been together on this deal for a long time and went back a lot of years before that. A major part of my deal was that only I took the heat. I wasn't going to name the people that moved what I made. I was responsible for them, and I was going to protect them. We agreed that this was Frank and my deal alone.

After our discussion, we went to a jewelry store, and I bought a President's Gold Rolex to announce my "retirement" from the business. Frank bought a silver one, and I also bought a Gold Ladies' President for my girlfriend. Then we went to a car dealership, Reedman's on the strip, and both bought new Lincoln Town Cars. If it was my last day living the life, I was going to live it.

Despite all of the agreements and reassurances, I didn't trust the government. I figured it was better to be prepared than taken by surprise. I wasn't worried about myself. I had survived repeated prison stays, and being institutionalized never really leaves you. I had no interest in doing a bit just because I could. I knew that I had to plan for the welfare of my son.

Though I was over marriage and had been fine living with my girlfriend for eight years, I asked her to marry me. My son's mother had drunk herself to death, and he had no place to go. We were married on January 31, 1987, and it was quite a wedding. Both Agents Tyler and Sweeney were in attendance. Frank was my best man.

After the wedding, we moved to the Gulf Coast, bought a home, and I began to prepare to be sent to prison. My wife's two other sons were familiar with flooring and installations, so I bought an interest in a local carpet store, and they went to work there, looking out for my investment.

During this same time, I was summoned to Scranton for a presentence investigation. The guy I met with was a real mountain hick. From the start, he showed nothing but contempt. I explained to him that I played a role as a chemist to lure the heavies in who were importing chemicals into the country. He pressed me for agents' names, whom I had worked with, and who knew what. But I wouldn't give him any; I told him about the major bust I had been in on in 1982 there in the Scranton area and also about my work with the New Jersey task force in the summer of 1983.

All he wanted to know about was how much money I made and how often I bought a new car. I told him I bought or exchanged new vehicles several times a year. He got these tortured looks on his face wanting to know why. I tried to explain how living the life works, but he obviously couldn't wrap his mind around it. I also tried to explain that there had once been a contract out on me, and I was sure those guys knew that I was back in the area, but I refused to give anybody up.

My sentencing took place in the late summer of 1987. I arrived at the federal courthouse in Scranton for the grand finale. We waited around all morning for the judge to get to us. Some of my family had come with me to show support, and we all went over to lunch at a nearby deli. I remember thinking, *I hope I'm still a free man by dinner.*

Court reconvened after lunch, and the insanity began. I was taken to stand directly in front of the judge, and Agents Tyler and Sweeney were standing behind me. The judge started asking me what I was doing with all of that equipment.

I answered, "I was role-playing."

"What does that mean?" he replied.

"I operate as a chemist and portray the lifestyle in hopes of luring in the big fish who import the chemicals."

I later learned from my family that during this time, the agents behind me were shaking their heads, indicating what I was saying wasn't true. I couldn't see them, and there was no verbal denial that I could hear or defend myself against. When the judge asked me who the agents were that I worked with, I just stared at him. None of them spoke up.

The judge addressed the FBI and said, "I see you guys ate out and did a lot of dinners together. Who initiated those?"

Judy responded, "Him some. Us some."

I could see that the judge was starting to get pissed, and I was getting scared. The last thing you want is your sentencing judge to get pissed off just as he's about to sentence you.

Finally, he said, "I can't go along with this recommendation of no time. I sentence you to three years in the Bureau of Prisons and a fine of two thousand dollars. That sentence is to be followed by two years reporting supervision."

The judge kept talking, but I was so upset, I missed most of it. I knew there was no more good time like there was in the early '70s when I did my federal bit before. Back then, a three-year sentence with good time off was twenty-seven months with an opportunity to earn additional good time off of your sentence. But in 1987, three years was thirty-six months, day for day.

That's when I heard Judy say, "That's not so bad."

I thought, *Yeah, you're not the one doing it.*

That's when it registered to me the rest of what the judge said: "I'm suspending two and a half of the three years. The fine and two years' supervision stand."

My mind started racing. Okay, so I have a six-month sentence, and that will call for a minimal level camp. I'll also qualify as a low-risk factor, so I'll be able to go home and wait for reporting instructions. A sudden wave of relief came over me. I didn't want to abandon my son, but the math has improved now. The sentence of six months to serve and two years' supervision was really much better than five years' probation. I had no intention of breaking any laws, but probation in the long run can be difficult. Just an argument with your wife can get you violated.

Jeff, my attorney, asked the judge if I could return to the Gulf Coast to my family and new business until reporting day. He also requested that the judge recommend I be placed at Maxwell Air Force Base in Alabama about four hours from my home. The judge said he would recommend it, but the decision would rest with the Bureau of Prisons. I headed home to Mississippi.

CHAPTER 37

Frank's Tragic End

Frank the Beard was given five years' probation for his part in this mess. Before I left for the Mississippi Gulf Coast, I told Frank he should take his millions and follow me down. I knew he was having problems with his liver; but with his money, he could get the best care available and buy a big boat to live on. I told him that everything that had happened was a sign that living the life was over of us, that he needed to get away from the city. The Feds were certainly not his friends, and he needed to write it off as a marriage gone bad. I even offered to hold a hundred grand for him. It would never be touched and would always be there if he needed it in a hurry. He declined, saying, "I'm good."

Frank should have read the leaves and found a way to disappear. The government is everywhere, but, hey, out of sight out of mind can be a blessing.

I reported to Maxwell Air Force Base in September of 1987. We drove up the night before and rented a hotel room in Birmingham, Alabama. The prison compound is at the rear of the base, and we made a test run to make sure we would be on time the next morning. We had dinner in one of the nice downtown Birmingham restaurants and made it a point to retire early. We tried to make enough love to last us for six months. The next morning, she dropped me off at the entrance to Maxwell Prison Camp, and I resumed life as an inmate for the fourth decade.

Maxwell was about the nicest joint I had ever been in, and I still knew how to do time. I was five feet eleven inches and 220 pounds and had always lifted the iron since I had done my time in Terre Haute in the early '70s. Back then, it wasn't a regular occurrence for a weight lifter to come off the streets. I later learned that the other inmates had thought I had transferred from another prison and were watching me. I knew the game.

Another inmate had turned himself in at the same time that I had. I could tell he was a first timer, so I took him under my wing. He was ranting and raving in the holding area. I told him, "You can't go into population carrying on like that. You'll have a problem." I told him to hang out with me, and I would teach him what to do and not to do.

That first day, we walked out to the yard. I took him over to the weight slab and told him to stay close by so the other inmates would think he was with me and not alone. I put 315 pounds on the bench and started knocking out sets of twelve and fifteen reps. I could see several inmates shake their heads with approval. Later on, another inmate came up and asked my name. When I told him Jack. He laughed and said, "Good enough, Weight Shack Jack." And so it was the rest of my stay.

Maxwell is a low-risk or minimum-security facility, so not much went down there. Most of the guys are doing short bits or are at the very end of a longer term, sort of like me during my last months at Terre Haute. My new buddy and I hung out. He needed me to show him the ropes, and it gave me somebody to talk to that I knew wouldn't be getting into any hustles or causing me extra time. Quiet and easy, that's how I wanted to play it. There was only one time I thought my young protege would get me into shit.

One afternoon, an inmate came to me and asked if my buddy was my son. I responded, "No, why?"

He looked relieved at first and then he got cocky. "Because I'm going to fuck him up."

I told him, "You're not going to fuck up anybody." Then I really challenged him in a serious way. I stepped in close so no one could hear and got up in his space. "If you fuck with that kid in any way,

I'm ready to get transferred after what I'm gonna do to you. I've done time in them all, and it don't make a shit to me where I do my bit."

That was enough to take care of the situation. This guy just thought he was a tough con. I did have a long talk with my young friend about smarting off to other cons. You can't go around disrespecting other inmates.

I won't say my young friend's name because he's now an accomplished businessman on the Gulf Coast with a great family. He really made something of himself, and I hope it was partly due to my influence. I tried to do for him what some of the guys had tried to do for me in Terre Haute fifteen years before. Needless to say, we do not run in the same circles, but I run into him from time to time, and he always tells me how grateful he is to me for looking out for him.

Just because I was no longer hustling and trying to stay in the life didn't mean I had forgotten how to maneuver. The first thing I did after getting established with the other cons was to start working on a transfer to Gunter Air Base. It's a school for air force trainees about twenty minutes away. I had heard it was the minimum security of all minimum securities and the place to go. I told my young protege about it, and he got transferred there right after me. Gunter was awesome. I got a job driving a truck for the grounds-keeping crew. We even got to eat with the air force guys in their dining hall.

The next step was to start writing my sentencing judge. I apologized for not responding to his questions and told him if I had known what was going on behind my back, I would've been more forthcoming. I told him that my six-month sentence meant my missing Christmas and New Year's with my young son—the first time since he was born—and asked him to reconsider, so that I could be home for the holidays. I also recounted my youth and told him how I had been incarcerated for twelve or thirteen of my first twenty-three Christmases. I needed things to be different for my child.

Several week later, I received a response from the judge's law clerk, informing me that the majority of my sentence was being suspended and setting me a release date of December 12, 1987, only a few weeks away.

During this time, I had been helping my young protege write to his sentencing judge. However, when he heard back, the judge had terminated his sentence effective immediately. He was going home the next day. I cannot tell you the ribbing I took from him that he was getting out before me. I was happy to have a positive effect on him.

When we were working on the grounds crew, we could look through the fence and see a bar across the street from the base. We talked about how good the food they cooked smelled and how good a cold beer would be. When my wife picked me up, we drove around to it. As we got out of the car and walked to the door, I could hear a chorus of cheers from across the street. I turned, and there was my old work crew gathered near the fence, yelling and laughing. I gave them the thumbs up and went inside.

Frank the Beard didn't fare so well. He wanted so bad to stay in the life that he got hooked up with my old crew that I had put away for manufacturing. As soon as they got out of prison, they had a sit-down with Frank, who had gotten my address in Mississippi. The meeting was to arrange a hit on me. The Feds must have had somebody in there wired up because one day, out of the blue, I got a call to report immediately to my probation officer. When I got to his office, he told me what had happened and had two guys from the Marshal Service ready to take me into the witness protection program. There was no doubt the contract was out there. I just told them, "No thanks. I'm good," and I walked out.

I went home thinking, *If they come for me, they better have said goodbye to those they hold dear.* Being a convicted felon, I had limitations on how to protect myself. However, my wife was legal, and there was still a part of Bojack deep down inside me.

During this same time, Frank also violated his probation in a deal with Jimmy "Skinny Jim" Kennedy. Frank claimed that Jimmy owed him eight grand, and Jimmy said it was financing for a drug deal. However, the Feds had everything on tape, and the jury believed Jimmy. Frank got popped for twelve years to run wild with the five years he already had for a total of seventeen years, day for day.

To add insult to injury, when Frank tried to hire Jeff Miller to represent him, he told his sister about all of the stashes of cash and to go get a hundred grand for Jeff. She later called Miller and told him there was no money. The boxes were empty. There was no money. Frank was sent to Sandstone Prison in the cold country of northern Minnesota where he died of liver disease.

After he went away, his sister and brother-in-law started living large. They traveled all over, started driving Cadillacs, and even bought a racehorse. I guess what goes around comes around.

AFTERWORD

After being released from federal prison on December 12, 1987, I finished my two-year postrelease supervision and never broke the law again. In 1990, I became a bounty hunter, and over the last thirty years, I have tracked down hundreds of fugitives all over the United States. I have brought in murderers, rapists, child molesters, and men indicted under the habitual offender laws who were facing life without parole as three-time losers. Often, these thugs would get my number and call me up, saying if I came after them, they would kill me. I'd just tell them, "Well, you have a serious decision to make because I'm coming."

Although I can't vote due to being a convicted felon, I have worked on the campaigns of sheriffs, prosecutors, and judges, helping good, honest people to get elected. I count these people among my friends and have earned their respect. I gave up the name Bojack when I decided to turn my life around. Today, all of these people know me as Mr. Jack. That's even the way I'm addressed in court. One of my closest friends and cowriter is a long-serving Mississippi Supreme Court judge. He and his wife take me to dinner for my birthday, and I've celebrated Thanksgiving and Christmas in their home with their extended family.

That's a long way from being a hungry eight-year-old surviving on the mean streets of Philly.